D1463130

JENNIFER
F·E·V·E·R

ALSO BY BARBARA GORDON

I'm Dancing as Fast as I Can

Defects of the Heart

BARBARA GORDON

JENNIFER F·E·V·E·R

OLDER MEN / YOUNGER WOMEN

HARPER & ROW, PUBLISHERS ◇ New York

Cambridge, Philadelphia, San Francisco, Washington
London, Mexico City, São Paulo, Singapore, Sydney

JENNIFER FEVER. Copyright © 1988 by Barbara Gordon. All rights reserved. Printed in the United States of America. No part of this book may be used or reproduced in any manner whatsoever without written permission except in the case of brief quotations embodied in critical articles and reviews. For information address Harper & Row, Publishers, Inc., 10 E. 53rd Street, New York, N.Y. 10022. Published simultaneously in Canada by Fitzhenry & Whiteside Ltd., Toronto.

FIRST EDITION

Designer: Ruth Bornschlegel

Copyeditor: Marjorie Horvitz

Index by Joan Halladay for Riofrancos & Co. Indexes

Library of Congress Cataloging-in-Publication Data

Gordon, Barbara,
  Jennifer fever.

  Bibliography: p.
  Includes index.
  1. Adultery. 2. Mistresses. 3. Middle-aged men—Sexual behavior. 4. Single women—Psychology. 5. Runaway husbands—Psychology. 6. Rejection (Psychology). I. Title.
HQ806.G66   1988   360.7'36   87-46140
ISBN 0-06-015936-7

---

88 89 90 91 92 RRD 10 9 8 7 6 5 4 3 2 1

For Jane Richmond and Richard Bachrach

Contents

The names and identities of all the people interviewed for their experiences have been changed, with the exception of Jane Spock, Dory Previn, David Rothenberg, Jane Richmond, and Joby Baker, who have graciously agreed that I may use their real names. The professionals, doctors, psychotherapists, lawyers, and others interviewed for professional opinions have agreed that their real names may be used, except for Jack Halsey and Alfred Borne, which are not real names.

1

The Quest

It was a June afternoon, and I was standing near a swimming pool dramatically situated sixty stories high above New York City. My mind was slightly numbed by this unlikely, almost supernatural setting—the smell of chlorine, the dizzy-making altitude, the sound of Tina Turner filling the domed rooftop space, through which almost all of the city could be seen. The view presented Manhattan, sparkling in all its majestic beauty, concealing all its flaws.

I suddenly realized that for some time I had been engrossed watching a young woman perched at the edge of the pool, tucking a cascade of hair into her bathing cap. She raised herself, stretched languorously, and, graceful as a cat, started for the other side of the pool.

She had an extraordinary body, one that sang out, advertising the hours of work and care that had made it the smooth and sleek-looking machine it was.

I studied the people resting in chaise longues near the pool. Although it was a coed club, there seemed to be only men in their forties and fifties present. The young woman and I were the only females around. I noticed a man peering at her over his *Wall Street Journal,* another staring intently over a glass of Perrier, and another . . . All eyes were fixed on her as she plunged into the pool. Their expressions were so filled with lusty admiration it would not have surprised me if the men had burst into applause.

Why this incident affected me so profoundly I don't know. At the moment there was no great love in my life, but there had been a few months before, and from experience I realized there would be again. I know I wasn't thinking of December—which seemed ages away from that early-summer afternoon—when I was facing a birthday that would quite literally make a midlife woman out of me.

In the past, older men and younger women were just there. Not everywhere, and not all the time, but there like autumn leaves, like spring training, occurrences that were woven into the fabric of our lives. I wondered why on this particular day the spectacle struck me so deeply.

I do remember that even as I eyed the splendid body of the young woman and the men eyeing her, I imagined the time and labor she had expended to achieve her magnificence. I observed it all with a sense of irony. For I, too, had spent time working on myself, but I had concentrated on internal repairs. So on that hazy June afternoon, at last I knew who I was.

Millions of women had done it—gambled and grown. Giving up old dependencies, we recreated ourselves into what felt like a new incarnation. At first skeptically, we had thrown aside old assumptions and taken to heart the new slogans of our generation, and discovered they were true, and not just the syrupy evangelical maxims of *Reader's Digest:* That to know oneself and to like oneself made it possible to love and be loved. That it was healthy to take that journey and reach the point where, like the proverbial tree in the forest, you knew you were there, even when there was no one around to hear you or see you.

It had taken a while, still for some months I had considered it essential time, survival time. But that day a voice within me asked, "Too long? Did it take too long?"

I had, I thought, taken reasonable measures to ward off or conceal signs that the years were flying, leaving unsightly mementos in their wake. With a sudden jolt I wondered if by concentrating on internal growth I had not been sufficiently vigilant, and perhaps the years had indeed taken their inevitable toll.

I also wondered if other women had experienced this uneasy realization. After getting degrees, jobs, better jobs, more pay, and even after aerobics, more aerobics, sweating to the voice of Jane Fonda, stretching to the cadence of Raquel Welch, did they discover that if they now found themselves alone but readier than ever to enter the game of romance, they no longer met the entry requirements?

It was marvelous and about time that we were becoming Supreme Court judges and brain surgeons, running for governor, becoming mayors, corporation presidents, and bankers. But even if we insisted we were at the peak of our form, in our prime, and just when we understood the intricacies, the philosophy of the game of romance, could we play only if we entered the old-timer's game? Disqualified, too much time on the meter, out of the running?

It's the altitude, I told myself. It's insane to be swimming in a pool thousands of feet in the air. It's not normal. I'm letting this tiny moment in time color all my thinking. I reminded myself that at least some of us had discovered that all that leaping and growing had caused something else to happen, something we hadn't counted on. Many of us were no longer victims, passive, waiting for a man, any man to come along and rescue us from ourselves. No, we had become a choosy lot. We hadn't done all that growing without developing a sharp editorial sense: we had strong likes and dislikes, had developed preferences about work, health, books, movies, food—how could we not have a pretty clear idea of the kind of men *we* wanted to play with?

I also reminded myself of women I knew who, though no longer nubile, were having relationships with men for whom youth, obviously, was not *all*.

Admittedly we were being told that for the thirty-five million of us midlife women—the fastest-growing group in the population—things were changing. Weren't there five or six glamorous over-forty film stars and several attractive media heroines who had acknowledged they were over fifty? And wasn't there a new perfume named for an over-forty French actress? And weren't the papers filled with stories on older women being adored by men, younger men? I wondered, did that mean that middle-aged women were becoming acceptable? With men their own age? Still I heard it everywhere: Good times are just around the corner.

The young woman was now leaning over, drying her long hair, and I looked away, through the transparent bubble, past a sea of cement, and spotted the tower of the RCA Building flirting with the clouds. I remembered myself at a younger age, when older men had been attracted to me and several fell in love with me. And I with them. In *that* building.

My eyes zoomed in on the young woman, who now was sitting on the edge of the pool chatting easily with a gray-haired man who had just joined her. I hoped I seemed as neutral as a camera, a disinterested party. In the twenty years I was a documentary film-maker, I was always an interested party—an interested party who happened to be investigating the plight of Vietnam veterans, of tenants in buildings run by slum landlords, of émigrés from the CIA, or the rights of ex–mental patients, frequently aiming my cameras at the disenfranchised in our society.

I saw myself in both worlds, then and now. The allure of young flesh and the appeal of an experienced, older, wiser man: Was that what it was all about? When I was younger, playing the other role, I was sure I had the answer. Now I wondered if other women over forty sometimes felt like aliens?

A cursory observation on a summer afternoon had turned into mild curiosity, but as I watched the sleek young woman and the gray-haired man gather their towels and head for the locker rooms, I was seized by another emotion, something I couldn't define.

Why? I wondered. Why was it so startling years ago when Charlie Chaplin, or Justice William Douglas, or Senator Strom Thurmond married women twenty or thirty years younger? And why today is it less startling?

Was it simply sexual? Freudian? Cultural? Economic? Was it merely a game? And if it was, had the women's movement changed the rules of that game? What were the men seeking? And the young women, did they imagine a time would come when they might struggle to remain the neutral observer? How did a woman of my generation feel when her husband left her for a younger woman?

Soon I was embarked on a quest that would take me across America and back in time, as well as on some unexpected jour-neys—to the biblical court of King David and to modern divorce courts, and to the surgeons, therapists, and attorneys who minister to the protagonists themselves. I took my tape recorder to those who responded to my advertisements, phone calls, networking efforts, and asked them endless questions. Because I am a woman of a certain age and was once cast in the younger woman's role in this particular drama, I was an interested party as well as an investigative journalist.

Just as a documentary film tries to blend facts and feelings into something called personal journalism, this book is one person's vision, a documentary, not a sociological tract, nor does it pretend to reflect an exact scientific sample. But as in a documentary, the words of the protagonists are recorded as they said them to me. And as in a documentary, through the prism of my particular lens.

I was amazed, after researching the historical roots of this eternal triangle, at how *eternal* it is. After listening to the voices of the men and women again and again on the tape recorder, I was reminded that some of us, in the bumpier moments, when the human condition doesn't feel very human, must deal with what Tennessee Williams described as "the cruel deficiencies of reality."

In the crunch, we all wage a battle for time—a few more years—trying to protect or protract a certain feeling about ourselves: a sense, a look, an attitude. We are in the biologically unique position of being mortal and knowing it, and we struggle not only to stay alive but *feel* alive. Hyper-alive.

The struggle to feel alive, however, for both men and women, is an individual battle. And a big discovery was that *what* those "cruel deficiencies" are, and *how* we wage that battle, have vastly different meanings for each of us.

I set out to discover how that battle is being waged today, and what in the twentieth-century atmosphere is changing the rules of the game.

2

The Jennifer

I have a favorite joke.

An eighty-year-old man tells his doctor, "Doc, I've got good news. I've met a beautiful girl. She's twenty-five; she's fabulous; the sex is great; I've never been so happy. Isn't it wonderful?"

"Yes, but I must warn you," the doctor replies sternly, "you must face reality. You are eighty; she's twenty-five. You must be prepared for illness, even a heart attack."

The old man nods, shrugs his shoulders, and answers:

"I know. If she dies, she dies."

"Youth is wasted on the young."

Hardly.

Despite the fact that the words of George Bernard Shaw have been passed on like fine silver from one generation to another, Shaw was slightly mistaken. Youth isn't *always* wasted on the young. In 1980s America, youth is the highly valued currency of the realm. Worshiped and adored, the young are considered the repository of vigor, sexuality, beauty, and go-getterism—all the glittering attributes our society holds dear.

Those who no longer bask in that sweet light of adoration—the bright golden glow our country casts on its young—may suffer great despair about the tarnishing defects time inevitably visits on us all.

And it's Dante, not Shaw, who best describes the cold realities of middle age: "In the middle of the journey of our life, I came to myself within a dark wood where the straight way was lost. Ah, how hard it is to tell of that wood, savage and harsh and dense, the thought of which renews my fear. So bitter is it that death is hardly more."

Who has not experienced a whiff of mortality in the not so incipient bulge at his middle or a sudden sprinkling of brown spots on her hands, or awakened one morning with a leaden feeling of world weariness, rather than the thrill of adventure that marked the not so distant past?

For a woman these bulges and saggings are accompanied by a series of acutely distressing symptoms that signal something much more critical than a frantic and costly battle with cellulite and wrinkles. They mark the loss of a fundamental part of her identity. She may draw on a number of external solutions to camouflage the changes in appearance that blatantly reveal the passage of time. But there is nothing she can do to retrieve the particular status and comfort that come from knowing she is still in her childbearing years. It's a feeling, a sense of herself that is altered *even* if she has already had children, or never had them, *even* if she doesn't wish to have children in the future.

While men experience considerable midlife anguish they generally don't suffer a rupturing of a basic part of their identity. A sluggish libido may indicate a waning appetite, but unless a man suffers complete impotency, his ability to plant a seed remains intact. Picasso, Pablo Casals and Charlie Chaplin all fathered children after they were sixty.

However, his lackluster sexuality and fears of impending impotency can devastate a man's sense of virility. He may realize with considerable anguish that his life has not lived up to his youthful aspirations and ask himself the question that is the anthem for all midlife sufferers: *Is that all there is?*

A man may treat this tempest as a fleeting nuisance, easily assuaged by counting his blessings: love for his wife and children, the rewards of his chosen career. Or he may try to energize his life by changing careers, taking up a new hobby, jogging, a racy new sports car, or if he can afford it, a trip around the world. But another man may suffer such crippling anxiety that the gloom of failed

expectations, dreams denied, and portents of mortality may con-
spire so that all his waking hours are tinged with the grayness of
regret.

How each man responds to the particular challenges middle age
presents to his self-esteem and sexual identity differs, depending in
part on how he has faced other challenges in his life. While there
are many responses a man may select to ease his suffering, he may
be convinced, as many men are, that even if his suffering stems from
disappointments with his work, or the anguish of dying parents, the
best antidote for his pain is sexual experimentation.

There is a variety of sexually stimulating solutions available to
him. In his quest for sexual and psychic rejuvenation, man has
resorted to everything from hundred-year-old eggs to glandular
extracts mysteriously derived from the intestines of endangered
species.

For generations, men have relied on an aphrodisiac that comes
in human form: novelty. Sex therapists report that for some men
suffering from sexual problems, a new woman can be an effective,
if temporary, solution.

One aphrodisiac men have turned to for generations, which
offers middle-aged men a special kind of novelty, also comes in
human form: youth.

She arrives with her own set of mythology and jokes, with a
claque of ardent supporters and an angry army of opponents.
Recommended by ancient doctors with the certainty and sanctity of
medical wisdom, and by contemporary doctors with a wink of male
camaraderie, she is what I call a *Jennifer*.

Jennifers are sought by the man who *knows* in his core, in that
inner place where facts, folklore, imaginings, and fantasy blend into
something called wisdom, that the only antidote for midlife angst
is a younger woman in his life. In his life, on his arm, but preferably
in his bed.

How long has man cherished a belief in the magical powers of
a Jennifer? While its origins are unclear, we're safe in assuming that
she has been around since the first caveman left his wife and chil-

dren to play around with a cavette, before nesting with her and fathering another brood of cave children.

The reference to our less intellectually developed ancestors is in no way a comment on the intelligence or lack of it in a man or his Jennifer. Older women often seek comfort in the notion that Jennifers are, in the main, stupid, ditzy and uninformed. But intelligence and beauty are not standard equipment. A certain amount of innocence, a certain lack of cynicism, a certain propensity for docility, may or may not be present in a Jennifer. Brainpower, joie de vivre, and a sense of humor are all optional. The only prerequisite is youth.

Curiously, a Jennifer is viewed as both a symptom and a cure. Like many remedies, it may be highly effective if only because the belief system that it will work is so strong. The benefits may sometimes be only temporary, the side effects more long-lasting than the cure. (Jennifer Fever does not necessarily mean marriage to a Jennifer. Men have been known to live with Jennifers serially, without ever marrying one of them. Still others manage to remain married and enjoy only stolen moments with a Jennifer.)

But statistics from the U.S. census reveal that there are millions of American men who choose to add a younger woman to their lives, and they *do* marry them. The first time around, American men marry women close to their own age, but in second marriages they marry women five or more years younger. If a man is in his forties when he decides to take the plunge again, it is likely he will marry a woman ten or more years younger.

For the last fifteen years, the most popular name for girls in New York state has been Jennifer. While national figures are not available, statisticians believe that for some time, Jennifer has been the name of choice for young females throughout the country. Therefore I have chosen to call the condition of men becoming involved with younger women Jennifer Fever.

It's not clear why the name Jennifer has captured the imagination of Americans. When the name first broke into the number-one spot on the American hit parade of names, one of the most popular books—later a movie—of the time featured a heroine named Jennifer. *Love Story* broke records at the box office and also broke the hearts of the audience when its beautiful, quirky heroine, Jennifer Cavilleri, played by Ali MacGraw, died at an early age in the arms of her husband, Oliver (Ryan O'Neal). Unravaged by signs of her illness, untouched by the lines of time, she dies. Etched in our memory, forever young, forever beautiful, Jennifer Cavilleri lives and dies—a Jennifer.

For some young women, their love affairs with older men can be a grand passion producing its own kind of fever. If she has a high-power job, and even if she doesn't, a contemporary Jennifer certainly has greater economic and vocational opportunities than young women of the past. For a Jennifer, an older, richer man is no longer her only available means of economic support—her only passport to the fast lane of social status—as he was for women who faced more limited horizons.

As Diane Shevin, a twenty-nine-year-old insurance executive in Baltimore, told me, "I make as much money as men my own age. They expect me to always be selling, on top, successful, fearless, independent."

"Or perhaps that's what you *think* they expect?" I suggested.

"Maybe." She laughed. "Or what they think they *should* expect. Who knows? I do know that for me and my friends, older men are our salvation. Jeremy, my fifty-five-year-old lover, is my one safe place, where I can lean, relax, say I'm tired, say I'm scared, ask for help. He's so understanding, he loves to advise me and help me. He makes me feel special."

Without closer examination, one can't be sure, but Jeremy sounds as if he's been bitten by the bug. The virus primarily affects males, but Jennifer Fever dramatically disrupts the lives of those close to the afflicted as well as the men themselves. We will call these victims by association, the wives, *Janets,* a name popular for an earlier generation of women. When their husbands are seized by a particularly virulent case of Jennifer Fever, Janets are often abandoned.

Doubtlessly these soon to be discarded wives have experienced some whiffs of mortality on their own. But when they learn they no longer matter in their husbands' lives, what happens to their own apprehensions about aging?

The irony is that while the male is usually the same age as his obsolescent Janet, he is regarded as a prize—a classic model of inestimable value—by Jennifers and by society at large.

"A man, though gray-haired, can always get a wife, but a woman's time is short," wrote Aristophanes. According to demographers, America is getting grayer. Suddenly more attention is being paid to the aging American woman, and the mass media are quickly trying to revise the image of the graying American. Cynics may argue that this revisionism does not arise from a wellspring of authentic admiration or affection, but rather it stems from greed.

Those aging Americans have a bundle of spendable dollars at their fingertips, and a limited amount of time left in which to spend them. Whatever the motivation, there is no denying that the aging American woman is less ignored today than in past years. What this really reflects remains open to argument. It is a less than comforting irony to note that just when advertising and television are courting the Janets, thousands of their husbands are leaving them for Jennifers.

It may take the Soviet Politburo's gift for refashioning the formerly scorned into cultural idols to transform the graying American woman into the image of a zesty, sexy heroine of our culture. And there *are* signs that the tide is turning. Television shows with midlife stars *(The Golden Girls, Cagney and Lacey, Designing Women, Murder, She Wrote,* and *Kate and Allie)* have ranked among the most popular programs in recent years, and Barbara Walters, Diane Sawyer, and Gloria Steinem are prominent examples of women over forty who have proved that age is no barrier to sex appeal. Yet for all the hopeful signs, there is still a long way to go.

The "Golden Girls"—Bea Arthur, Rue McClanahan, and Betty White—are a hit. That's progress. That they live together and spend much of each half-hour episode bemoaning their manless state, plotting how to boost their personal ratings with men, is not.

Angela Lansbury's portrayal of fiftyish mystery writer Jessica

Fletcher makes *Murder, She Wrote* a favorite for millions of devoted viewers. Progress. But apart from misty memories of her long-deceased husband, Jessica's only male relationships are with the astonished sheriffs and detectives she beats to the punch each week, when she sniffs out the clues and nails the murderer.

Those contemporary stars, like Jane Fonda, Cher, Linda Evans, and Joan Collins, who are over forty and still playing sexually alive heroines are glamorous exceptions who merely prove that for a woman that age to be considered sexy, she must be almost aberrantly beautiful and youthful for her years.

One thing is certain, as the opinion-molders—advertising copywriters, film producers, and network programming executives—snap and click, and press their respective buttons: Refashioning the image of the middle-aged woman into a lusty, sexually alive creature will take some doing. Like generations of women before her, she has been struggling to refashion herself into a creature valued by society. She knows the words society has devised to describe her: hag, witch, shriek, harridan, shrew, virago.

On the screen, the men of *Star Trek*—Captain Kirk and Mr. Spock—are charged with this awesome task: "To boldly go where no man has gone before."

But offscreen, the actors who portray Captain Kirk and Mr. Spock—William Shatner and Leonard Nimoy—made headlines last year when they reportedly chose to less boldly go where millions of men had indeed gone before: into the arms of a younger woman.

Pictures of a vigorous, adventuresome, seventy-five-year-old President astride his favorite horse, cantering across the rocky terrain near Santa Barbara, barely a few months after major surgery, certainly enhance the image of the aging man.

But the image of the midlife male has always been of someone living in a perpetual prime. Impervious to time, he remains, regardless of his age, the energetic star forever appearing in the main event of his life. He is perceived as thriving, bedding, wedding, and fathering. Older, wiser, the lines on his face are hard-earned creases that are part of his allure, assets that contribute to his craggy charm. All his experience—on the battlefield or ballfield; in the bedroom or boardroom; with women, colleagues, children, and enemies; his education, wars, marriages, divorces, even maladies—can add to his attractiveness, enhance his sexuality. He can be mentor, teacher, and lover, respected for all he has survived, all he has learned, for all his years.

While their female co-stars of ten or twenty years ago (Myrna Loy, Doris Day) were likely to be cast in interesting character parts peripheral to the arena of romantic action, male film stars like Cary Grant, Kirk Douglas, and Paul Newman slipped into their sixties and continued to portray romantic leading men without missing a beat.

Still, some of the men I spoke with cannot imagine being discussed in the same breath with Paul Newman. They feel more like Jerry, the middle-aged hero in Paddy Chayefsky's 1957 play, *Middle of the Night,* when he said, "My God, I'm fifty-three years old, I'll be an old man with white hair pretty soon, my life is coming to an end. I know it sounds irrational but . . . I'll tell you something. It's important to me that a young girl finds me attractive. I didn't know it was so important, but it is important."

Today many men who share Chayefsky's sentiments are actively involved in combating the ravages of time with vitamins, jogging, plastic surgery, or, like Chayefsky's hero of 1957, Jerry, with a Jennifer. In that sense, 1988 is very much like 1957. It remains a cardinal fact of the conventional wisdom that when we speak of sex, flesh, lust, the basic primitive physical attractiveness of men and women, men have a longer shelf life than women.

Women don't surrender to this assignation to obsolescence without a fight. We plump our creases away with pots of expensive creams or inject them with chemicals, or we go under the knife. Batteries of nutritionists and a blitz of exercise coaches are consulted regularly. Countless questions emerge: To face-lift or skin-peel? Implant or inject? Stretch or tone? Silicone, collagen, estrogen. Men grow sideburns, women get side effects.

Sometimes the Janets being tossed about in the fallout of Jennifer Fever must face a melancholy reality. All the wonders of surgery and the miracles of chemistry do not a Jennifer make.

Increasingly men are feeling the need for plumping and injecting too, but when they do, plastic surgeons report those efforts are less a desperate last gasp at keeping their mates and more often an attempt to look young on the job, be competitive with other men at work and at play, be with it, feel and stay *alive.*

And what does alive mean to a man? You guessed it. If the gods had a trick up their sleeve when they designed women, they kept a trick or two reserved for men. If the whole world views a man as a catch, as gorgeous, sexy, and desirable, and women fall at his feet and into his bed, once he gets them there he must literally, physically, demonstrably give a sexual performance.

Even those men who live in a rarefied atmosphere, jetting around, taking over corporations, sending in the marines, winning awards, amassing millions, having easy access to the powerful and glamorous, and an endless pool of beautiful women from which to draw—even those men may find sexual performance is a problem.

There is no artifice, no act of guile, that can help a man simulate virility. Worse, he cannot hide his failure, especially from himself. As Karen Horney observed:

"The man is actually obliged to go on proving his manhood to the woman. There is no analogous necessity for her. Even if she is frigid she can engage in sexual intercourse and bear a child. She performs her part by merely *being,* without any doing, a fact that has always filled men with admiration and resentment."

Writer Shirley Eskapa goes further: "The differences between male and female attitudes toward sexuality are enormous. Men's fears about sexual performance are so great, there isn't even a female linguistic equivalent for the word 'virility.' Men fear the loss of virility as much as they fear dying."

A woman may develop wrinkles and cellulite, lose her waistline, her bustline, her ability to bear a child, even her sense of humor, but none of that implies a loss of her sexuality, her femininity, in the same sense that a loss of virility means a loss of manhood.

From the onset of menopause, women, knowing how they are perceived by others, or *believing* they know, often *feel* the loss of their womanhood.

Lurking behind Jennifer Fever is the cosmic trick the gods

played on humans when they designed us. Men, who *have* to demonstrate their virility in the sexual act, can procreate forever. Women, who can perform sexually forever, lose the ability to bear a child in the prime of their lives. It is this evolutionary quirk that can create havoc between men and women.

The cosmic trick was millions of years in the making. I wondered about the first outbreak of Jennifer Fever. Where did it originate, and what atmospheric conditions were favorable for its growth? I also wondered how the double standard of aging ever got started in the first place.

3

A Separate Species

"It's unfortunate but true. Women have an actual menopause. They involute. They aren't as curvy as they once were. They aren't as juicy as they once were. They get older faster; bags faster; grayer faster. As men age, they just look more like themselves; they become themselves intensified, not older," sixty-two-year-old Jack Halsey was saying.

I was sitting silent as a stone, trying to be a neutral camera, trying to be unfeeling. Expecting an objective view, I realized I was hearing the party line, the one I had hoped was becoming a cultural artifact.

It was my first interview, and I had set out with optimism. Jack Halsey was waiting for me in the bar of his hotel, and I spotted him instantly. A tall, stocky man standing at the edge of the bar, he was dressed in a pastel seersucker suit and was deeply engrossed in the Michelin guide to New York.

Slightly stunned by his opening remarks, I plowed on, asking about his patients' opinions rather than his own. "Based on your experience as a physician, what's going on in the minds of the men you see in your Richmond practice? Is the conventional perception that middle-aged women lose their sexual attractiveness diminishing?"

"Not at all," he said, handing me my drink as we headed toward a corner table. "It's a sad fact, but nature designed us so that it's inevitable."

"What's inevitable?" I asked.

"You can't tell the difference between a man of forty-five,

fifty-five, or sixty. It's true, today a fifty-year-old woman can do something about it—have the cellulite removed surgically, dye her hair, get a face-lift, but she should know going in, or she is doomed to disappointment, that after all that work she's *still* only going to attract a man in his seventies. Late seventies."

"Oh, really?" I said sweetly.

"For many women I see in my practice, that's a real problem. They have this expectation that after investing all that time and money, suddenly they're going to be attractive to men their own age. It's just not true."

I was taken aback by the brusque, confident way in which he leveled this indictment at an entire generation, *my* generation of women. I was even more surprised by what followed.

"My marriage was a horror for years, but my wife said she couldn't face the disgrace of divorce. I decided to try to make her happy even though I knew the marriage was a mistake. We had two children. Then I was unfaithful a couple of times, but I didn't want to be or do that," he said with a smile. "Finally I got divorced, at forty-four, and that was the year I married Betsy. When we met, she had just turned twenty-one. With her I felt very romantic, very tuned into myself. It was instant, when I laid eyes on her: I wanted a baby with her."

I must have looked puzzled, because he went on to explain. "You see, that's always been a signal with me that this is it. A young woman is a new chance." I heard him say it, although it sounded as if he were far away, or maybe that was only wishful thinking on my part. "It's starting over; it makes a man feel he is winning and attractive, powerful and dynamic."

"Has it worked out?" I found myself asking.

"You bet. We've been married eighteen years."

Later that day I went to the office of Raoul Felder. A well-known divorce attorney in New York, he has been married for over twenty years. In divorce actions, he is frequently the legal counsel for the Janets who have been abandoned for Jennifers. Felder, who is fifty-two, states the matter with the brutal, hard-core pragmatism necessary for his work.

"You can get your eyes done," he began, "but there's nothing like the physical laying on of hands, nothing like the sexual injection of vital bodily fluids. That's the nearest thing you can get to that doctor in Switzerland who will inject you with life-prolonging sheep cells."

Oh God, I thought, steeling myself for another session like the one I had with Jack Halsey.

"So they get a young girl, it's a highly choreographed game. She plays a game, she says things that are bullshit, tells him gobbledygook which the girl knows is bullshit; the guy knows it's bullshit, but he listens to the girl and everyone knows it's bullshit and that everybody is kidding everyone else."

I smiled, my apprehension fading. Then with an expression of disdain, he remarked, "She says, 'Oh, you're wonderful,' and she's running her hands through imaginary hairs on his bald head. They both understand there are no hairs there and he's not wonderful, but he's paid his dues, and that's what he gets out of it. A certain percentage of the men want Jennifers full-time and they get them. The men are happy for three years, but they still keep aging, and so now we have this phenomenon of serial marriages."

A contemporary man speaking about a Jennifer often uses language that is urgently and precisely modern—words pulsating with the rhythm and vocabulary of today, ideas laden with conflicts and choices that can only be those of a modern man, circa 1988. But at other moments, his words seem to echo through time, resonating with ideas and emotions that sound so familiar, many women may view them as clichés. For the men I spoke with, however, they are authentically experienced emotions. Each man states them as if he is the first man in the world to have made the discovery that his Jennifer incorporates all the life-enhancing benefits of a drug; a tonic for mind and body.

To many observers, both the man and the Jennifer are embarked on a singularly practical arrangement. One hears the criticism that older men and Jennifers are merely expressions of the old power dominance game, the father-daughter complex, or mentor-student arrangements. As author Joseph Heller quipped, "When I see a couple where one member is much older than the other, I know there's something wrong with *both* of them."

It may be that at times Jennifer Fever, like all relationships, offers secondary gains of psychological satisfactions, satisfactions that may not feed the healthiest part of either the man or the Jennifer.

But I discovered that when a man talks about a younger woman, however practical her value may be in his life, he rarely speaks with the chilling pragmatism which many people think they detect in the newspeak of yuppie love. No, a man talking about a Jennifer conjures for me a time when the world was young, when men believed in magic and miracles, when young virgins were thought to possess the wonders of a Michael De Bakey long before there was a Dr. De Bakey or a glimmer of an idea of open heart surgery; of lower blood pressure before beta blockers or stress tests were invented; of longevity, even when the expected life span for a man was forty.

The conventional wisdom is that a Jennifer is merely an antidote to the all too familiar litany of men's midlife fears and anxieties. Or that one or both of the partners in what sociologists call "age discrepant" relationships is reliving the imprint of an earlier time: a fixation on a mother or father which remains unsolved, and is relived in choosing an older or younger partner. But there is one recent explanation that seems remarkably fresh:

Psychologist David Gutmann writes that midlife men and women become involved, quite unconsciously, in a kind of gender swapping, which can have a profound effect on a man's susceptibility to a Jennifer. At midlife, he observes, men begin to feel more tender, more passive, more sensual, qualities they had repressed in their earlier years, when they were focused on building their careers and creating their families.

This sudden burst of passivity can be most disturbing to men and may reach crisis proportions when it is exacerbated by corresponding changes in their aging wives, who, Gutmann says, "generally become managerial, achievement oriented, and relatively tough minded, taking over the 'masculine' qualities that men surrender. In his earlier years, the husband can externalize . . . the discrepant 'feminine' side of his own nature through indulging and sponsoring his wife's femininity. But as women become more assertive . . . the aging husband . . . begins to sense, usually with some discomfort, that so-called feminine traits are a feature of his *own* internal landscape and not exclusive to his wife."

A middle-aged American man can panic when his wife no longer plays out her "traditional, dependent role." In traditional cultures, Gutmann says, the aging man is encouraged to be passive, a wise man communicating with the gods, and "need not make some final choice between active and passive, the 'masculine' and 'feminine' sides of his nature."

But in our society there is no conventional substitute. A man may come to terms with his own passive, "feminine" side—a tricky business at best, in a culture that was galvanized by the conquest of the tiny Caribbean island of Grenada, adores Rambo, idolizes Clint Eastwood, worshiped John Wayne, and was so seduced by the derring-do exploits of Ollie North that it turned him into a folk hero in a period of seven days.

Or, Gutmann says, a man can resort to "pathologic solutions— alcoholism, driving himself into workaholism, or developing psychosomatic symptoms, including the heart attack so prevalent at midlife."

On that point Gutmann makes this intriguing observation: "In effect, the patient brings his denied passivity to the one major institution in our society that recognizes and even insists on a dependent stance—the hospital. It is as though the diseased organ plays the role that his wife now refuses to play. By becoming a patient, the middle-aged man says, 'It is not I, but my diseased organs that ask for help.'"

The midlife crisis may not result in a heart attack; rather it may cause panic, anger, anxiety, and depression. One way a man can deal with all this is by selecting a Jennifer. Gutmann observes: "Men relocate their feminine side in a new external vessel by discarding the now autonomous wife—a wife who further brings out the husband's frightening succorant needs—in favor of a still dependent, still adoring younger woman. Through her, these older men hope to both live out and cordon off the discrepant, questionable aspect of their own nature."

His conclusion offers an unusual explanation for Jennifer Fever: "The reason older men leave their wives for younger women is *not,* as is commonly believed, primarily to enhance sexual potency, but rather because the middle-aged wife now refuses to live in her husband's shadow."

Of course, many middle-aged men have been known to leave wives who were quite content to live in their husbands' shadows, who were willing to continue playing the adoring wife. Gutmann wasn't blaming the wives for wanting to come out of the shadows, but describing the inability of men to cope with them when they *do.* His theory provides one clue to why Jennifer Fever is not just the unconventional behavior of unconventional men, like Charlie Chaplin, who many considered to be a bit outrageous anyway, or Justice Douglas, whose behavior was insulated by his lofty position on the Supreme Court.

Today, when a man who sells insurance in Cleveland goes through his bout of midlife passivity, his wife will probably not be eager to live out her old role, baking cakes and playing the adoring woman so he can continue to keep his more feminine side at bay.

I asked other psychoanalysts if they had observed this terror of midlife passivity in their male patients. Dr. Donald Aaron, a New York analyst, appears to be in his early forties. A small smile cracked the veneer of his impassive expression as he listened to Gutmann's theory.

"That's a very sophisticated argument," he said, "and I don't think most of my patients are aware of it on a conscious level." Dr. Aaron hesitated and then continued thoughtfully: "Still, I think Gutmann has a point. Men and women going through the bodily and endocrinological changes of middle age can lose the 'bolstering' of their sexual identity, which they receive from feeling, looking, and acting whatever our culture defines as 'feminine' or 'masculine.' Without that bolstering, a man who experiences some reduced sexual potency may process those failed sexual episodes so that he experiences other aspects of his personality as 'feminine,' feels a kind of softening, a tenderizing of his entire persona.

"Rather than accept this duality and celebrate his ability to feel other sides of his personality," Dr. Aaron explained, "he feels terror. A 'Jennifer,' " he said, smiling, "can quiet that. Less demanding, more adoring, she can make him feel more 'masculine' and silence those gnawing, distressing emotions he labels as feminine."

Other psychologists thought it was an intriguing possibility but that most patients wouldn't be able to articulate it because it is so subtle, and so frightening to the patient. On one matter they all agreed. Today, after years of struggle, a woman who asserts the "masculine" or "active" side of her personality is likely to receive more support and encouragement from society, friends, and family than a man who tries to live out his passive or dependent side.

But few men are aware of this form of midlife angst. When they view their relationships with younger women, they don't see themselves through the prism of sociology or psychology. What they know, and what they are eager for you to know, is *how* they feel.

Tom Carpossi, a fifty-nine-year-old Phoenix accountant, recently married twenty-nine-year-old Carol. Short and wiry, Tom had blond, wispy hair that glistened under the harsh light in his office. He had delayed seeing a client, he told me, because he wanted to talk about his new life.

"She walks into a room, she lights up a room, other people don't. She brings joy to me every day," he exclaimed. "I love her enthusiasm, her sense of adventure, her willingness to try anything. Her energy inspires me, keeps me young.

"Friends who haven't seen me in a while say, 'Tom, what's happened to you? You look fantastic.' They don't believe me when I say, 'No, it isn't plastic surgery. It's Carol.' "

Maurice Gerard, a sixty-year-old real estate lawyer in Phoenix, added a personal revelation of his own:

"Sure a middle-aged woman can get a face-lift, a tan, can dye her hair, and she can look great. But that's not what a man wants, not what *this* man wants. I want romance. I want to *want* to send flowers."

Realizing that he had raised his voice, he brought his head closer, and continued: "I want someone young to love me. I want someone young and fresh and new to be attracted to me, I don't want a forty-five-year-old woman who looks great for her age, young for her age. No matter how great she looks, she's still forty-five," said sixty-year-old Maurice Gerard.

A young woman reading sentiments like these may breathe a

sigh of relief and feel unmoved. Then she may grow uneasy, and become aware of a gnawing sense of dread, thinking to herself: Someday that could be me they're talking about. But she is years away from that, vows to work harder in the gym and never to eat french fries again. That kind of dread has inhabited women's psyches for generations.

But midlife woman may experience something worse—a kind of numbing depersonalization, which can make her feel like a member of a neutered minority. In a sense, it is a feeling that has nothing to do with age. Rather it is as if she has *no* gender. Not young, not old, she is merely sexless. A separate species.

It *is* comforting for midlife women to know there are many men who appear to be Jennifer-proof—men we will meet in a later chapter, who are immune to the kind of thinking that labels a woman as sexless because of her age, who believe that women remain sexy and appealing as they age, and cannot understand the man who is attracted only to younger women.

But when the man who is not immune ticks off the wonders of a Jennifer, he is entering the stream of time, dipping into a reservoir of emotion and prejudice, without knowing how vast or how deep that reservoir is, or how it got started in the first place.

Neither did I—in the beginning.

4

"It's Not Freud, Darling, It's Darwin"

Was it inevitable, as Jack Halsey told me it was, that women inexorably, inevitably, and helplessly lose their sexual attractiveness as they aged? And what else had he said? Ah yes: if women didn't face that fact, they were "doomed to disappointment." I would not and could not accept such a bleak condemnation. Nor did I believe that most men felt that way.

I was in Denver, exploring the various psychological explanations for men's attraction to Jennifers with a well-known painter I will call Lee Kalder. Sixty-two and divorced, Lee works at home, and invited me to have lunch in his apartment.

He insisted I sit on the kitchen stool while he tossed the salad, taking occasional peeks at the chicken pot pies through the oven door. We were talking about Jung, who believed we all harbor male and female sides in our psyches. This supports David Gutmann's notion that at midlife we experience an intrapsychic battle when the side that has been latent for many years struggles for its time in the sun. And we talked about Freud, who viewed age-discrepant relationships as attempts to remedy or relive an old, unsolved problem with a parent.

Carefully measuring the oil and vinegar into the salad, he announced suddenly and with just a touch of exasperation, "It's not Freud, darling, it's Darwin. What nature has put into man, what Darwin has put into man, is to be attracted to women of childbearing age. When a woman passes that age, it becomes an intellectual thing, but evolution is not on the side of that woman as a sexual object." Lee's expression was serious, earnest, when he added, "I'm laying it on the line. I'm telling you about evolution—what it does to trees, bushes, flowers, and animals. It's something you can't escape."

Evolution? Darwin? I was prepared to discuss Jung, Freud, Oedipus, angst, fear of dying, fear of living—not trees and bushes—and Lee Kalder sensed my confusion.

"We're talking about hard-ons. *Hard-ons.*" He paused for emphasis, handing me the salad bowl, asking that I follow him and the chicken pot pies into the dining room.

"Evolution says to a man, 'Wouldn't you like to fuck this young woman?' He wants to, not because he wants children, but because Darwin said you are going to be attracted to this kind of woman. It's what keeps the species alive."

I wasn't prepared to view a man's attraction to a Jennifer as a gesture of altruism; nor could I interpret the sexual act between a man and a Jennifer as a philanthropic bequest to the survival of the human race.

"When middle-aged men speak to me about their Jennifers, it's not keeping the species alive they're interested in," I protested, as he filled my wineglass. "As for fertility, most of them don't want any more children. Some of them are grandfathers, for God's sake!"

"I told you, I'm not talking about men wanting a child," he replied, an expression of annoyance flickering across his face. "I'm talking about instinct. Birds do it; animals do it. It's as old as time. It's Darwin. It *is* what keeps the species alive. And that's what your Jennifer Fever is all about."

I was beginning to see the logic. *Man always lusts for what he lusted for when he first lusted.*

In the interviews I conducted with eighty men, from the age of forty to seventy-six, only one other man mentioned this notion of "sexual memory." And when he did, it was a vastly different sort of sexual memory than the one Lee Kalder was talking about.

Jed Rolphe teaches twelfth-grade English at a high school in New Jersey. A chunky, graying, soft-spoken man, Jed told me, "A man in his fifties goes through hell, and that hell has mainly to do with sex. One reason he's drawn to a Jennifer is because of sexual memory."

Fresh from my interview with Lee Kalder, I thought I understood, and quickly replied, "I know: the memory of all those young girls he was attracted to when he was first aware of being attracted to anything."

"Not at all," Jed said. "A memory of his mother."

"His mother?" I asked, puzzled.

"When a boy is twelve or thirteen," Jed continued, "and he begins to feel all those stirrings, all those startling sensations, his mother, her hair, her smell, her body, are all tremendously seductive. That image of her remains in his memory. His mother—frozen in time, attractive, supple, warm, loving. He never forgets that. So when he's in his fifties and sixties, that's the sexual memory he remembers. That's why men of fifty and sixty are drawn to younger women."

Some of the women I spoke with agreed that sexual memory might play a role, but not as much as Lee Kalder or Jed Rolphe contend. Others, upon hearing the Darwinian Defense, said, in a word, "Bullshit."

One feminist responded this way:

"Why can't they be honest? The culture says youth is where it's at, and they want to screw it. Let's face it, youth *is* more attractive. I prefer the way young men look; I like to look at their firm bodies. I don't like potbellies or wrinkles, either. As for the continuity of the species—give me a break. When they're screwing Jennifers, they don't give a damn about the survival of the species. And fertility? All they think about is how to prevent it. Why do they have to bring Darwin into it?"

But Lee Kalder had pointed me in the right direction. Does sexual memory, that inextricable force which he contends draws men to fertile women, play a role in the sexual behavior of other animals?

Just as this phenomenon has not been studied in depth in humans, it has not been examined in other species. However, the data available reveals that it is not generally observed in animals. In fact, our closest relatives on the evolutionary family tree—the primates—take quite the opposite attitude toward young flesh.

According to the noted biological anthropologist Sara Blaffer

Hrdy, "There is a difference between humans and nonhumans with regard to the attraction of older males to younger females. For humans there is infatuation with nubility, and the standard of beauty is *youthfulness at the beginning of adulthood.* This is not true for primates. Male primates are not attracted to younger female primates. They prefer middle-aged, older, or 'dominant' females. These *females* are more experienced and their infants have the higher survival rates, which would be a principal motivation on the part of the *male."*

But Dr. Hrdy reports there are Jennifers in the primate world as well: "This fact does not stop young females from doing all they can to advertise their sexuality. Young females who have not yet had offspring often exhibit larger sexual swelling."

Dr. Hrdy speculates that this develops because it is their "best crack" at attracting a male; however, she says that despite all their wiles and the brandishing of their sexual charms, these young nubile females are still less attractive to the males.

If a male animal should develop an attraction for a young female within the confines of a monogamous species, Dr. Hrdy reports, older female primates have devised ingenious ways of making sure their males adhere to the rules of monogamy:

"One way or another, females in these species deploy themselves so there is only one breeding female in each territory or group. Any prospect of cheating would be precluded by fierce antagonism among females of breeding age. In most monogamous species, rival females are physically excluded from the territory by the aggressiveness of its mistress. In many cases where the presence of other females *is* tolerated, the integrity of the breeding unit is maintained by the suppression of ovulation in subordinate females."

While many female Homo sapiens may find these methods of enforcing monogamy of little practical value in their own lives, they might wonder what life would be like if such skills were part of their sexual bag of tricks. Would the integrity of their breeding unit be maintained if these methods were part of the legacy passed down to them by their evolutionary sisters?

Sociologists and psychologists agree that the menopause has

profound emotional implications for both men and women. Soci-
obiologists, however, have divergent views on the subject of the
menopause in primates. Dr. Hrdy, in the minority, argues that the
female menopause may be observed in some primates, but the majority contend that the menopause is a phenomenon experienced
only by human females.

There is general agreement among scientists that primate literature is so diverse that adherents of *any* position on male-female
relationships can find corroboration for their beliefs in studying one
species or another. As Dr. Hrdy writes, "Primates live in pairs,
harems, unisex bands or . . . as solitaries," and in sexual relationships, "females can be dominant, subordinate, equal, or not interested."

Still, with all the diversity of mating patterns, the phenomenon
of males abandoning their sexual partners for younger females
seems to be a uniquely human condition. For the birds and primates,
gibbons and ravens, who are monogamous, or exclusively pair
bonded, adultery may take place from time to time (sometimes
initiated by the female). But it's rare for a mature male to abandon
his bonded mate for a younger female.

Professor Allison Jolly of Rockefeller University emphasizes the
reason Jennifers don't play a significant role in the sexual relations
of other species: "Since in the majority of species the female can
continue to bear children practically until the time she dies, there
is little incentive for the male to leave her."

Few men who left their wives for Jennifers said they did so
because their wives could no longer bear children. But it's intriguing
to wonder: If women remained fertile as long as female primates, as
long as a man, how would that affect his desire or need for a
Jennifer? My guess: It wouldn't change a thing.

For years the field of sociobiology was dominated by male researchers, and Lee Kalder's sentiments were echoed by the majority
of biologists. But as feminist and novelist Marilyn French has written, "In the past . . . researchers found what they wanted to find and
concentrated on species that demonstrated monogamy, male dominance rituals or seeming male dominance of females. More respon-

sible research performed recently has modified and sometimes in-validated the conclusions reached earlier."

Sociobiologist Nancy Tanner questions the whole notion that it is male primates who exclusively determine the rules of the mating game. Professor Tanner, whose landmark work *On Becoming Human* focuses on the role of the female in human evolution, reports that it is often the females who determine the mating partner. Recent studies have shown that "among chimpanzees [the animals closest genetically and structurally to human beings], those males who have the best chance of reproducing themselves are those who are *chosen* as consort by a female, and it is the *female* who initiates sex."

As for Darwin, Professor Tanner concludes that his theories on sexual selection have been misrepresented for years, and that while most attention has been focused on "competition among the males for the opportunity to copulate," Darwin also discussed the "selection of males *by females,"* which has been largely ignored. "Most writers have either ignored female choice or considered it trivial."

Apparently the notion that Jennifer Fever in humans is merely another evolutionary expression of sexual selection, as if an essential part of man's primeval programming—something in his DNA drawing him relentlessly or unconsciously to fertile females—is not borne out in recent studies of the sexual behavior of primates, though it is valid perhaps in some species.

So biology plays a role, but even if it doesn't provide the answer to the origins of Jennifer Fever, it's still important to note that among the highest order of primates, there are many men like Lee Kalder who *believe* it does.

Lee Kalder's concept of "sexual memory" stirred some memories out of the dusty recesses of my mind. When I was younger, playing my Jennifer role with an older married man, fear of losing him to a younger woman was not the issue. I thought I might lose him to his wife, to years of shared pleasures, to a house resonating with the sounds of children's laughter, to Thanksgivings and Christmases, to guilt and responsibility. But I was younger, more plugged into his work, the "meat" of his life, more adoring of the "nowness" of him, and in the insufferable arrogance of youth, I thought that was enough. My youth was enough.

Recently a twenty-eight-year-old woman who is involved with a married man fifteen years older than herself told me, "I can imagine it must be real traumatic for an older woman to lose her husband to a younger woman, real traumatic."

But it was as if she were speaking of a distant misty time and a woman she would never be. Her belief system was fueled by the same assumptions shared by a majority of younger women: An older woman who loses her husband has done or not done something to drive him away. Too interested in her career, not interested enough in his, she did not keep up with him. Time had worn her down. Time would never do that to them.

Another memory. My mother's birthday: I don't recall all the details, but I do remember my father's laugh and the wink he gave his friends when he quipped, "I think I'll have to trade her in for two twenty-year-olds." Today I know that joke has its roots in the seventeenth century, but the stab of pain I felt then was so sharp I had to turn away. Still, no matter how deep my pain, or profound my identification with my mother, it was not me. Would never be me.

One other memory was prodded out of retirement. My mother in a department store, trying on a dress, frowning, putting it back on the rack, shaking her head, telling me, "Too matronly."

Just as a song can rekindle fond memories, so a word can evoke happiness, sadness, or fear. When I was a child, of the most frightening words, along with death, devil, ghost, hospital, and operation—or any of the other words that can create terror in the minds of children—"matron" was high on my list. Or at least I think so now.

Doubtless this stems from something more than my mother's unhappy expression when she used the word. More likely it is because in the movies I grew up on, the woman in the prison who treated the inmates so horribly was called a matron. In those same films, the kindhearted nurse was pretty, and young, in love with the kindhearted prison doctor, who sometimes took her in his arms, and they dissolved in happiness. The nurse knew sexual splendor, and she was never called a matron.

Later I would see "matron" used in a way that had nothing to do with prisons or dresses. On the society page, I read that "a Palm Beach matron" gave a party, and it seemed to have nothing to do with prisons. In those Ms.-less days, we quickly assimilated the fact that a man remained Mr. whether married or single, young or old. A girl would grow up to be Miss or Mrs. But whatever a matron was, clearly she had nothing to do with romance, nothing to do with men.

Some childhood associations die hard. Years later, although devils, ghosts, and skeletons have been neutralized, whenever I hear "matron" I still see the black muslin, tight lips, and beady eyes, the ferocious bun at the nape of a thick neck, and the crack across the face the matron of my memory would deliver to any man who offered her a night of sexual splendor.

So for women, the myths and the jokes, the words and the winks, burn themselves on our psyches, even when we are not aware, even when we think we are immune. If men have a sexual memory which gives license to the desire to have love, sex, and the admiration of younger women, so we women have a sexual memory of our own. I don't mean we are constantly in search of attractive, virile young men, or that we necessarily want that kind of man for the rest of our lives.

Rather we are recipients of a psychic programming, in which we record in some preconscious way the alarming fact that we will die twice. Shortly after we learn that we are mortal and, impossible as it is to believe, a time will come when we will no longer *be,* we learn another dark truth: We will die a second death, the one that comes when men—not all of them, but many of them—no longer find us physically or sexually attractive.

But did we think it had to be that way? Or that it all started with Darwin? I don't think so. The reasons men seek a relationship with a Jennifer change from generation to generation, but the idea is as old as time, *human time.* Yet there is evidence that it was divinely inspired—by some nudging from the gods.

5

Man Was Not Meant to Live Alone

It's not Freud, it's Darwin. It's not Darwin, it's Jung. It's not Jung, it's Freud. As the weeks went by, I sometimes felt like a ball being bounced from one great thinker to another, and then to another, each having said something that might explain Jennifer Fever.

As fifty-eight-year-old Denver dentist Bill Epstein ticked off the wonders of the twenty-four-year-old Jennifer he had married, I realized his sentiments had their genesis long before either Darwin or Freud had written their seminal works, thought their profound thoughts.

"Every patient tells me, 'Bill, you look so terrific,' " Bill Epstein was saying. " 'You look so young, so happy. What's going on?' "

"What *is* going on?" I asked.

Words pouring out of him, Bill Epstein stood up from behind his desk, as if he wanted me to see all of him, all of his radiant new health. "I know it's because of her," he explained. "When I met Sara, it was like somebody throwing spring water in my face. I suddenly feel great, my circulation is going. People tell me I radiate health; they can feel it, just looking at me.

"I'm alive. Intensely alive." He picked up a picture from his desk and smiled. "Just seeing her, looking at her pretty blond hair, those blue eyes. You've just met me, so you can't judge, but I never looked like this, felt like this, and I know it's because of her."

For weeks I had been dwelling in Great Books Land, and I decided I should reread what many consider the greatest book of all time. It was then I realized that when Bill Epstein talked about his twenty-four-year-old wife, making her sound like a one-woman resurrection kit, he echoed the same sentiments and the same expectations the ancient Hebrews had toward young virgins. Today's Jennifers don't have to be virgins and seldom are, but men still believe they have magical powers. Because of her piety and innocence, and because she was supposedly free of lust, the ancient Hebrews endowed a virgin with miraculous charms.

Consider the case of King David. David wasn't as lucky as Bill Epstein. When he was very old and ill, his servants, attempting to help him, covered him with clothes, but still "he got no heat."

What did they do? Why, they searched for a young virgin who would cherish him, and "lie in his bosom so the king would get heat." They found a beautiful maiden, Abishag, and brought her to the King, and she "cherished the King and ministered to him, but the King knew her not."

Perhaps King David was too old and frail to receive help, even from a beautiful maiden like Abishag. But in the eyes of the men who wrote the Bible, she was the last best hope, a kind of human Lourdes. Despite her failure to rouse David's sagging spirits, Abishag lives on in the hearts and minds of men.

In the 1960s, when the United States was seized by its most extreme infatuation with the young—their music, their clothes, their sexual freedom—Arthur Koestler labeled this youth worship, which bordered on mystical reverence, the "Abishag Complex." Just as Abishag had failed to revive King David, Koestler doubted that what he believed to be a drugged-out youth culture would redeem America, liberating it from its "conformism and competitiveness . . . and subjection to the mass media."

At its worst, America was not in the terminal condition of King David. Nor was there reason to believe the country was in disfavor with God. Even those who believe in an omniscient deity, with the exception of a few hard-core evangelists, can't be certain that "God is on our side." As for me, I think the jury's still out. If there is a God, he or she is far too busy keeping the planets from colliding with the sun to find time to develop a rooting interest in any country. But we know King David had a long history of serious problems in his working relationship with God. Throughout his life he had a weakness for the charms of attractive young women. And David *had* been implicated in the most notorious case of adultery in the Bible, his steamy love affair with Bathsheba.

Bathsheba was no virgin, but she was young, and beautiful, and *married;* yet according to the laws of that time, a man couldn't marry a divorced woman. Still David took her to bed, and when she became pregnant, he knew the child was his. He decided to pass it off on the husband. David then put Uriah in the most dangerous battle zone so that he might be killed, enabling David to marry the beautiful widow.

"The Lord was displeased with all that King David had done, and from that moment on, David's career was plagued with bad luck." But if God looked with such disfavor on him, and it was written that God showed his disfavor in the ill fortune that came to the children of such liaisons, one cynical observer wonders why this "does not prevent the son whom he has by Bathsheba, King Solomon, from ruling after him and having the largest harem recorded in ancient history . . . and from building the Temple at Jerusalem, the most sacred relic of the Jewish religion."

Some punishment.

Lurking in the David and Bathsheba story is another expression of Jennifer Fever, which has survived the test of time and has ironic meaning for us to this day:

"Failing old men who are waging their own battle against impotency and hating younger men for their sexual potency arrange to have young men killed in wars engendered by the old men."

The portrait of the voracious, sexually aggressive woman has lived on as the "Delilah Myth" for centuries. Ironically, the picture of the virility-sapping Delilah coexists with the opposite picture of the older woman—a neutered, maternal figure who has no interest in sex at all.

But of course the Bible was written by men. And because it was written by different sources and gathered over hundreds of years, it cannot be considered a true reflection of one period of time. With that caveat, it's still our best source of information as to how the ancient Hebrews viewed Jennifers and Janets.

With wars and tribulations everywhere, the survival of the Hebrew people was always an issue. Men needed women who could survive childbirth, and that their children survive. It was crucial for men and women to marry early, and parents tried to marry off both sons and daughters close to the age of puberty.

A high death rate for women during childbirth and an equally high infant mortality rate were grim facts of everyday life. At first, polygamy was necessary to keep the family line alive. But having many wives was a costly business, even then; and polygamy wasn't universally practiced. After a time, when polygamy became more economically feasible, undeniably it was lust as much as survival that fueled men's desire to have many wives.

For example, Solomon, who had seven hundred wives, three hundred concubines, and countless female slaves, had something more on his mind than leaving an heir to the family name and fortune.

If a man could have a concubine or a new wife who wouldn't threaten the serenity of his household, and who would be a symbol of his wealth and prestige, it's easy to understand why we find few references to wives being abandoned for Jennifers.

After several generations, one man—one wife became the law of the land. Despite the emphasis on family and progeny, passage after passage of the Old Testament is replete with a heady appreciation of the sheer joys of sexuality. God recognized the power of physical love when he declared that man will cling to his woman, "and they shall become one flesh."

While some scholars believe "one flesh" signifies marriage, or a child born from a marriage, Phyllis Trible, Professor of Sacred Literature at Union Theological Seminary, suggests it is the "one flesh of sexual communion between a man and a woman. And it is a celebration of sex."

There are few celebrations of explicit sensuality that match passages of the Song of Songs: "Oh that he would kiss me with the kisses of his mouth . . . My lover put his hand to the latch and my womb trembled within me."

But God warns man to be wary: "He follows her, as an ox goes to the slaughter . . . he does not know that it will cost him his life."

Men must be vigilant and remain loyal to their wives: "Rejoice in the wife of your youth . . . for why should you, my son, be enraptured by an immoral woman and be embraced in the arms of an alien bosom?"

However, in order to become *that* wife, your best shot in the marriage and mating game was to be a virgin. Virgins were the brides of choice, and if a man discovered his wife was not virginal, he could make a public complaint and she would be stoned to death. Two of the Ten Commandments forbid adultery, but generally only women were punished for transgressing.

Earlier, Lee Kalder said that even without the need "to be fruitful and multiply," a younger woman's fertility was a central part of her sexual appeal. The story of Sarah and Abraham is a wonderful example of how that issue was handled by the Hebrews:

After many years of marriage, Sarah hadn't given Abraham a child. So she gave Hagar, her Egyptian maid, to Abraham so she would bear a child. Abraham was eighty-six years old when Hagar bore Ishmael. Of course, this created problems between Hagar and Sarah, and Hagar was banished.

"The story opposes two women around the man Abraham . . . Even at a time when fertility was a crucial asset for a woman, Hagar is powerless because God supports Sarah."

Despite the conventional notion that women were merely pieces of property, despite Hagar and the years of Sarah's infertility, the bond of marriage was highly valued, strong enough to survive the tests of time.

With all the lofty valuation of the marriage bond, other adages from the writings of the ancient Hebrews reveal that men were still drawn to younger women.

"When an old man takes a young wife, the man becomes young and the woman old."

"The old and the young should not be joined in marriage, lest both the peace and the purity of marriage be destroyed."

"There is a substitute for everything except the wife of your youth."

"What you become accustomed to do in your youth you do in your old age."

Confusing? Obviously, in the eyes of their God, as in the eyes of Hebrew men themselves, their attitudes toward women—Jennifers, Abishags, and Janets, Bathshebas, Hagars, and Sarahs—created a complicated web of inconsistencies. The same God who said, "It is not good for man to be alone," and created Eve as his companion, went on to warn man that just as Eve led Adam into sin, so all women have the ability to corrupt and bring sin into the world.

The same God who said, "Rejoice in the wife of thy youth," rewarded many of the kings with an abundance of wives and concubines, and did not punish them for being "embraced in the arms of an alien bosom."

Christianity would drastically alter ideas about sexuality for sexuality's sake that had been acknowledged by the Hebrews. According to Dr. Bernard Murstein, to the Hebrews, virginity was important only *before* marriage, and to continue that state beyond youth was considered a "frustration of divine will." Under Christianity, the rules of the sexual game were changed. "Virginity became exalted for all, male and female, polygamy was abolished and sexual relations were condemned except for procreation. Chastity was in, for both sexes.

"In practicing monogamy exclusively, the Christians went no further than the Greeks. . . . However, in declaring marriage indissoluble, they strengthened the position of women . . . male adultery was for the first time officially condemned as much as female adultery."

Jesus took a dim view of a man leaving his wife for another woman—young or old: "Whoever shall put away his wife and marry another commiteth adultery against her . . . and if a woman shall put away her husband and be married to another, she commiteth adultery."

But when a woman accused of adultery was brought before him, and the crowd clamored for her to be stoned, Jesus uttered words that have been etched permanently into the world's collective memory: "Let him among you who is without sin cast the first stone." The crowd backed away, and Jesus spared the life of the woman.

Certainly the most profound effect of Christianity on men's attitudes toward Jennifers stems from its being a religion founded on the adoration of a woman who combines fertility and virginity, innocence and motherliness, saintliness and worldliness. There would always be wicked prostitutes and adulteresses, sexual sirens luring men into temptation, women worthy only of contempt. But there was Mary—and women were also blessed mothers, sexually immaculate, madonnas, saints, objects of reverence and adoration. The Good Mother. The Holy Mother.

According to author Francine du Plessix Gray, in some Catholic countries like France, where, historically, older women have not been treated as a breed apart—sexual undesirables—the carryover from the adoration of the Virgin Mary has played a significant role in shaping more favorable views of older women. Still the idea of a virgin mother, desexualized and saintly, has doubtlessly been responsible for some men's desexualizing their own wives after they give birth. The whole Madonna-Whore Syndrome—there are women men worship and women men make love to—has its origin in the worship of the Virgin Mary. The repercussions of this worshipful attitude toward the virgin mother dovetails, as we will see, with some fundamental aspects of male psychology.

If the genesis of Jennifer Fever isn't to be found in Genesis, we do find references there to both the wonders of a Jennifer and the joys of marriage, of a man remaining loyal to his Janet, "the wife of his youth."

In another heaven, the adoration of youthful beauty *is* pervasive, to the point of being an obsession. Through the eyes of gods and goddesses I discovered sentiments about Jennifers and their older lovers that make the words of the Old Testament prophets and the New Testament apostles seem nothing less than schizoid.

6

A Woman's Time Is Short

After the Old Testament and the New Testament gospels what I needed to do was hear from a twentieth-century apostle.

Contradicting the Cary Grant syndrome, which presents the stereotype of men clinging to, even growing in attractiveness as they age, time had been less kind to Sam Toffler than it had been for Cary Grant. A tall, ruddy, heavyset man of sixty-one, he looked much older. Spidery red lines created a patchwork pattern on his face, and beneath heavy lids his eyes seemed drained of color and light. When he heard about my book, he eagerly offered to explain why a man like him preferred a Jennifer to—as he put it—"charming as you are, women like you."

We met at the summer house of mutual friends and talked as he drove us back to New York on an overcast, oppressively clammy summer day.

"I want someone new and fresh, who knows me and loves me as I am today," he began, not taking his eyes from the road. "Not someone who knows I lied on my income tax, not someone who knows I cheated on my final exams. I've changed in the thirty years I've been married, I've grown in all kinds of ways. I'm filled with new ideas, bursting with new thoughts. Yet my wife still sees me as I was thirty years ago. I want someone who loves *this* Sam Toffler. All I've become, all I am today."

Suddenly his eyes were on me, looking at me accusingly. I realized this was a dangerous place for our conversation, so I was relieved when he shifted his eyes back toward the oncoming traffic. Frowning, he continued with a new edge to his voice: "I don't want someone who reminds me to floss my teeth, who tells me my socks don't match, tells me to go easy on the butter. I don't want a mother."

His hands gripped the steering wheel tensely, his voice tinged with anger, and after hearing the anger in his voice, I was relieved I hadn't urged him to keep his eye on the road. His expression was not angry, rather it was one of confused disappointment. As if part of him was wondering: How did it happen, when did the young woman I married thirty years ago begin to tyrannize me with care?

"I'm in the process of getting a divorce. The girl I'm marrying is young, much younger than me. And if my friends don't like it, screw 'em. As I told you, *I don't want a mother.*"

"I don't want a mother." Many women have heard that rebuke from a man at some point in their lives. Just as hurt and confused as Sam Toffler, they cannot imagine how they have earned the criticism. But psychologists believe the answer is simple. Men, they say, are more involved with their mothers than women are with either their mothers or their fathers. Loving them, leaving them, seeing the shadows of their mothers' positive or negative attributes in other women, is something men do, often quite unconsciously.

While many Jennifers may be searching for a replica of a parent—father or mother—in older men, few wives say they want a divorce because as their husbands age they see in them some negative picture of their fathers. Yet many men told me their wives had become motherly and were therefore no longer sexually attractive. What they craved was a whole new mating dance.

For some time I was unable to pinpoint the source of those particular kinds of emotions. Darwin, usually so reliable in explaining the origin of things, hadn't helped, nor had the ancient Hebrews. Freud grappled with the phenomenon, and Dr. Mara Gleckel, a New York psychotherapist, explained to me in analytic terms how and why it happens. A sensual, attractive woman somewhere in her forties, with shoulder-length auburn hair, she speaks with a rat-a-tat jet-speed velocity that is in striking contrast to the measured speech of the average therapist. We met in her office, just off Madison Avenue in Manhattan, where among her patients she sees Jennifers and Janets, as well as many men who are seized by Jennifer Fever.

"Why," I asked, "do men as they age see the image of their mothers in their wives? And yet women, while they may tire of a marriage or want their freedom, don't say it's specifically because their husbands became too fatherly?"

"It's very simple," Dr. Gleckel replied quickly. "The girl can identify with her mother and respond to her touch, caretaking and love. The boy must deny his dependency needs for the omnipotent mother and redirect his sexual drive to other females. He identifies with the powerful competitor, his father.

"As the boy gets older, he has to repress the erotic feeling he has for his mother, so he desexualizes her. In order to carve out new relationships with women, he must reject feelings for the woman he was dependent on, the first woman he ever loved."

"Scary, for a little boy?"

"It can be scary too, but it's crucial. All his future interactions with women will be colored by how his mother responds to his need to break away. If she allows him to separate, realizing it is a necessary part of his development, he is more likely to have healthy relationships with women."

"And if she doesn't?"

"If she's grasping or seductive and makes it tough for him, causing the boy to choose between his father and her, he will have problems. We often see in men a readiness to find parallels of their mothers' behavior in the women they become involved with. Real or imagined."

For a younger generation of women, raised on a you-can-have-it-all philosophy—career, man, marriage, children—where nurturing is only one of a laundry list of desirable female attributes, things will doubtless be different. But for hundreds of years, teaching women to be nurturing and maternal was as essential to their education as learning their ABC's. For these women, the Janets, this maternal quality often spills over into their responses to husbands and friends, as well as to their children. In fact, as Dr. Gleckel emphasizes, men often encourage their wives to feed and nurture the little boys they harbor inside their adult exteriors. At midlife, this nurturing woman may, in a man's mind, even *look* more maternal. This is a toxic combination of circumstances, which often leads to trouble, Jennifer trouble.

The little girl doesn't have this problem. She doesn't have to reject her mother and identify with her father in order to separate and forge new relationships with men. Most women, far from perceiving in their aging husbands shadows of their fathers, feel safe and protected, and aren't as psychologically threatened as men are by their aging wives.

Pursuing Freud's thinking, contemporary psychologists suggest how unconscious forces may propel a man like Sam Toffler to a Jennifer. Dr. Rita Ransohoff, author of *Venus Over Forty,* observes that the boy faces very specific dangers on his road to independence. When a boy infant is angry at his mother, he doesn't feel safe with those intense emotions. He may deny them and split those feelings off. He now has two visions of his mother: the good mother–fairy godmother alternates with the bad mother, who may have denied him gratification or who has angered him by the very fact that he is dependent on her.

But it doesn't end there. As a boy matures, his Oedipal wishes in relation to his mother are reawakened. If he retains negative emotional feelings toward his mother, he may fall back on that early defense, splitting. Then the picture of the good and bad mother reappears; women can be overidealized or an attitude of distrust and misogyny can take over.

Sometimes there can be a permanent split in a man's fantasies. Then, according to Dr. Ransohoff, "He will look up to his wife as a pure, good, asexual creature, and only be able to find sexual freedom outside his marriage, with bad women."

The major difference between a young boy's and girl's development, and the one that will have an "inescapable effect on the boy's fantasy life," Dr. Ransohoff describes this way: "He is borne by a woman . . . and emerged from the birth canal, and although the vagina will later become the goal of his sex desires, fantasies about that dark, mysterious place that so attracts him may remain as one source of his ambivalence toward women, ambivalence which finds ready reinforcement in our culture in the aversive myths about mature women."

To many middle-aged men, a Jennifer is a fantasy and remains just that, a fantasy. To others, she is a fantasy he is compelled to live out. According to Dr. Ransohoff, "A little boy must come to terms with sexual fantasies in relation to his mother, who is wonderfully appealing, so he represses these thoughts and idealizes the mother, and she becomes the good asexual fairy godmother or the pure and virginal mother of Jesus Christ."

One male fantasy specifically involves a Jennifer. Sometimes a man identifies with his mother's role and wants to play out that fantasy. Then he wants his wife to be a baby; he will be the good mother. "As in Pygmalion, he educates, trains, creates her . . . and like a mother, he identifies with her perfection, as does a mother and a child."

But most men do not, I think, want to be a mother to their Jennifer. Rather it's a question of wanting a woman who does not remind him of his mother at all. As Dr. Gleckel observed, "A Jennifer serves a double purpose: She's further away from mother, further away from death."

But where did this idea begin? I turned to the heavens; for in that pantheon where the gods and goddesses met and mated, there might be clues, seeds of attitudes that might still be reflected in twentieth-century affairs of the heart.

To my surprise, I found not seeds, not buds, but convictions in full bloom, which are still flowering today in the minds of men like Sam Toffler, as well as informing many other men's attitudes about Jennifers. Classicist Sarah Pomeroy, in her book *Goddesses, Whores, Wives, and Slaves,* examines the lives of women in ancient times. She writes that goddesses were expected to have sexual relations only with males of similar rank, other gods. But the gods were allowed to enjoy females of lower or mortal state.

Taking another cue from the gods, Dr. Pomeroy says that just as goddesses were given distinct attributes, Greek mortals were prompted to compartmentalize as well. This led to men's having an either/or attitude toward women. Different charms were to be found in different women. A woman was either Minerva or Aphrodite, brainy or beautiful, Diana or Hera, hunter or wife, *and* most important, either blessed with youthful sexuality or cursed with desexualized motherliness.

In the fourth century B.C., Demosthenes described the either/or situation best: "We have mistresses for our enjoyment, concubines to serve our person, and wives for bearing legitimate offspring." Perhaps that is what is meant when they say Greece is the cradle of Western civilization.

Somehow this either/or attitude didn't work the other way around. For thousands of years, women have believed, as an article of faith, that one mortal man could (and should) be all things: fatherly and sexual; intelligent and handsome; lover and husband; older but sexually appealing. And for just as many years, men have expected that of themselves. Only in recent years have men—sometimes at the urging of women—begun to free themselves from this burden inherited from the gods.

Dr. Pomeroy believes that the Greek view of women has survived for generations: "Psychoanalytic criticism of classical literature suggests that fear of mature female sexuality means these men could feel secure only with a virgin. This idea is very tantalizing and applicable to Greek male attitudes towards *mortal* women themselves. A fully realized female tends to engender anxiety in the insecure male; unable to cope with a multiplicity of powers united in one female . . . virginal females are considered helpful, while sexually mature women are destructive and evil."

The Greeks, like the Hebrews, believed that young virgins were elixirs for the mind and body. As we've seen, modern men have embellished on this dominant theme, adapting it to express in a twentieth-century way feelings about their mature wives as contrasted with the kinds of emotions engendered by a Jennifer.

For centuries, both history and literature reflect a polarity of thinking on the idea of older men consorting with younger women. During some periods it was considered laughable, improbable, fodder for the joke and limerick mill—the jokes made frequently at the older man's expense. But during the "golden age" of Greece, there was no polarity. Homosexual or heterosexual, to the Greeks youthful beauty was everything.

To appreciate the intensity of feeling Greek writers had about the raptures of youth and the related horrors of aging, it is important to note that according to Dr. Pomeroy the average woman of ancient Greece died at 36.2 years and men at 45. Death in childbirth was a major cause of early mortality of many Athenian women. Aristotle advised that the optimum age for marriage was eighteen for a woman, thirty-seven for a man. In fact, Athenian women married much younger, usually at about fourteen. The law mandated that the bride be a virgin, and the belief that young girls were lustful made early marriage desirable.

Aristotle didn't suggest early marriage for women for the reason Lee Kalder offered—that men are most attracted to fertile women. As Marilyn French writes, "He taught that male semen was the vital force that gave form to the inert matter of female menstrual blood. For centuries men continued to believe they were the true parent. The female's contribution to the child (beyond the houseroom she gave it and the nutrients her body fed it) came much later. The mammalian egg was not observed until 1827."

Unlike the Hebrews, Greek men were allowed only one legal wife, although they could have as many concubines as they could afford. Since women weren't offered any kind of formal education, their primary role was one of bearing children and running the household. Dr. Bernard Murstein, an expert on the history of marriage, concludes that "considering the insignificant role allotted to the Greek wife, it should come as no surprise that Greek husbands looked for escape in the arms of other women, and created an elaborate hierarchy of mistresses to fill the void.

"To become a high-class courtesan was actually one of the few occupations open to a woman at this time. Unlike her married sister, she was sexually exciting, better educated . . . and steeped in all the social graces." One poet observed there were many shrines to the courtesans, "but in all of Greece there was not one dedicated to the Greek wife."

It is Aristophanes who tells it like it was in ancient Greece, as far as women were concerned. In *Lysistrata,* the heroine is asked, "Does not a man age?" Lysistrata responds in words that women of all generations can appreciate:

> Not as a woman grows withered, grows he.
> He, when returned from the war, though gray-bearded,
> yet if he wishes can choose out a wife.
> But she has no solace save peering for omens,
> wretched and lonely the rest of her life.
> A woman's time is short.

That's it, rather simply—a woman's time is short. Classical scholars believe that Aristophanes was referring to both the early death rate of women and the belief that women lost their sexual attractiveness at an early age. He was merely agreeing with Euripides, who said, "A man's strength endures, but the bloom of beauty quickly leaves the woman."

Modern women may lose the bloom, but in recent times we have cultivated other strengths. Without the bloom of youth we are still people, still have strengths and assets. But that is now, and in ancient Greece women of *any* age were viewed as inferior to men, pieces of property that could be bought and sold. Aging women were often the targets of ridicule, described as "grotesque old hags, or insatiable nymphomaniacs chasing after desirable young men."

In another play, *Ecclesiazusae,* Aristophanes has a young woman aim these angry words at an aging female character known as the "hag":

> You . . . you've filled your face's cracks with white
> Where time has roughly hacked,
> Until you look a plaster corpse,
> Death's whore, in fact.

The hag, who is in competition with the young maiden for the attention of a male lover, gives this rather graphic response:

> . . . And if a lover ever you take
> I hope he's frigid as a snake,

Only a snake that you can't wake,
Though stroked and tossed that way and this,
A boneless snake that you can't wake,
Not even with the longest kiss.

Today, a woman's talent, intelligence, money, and status can be as seductive to some men as the bloom of youth is to others. While this can sometimes lead to other problems, in a way we have made enormous progress. Would the Greeks have recognized older women who have the generosity of spirit of Mother Teresa or Eleanor Roosevelt, the grace of Martha Graham, the talent of Louise Nevelson or Grandma Moses?

Probably not. The Greeks didn't merely extol the beauty of youth; they were repelled by how aging transforms a woman. As in this lament to the fading of a woman's charms:

"Before she was lovely skinned, spring breasted, fine ankled, fine lengthed, fine browed, fine locked, but she has been changed by time and old age and white hairs, and now none of her has even a dream of what it was before . . . not even an ape grown old has such a face."

Alexander Russell, a contemporary writer who lives in Tampa, was, of all the men I spoke to, the closest to the Greeks in his ferocious antipathy to mature woman and his adoration of young flesh.

"I can go all night," he said, smiling. "It's too hard to turn on a woman of, say, forty-five. Who wants to make love to a woman who looks like the inside of an overcoat, pockets flapping below her stomach. But ah, that delicious wiggling at the end of my stick when a young woman comes—it's magic, magic."

Most modern men do not share Alexander Russell's feelings, at least not to that degree. In fact, many men are fully aware that midlife women are at the peak of their sexual responsiveness, and as one man told me, "An older woman knows what sex is about much more than a Jennifer, who's just figuring out how the whole thing works."

Even in ancient times there were occasional exceptions. The

Roman poet Juvenal was wise to the cynical way his fellow Romans treated their aging wives:

"You'll find he loves the beauty, not the wife; let but a wrinkle on her forehead rise and time obscure the lustre of her eyes . . . and you shall hear [him] say pack up your trumpery, madam, and away . . . you give offense."

Ovid, in a rare and uncharacteristic mood, could write: "What does youth know? Look for a mature woman, not a slip of a girl."

Still these are clearly dissenting opinions. Because of their low status (most of them could not read or write), the women of ancient Greece left us little data—poems or diaries of their own—that would tell us how they reacted to the scorn that came their way as they aged. But Professor Amy Richlin, who has studied the sexual attitudes of men and women in ancient times, concludes that living in a society that married most women off at an extremely young age and "demanded marital fidelity, while men usually had access to prostitutes and slaves of either sex," probably all a respectable married woman could do was produce and raise her children and know that her sexual activity would be restricted to her youthful years.

For the Greeks, a Jennifer was often a concubine, who, offering entertainment and sexual refreshment, was one of the escape hatches available to Greek men wishing to avoid dreary marriages and the horrors of wives losing the bloom of youth. Frequently the Jennifers were Jeffreys, as we'll see in a later chapter exploring Jennifer Fever in the homosexual world.

These, then, are some of the seeds planted by the ancients. Some have died a natural death, blown away by the winds of time and the storms of historical change. Others, as we will observe, are still blossoming today.

The Romans embellished the major themes set down by the Greeks and Hebrews. For example, unlike the Greeks, a Roman man was officially allowed either a wife or a concubine; he could not have both simultaneously. Yet they shared the Greek abhorrence for aging women, and divorce was made easy. The Romans added something else:

"That the Romans appear sensual in comparison to the Christians is hardly startling. Roman religion, unlike that of the Christians . . . did not denigrate sex or the body. Sex was viewed as a natural and interesting experience which the gods endorsed strongly."

"Not even an ape grown old has such a face." "Death's whore." These ancient attitudes make the double standard of aging in our century seem positively benign. How can you compare a few wrinkles, ripples of cellulite, and shots of gray in your hair with being told, as Horace told the women of Rome, that an old woman "smells like an octopus or a goat, is a creature lusting in her grave"?

As I read the ancient documents, I could not help but see their reflections in our culture—reflections admittedly with a lower decibel count, veiled by a different vocabulary, and altered by the realities of our increased age span, scientific knowledge, medical advances, and social experience.

Still the long shadow of Horace and Aristophanes can be detected in television commercials grimly warning women to use this product to add youth to their skin or hair, that scent to add sensuality to their being.

Those ancient blossoms of attitudes have in our time formed hybrids, and men, too, are being urged to buy one product to look youthful, another to appear sexy. Today's women may wonder if modern men, who are now encouraged to surrender godlike prerogatives, who are increasingly being urged to admit their mortal frailties and share their human vulnerabilities, will develop a new appreciation for women who aren't as beautiful as Aphrodite, as swift as Diana.

And what about the men who are of a generation for which admitting mortal frailties is just too hard, who feel it's too tough and too late to change, and still labor under the conviction that they have to be Zeus, Mars, and Apollo all at once? Or the men whose cultural, family, or religious backgrounds make it necessary for them to view women only in an either/or fashion? For them, does the shadow of Aristophanes and King David remain as clear, and the echo of Euripides and Horace keep reverberating as sharp as ever?

7

"Oh, Johnny, You Park So Good"

For some men a Jennifer remains a private fantasy, stashed safely away in their imagination, appearing in an occasional dream. But for the man compelled to act on the fantasy, what was it a Jennifer offered, which was so undeniably, inescapably irresistible, and other women, older women, didn't?

I began this search while gazing at a Jennifer—taking in her sleek, finely honed body, all of her brimming with youthful radiance. Now the combined voices of the men I had interviewed made me look at her again, through a new prism, their very particular twentieth-century-male prism.

I was struck by the realization that it was the ironic combination of a Jennifer's obvious fertility, and at the same time her lack of motherliness, that mattered to men as much as her lack of wrinkles and cellulite. But I knew there had to be more. Lots more.

A phone call from my friend Jane Richmond led me to more. Jane returned from a weekend in Maine, and before she had unpacked, she called to report the following story: A well-known novelist, whom I will call John, recently married a woman twenty-two years his junior. Jane and her date were in the back seat as they drove to a party on a Sunday afternoon. As John pulled the car into the circular driveway of a rambling country house, the young wife touched her husband's hand and, with an expression of pleasure tinged with awe, exclaimed, "Oh, Johnny, you park so good!"

Jane laughed and I laughed, and while we both knew we could exhibit that kind of admiration for things men say, the way they think, and a hundred other feats they perform with such style and grace, we wondered if we could demonstrate that kind of admiration for the rather simple act of parking in a driveway.

Later I thought of my older lover. He had fought in North Africa—the same North Africa where Humphrey Bogart had seen combat in a movie whose name is lost in my memory. My lover thrilled me with his war stories; he was so knowing, so seasoned, so worldly. And when he ordered wine, our favorite was Sancerre. The way he said it—Sahnnnnn Saihrrr: it was as if he had planted the grapes himself in the vineyards on the Loire. When we discussed writing, he would talk of John O'Hara's dialogue, A. J. Liebling's wit, Flaubert's search for *le mot juste.* And it was as if he had been on a first-name basis with all of them—Bogie, the vintner, John, A. J., and Gustave. I'm sure I cooed adoringly, and of course my adoring must have made him adore me, making me adore him more, making him adore . . .

Today I wonder how his wife or any woman who deals with the day-in-day-outness of her husband and their life together can possibly coo about anything as I did. I also remember I did not think of her then. But that is another tale.

It seems that in the early stages—in the offices, planes, board meetings, conventions, and restaurants where late-night work sessions somehow get transformed into something more, or in the cool blue-gray mist, in the early-morning quiet, where through branches of trees and along dusty jogging paths the day's first Jennifer-spotting takes place—adoration is high on the list of essential ingredients that bind a man to a Jennifer.

Listen to Greg Fox:

"My wife and I were cast precisely in the same mold. We lived out the American script. She was a girl who sat behind me in history class in Kentucky. I went off to war, and when I came back we were married immediately. So we didn't really know each other. I think at that time we weren't capable of knowing each other in a way that wasn't superficial, compared to people today. However, it worked out pretty well; the script was sufficient for all of our needs."

Greg Fox is an insurance executive from Hartford, Connecticut.

Soft-spoken, fair-skinned, he is attractive in a gentle, non-macho way. He told me he was eager to be interviewed because at sixty-five he was unmarried and there were still things he wanted to discover about his failed marriage and his experiences with Jennifers, which led to his divorce.

"We did all the usual things," he explained, "the house in the suburbs, the three children, the career moves. If we had been just a bit more aware, if we had gone to marriage counseling for a few years, it's possible we could have sustained the marriage."

Ten years younger than Greg Fox, Bert Cooney, a rancher from Phoenix, is now married to a thirty-year-old woman. He sounds a similar note. "I was married for eighteen years—got married at twenty-five, a few months after I got home from Korea. I was lonely and vulnerable, and everybody else was getting married, so I got married. That marriage was just a lot of mistakes. With perfect hindsight, I can say no one should be married before he's thirty."

I heard it again and again.

The men returned from the war—from Anzio or Normandy, Guadalcanal or Okinawa, and some years later from Korea. Battle fatigued but victorious, they had survived bullets and bombs, shrapnel, air raids, and imprisonment, and they poured out of troop ships and planes. At last they had come home. Pinching themselves at the miracle that they had survived, they were desperate to catch up with their lives. Still in their early twenties, they had seen too much of death. They were alive and hungry for life.

Each man knew he needed to move fast to regain his step on the ladder; now it was *his* time, *his* crack at a piece of that big fat American pie.

He had stayed alive nurtured by a dream, the very specific American dream. For years that dream had been nourished by pictures tacked to barracks walls or plastered to the nose of a bomber— pictures of Betty Grable or Rita Hayworth—or whoever was that year's hottest female star. Each man had tucked away in a private place—etched in his mind, or stashed in his wallet—a personal version of the popular dream: a picture of a girl, young and dewy, innocent and waiting—the girl he had left behind.

He quickly married her, or if there was no young girl waiting, he soon found one. He had children, fast. He carved out communities of green lawns, spiffy schools, and country clubs from previously useless stretches of land and called them suburbs. He weathered interminable daily train rides that added hours to his days, but knew he was inching his way to a life greater than any he had ever dreamed of, a life that outshone those on the gleaming *Life* magazine covers he had looked at in foxholes and trenches.

Hundreds of thousands of them fell into domestic lockstep, pursuing the dream, never imagining they would find themselves engaged in another war—one that often evoked contempt rather than cheers, a war for which they would have *less* preparation, and *less* patriotic support, than they had for the wars they fought twenty-five years before. Undeclared, it was precipitated by the death of a parent or colleague, or a bout of high blood pressure; or it was provoked by the marriage of a daughter, or by losing a job they'd had their eyes on to a younger man. Whatever the cause, it was a war waged within themselves, the war of middle age.

Men who hadn't fought in the wars abroad also found themselves engaged in the war at home. Men's battles in the undeclared wars of middle age have interested writers of recent years as much as their battles in wars abroad. In the movie *Network,* Paddy Chayefsky's hero, Max, memorably portrayed by William Holden, plainly states the issues involved in these domestic confrontations:

"I'm beginning to get scared shitless. It's all suddenly closer to the end than the beginning, and death is suddenly a perceptible thing with definable features. . . . You've got a man going through primal doubts and you've got to cope with it."

Or as Bert Cooney reflected, "After attending the funeral of two friends in two weeks, I had the terrible feeling they were calling up my class."

Each man describes it in different ways. The past is receding more and more into foggy memories; the future looms more as an end than a beginning. But for men engaged in the struggle, one memory remains transcendently clear—the one of themselves as unburdened young men, facing limitless time in which to fill their shining aspirations, untarnished by the cruel deficiencies of life. A distant past and a shrinking future leave them only with an intense, insistent, urgent *present.*

Just as men arriving from overseas felt it was *their* time at last, so many of the men I spoke with believed that at forty-five or fifty-five or sixty, it was *their* last crack—or their first crack at doing something for themselves.

Psychotherapist Mara Gleckel summed up how many men of this generation feel: "He says to himself, 'OK, I've done it all, made some money, raised 2.5 kids, reached about as far as I'm going to get at work, because the younger generation's coming and they're beating down the door. And I'm scared.' "

"And their wives?" I asked.

" 'Occasionally it's a madonna complex,' " Dr. Gleckel continued, playing the part of the middle-aged man. " 'Wives are often mothers and aren't supposed to be sexual. And young women are. Maybe it's just that wives can't *remain* sexual. Anyway, my wife is more maternal toward me. But she seems happy, coming and going on her own. She doesn't sympathize like she used to when I complain about problems at the office. I don't even have her at home anymore to hear my gripes. I may even have a woman superior at the office telling me what to do. Another mother.

" 'I've got this little hernia thing, and an ugly varicose vein is throbbing in my leg. Everybody's dying, and I'm scared. I've done all I can, yet I'm disappointed. I hate the idea of dying disappointed.' "

"What about their children?" I asked. "Don't they receive pleasure from them?"

Dr. Gleckel smiled and shook her head. "Unfortunately, not always. The guy thinks, 'My 2.5 kids don't think I'm so great. In fact, they don't like some things about me at all. They say I'm money hungry or that I wasn't there for them. I can't even offer advice without their arguing that I'm criticizing them. Now *they're* getting divorces. Even my kids are disappointments.

" 'I'm hurting, lonely. Life didn't turn out to be what it was supposed to be; yet I did everything I was supposed to do. I went to *that* college because Dad wanted me to, law school because it was respectable—now what do I do? I've suppressed and denied *my* impulses, *my* desires, for as far back as I can remember—I gotta do something different.' "

" 'What's left for me?' " Dr. Gleckel asked. " 'I've got to follow *my* desires, start living for me. I can't depend on these other people to please me. *I'm* going to please me, I'm going to find someone who adores me. And why shouldn't she adore me?' "

Few of the men I interviewed acknowledged that they chose a Jennifer for sexual reasons or because they wanted to feel young. And even fewer Jennifers told me they were attracted to an older man for his money, power, or status. One thing that does draw a man to a Jennifer is his need to receive from her, and her capacity to bestow, adoration.

According to the men, many of whom were still married when they met younger women, adoration at this particular time in their lives is an emotional life raft.

Some men, like sixty-five-year-old Greg Fox, were unable to tell their wives all that was happening inside them—of this intense hunger for adoration, this desire for uncritical love. Greg Fox shook his head, closed his tired eyes for a moment, and began softly: "I wish I had been more honest with her," he said. "I simply couldn't do it. I don't know to this day, fifteen years later, whether she even suspected. One fears that the wife always knows or is told. I honestly don't know. I imagine a few years later our daughters must have spoken to her and she wasn't terribly angry, but we never had anything like a very honest discussion about it.

"I was forty-eight, and it's fair to say I was terribly stressed out from the business angle, and the character of my wife was such that she couldn't be of much help to me. My business was in trouble, I wasn't feeling well—the heart attack was only a year away—and she was terribly frightened. I didn't feel I was getting the support I needed. I think it's fair to say that I wasn't.

"And when this exquisite young woman in my office fell madly in love with me, it was something like a support. I was astounded. I didn't know how to handle it, didn't know what to do, but yes, it was good for the ego."

Greg paused as if he was considering how to continue, then,

flashing a wide smile, he proceeded. "She adored me, she absolutely adored me—I think the first time she laid eyes on me, as near as I could tell. And I was hardly aware she existed; she was somebody to type my letters and get coffee for me. From her standpoint I must have been quite awkwardly, stubbornly dense. After a while I began to be aware of these big eyes following me and this person attending to my every wish. I became avuncular, understanding, fatherly, even grandfatherly. I told her and myself this was a passing phase, that we had to wait it out with as much tolerance and understanding as we could muster. She wouldn't hear of it."

Raoul Felder took a less sentimental view of the adoration factor. Considered one of New York's most successful divorce lawyers, Felder has an office filled with valuable paintings and sculpture—trophies of his success in the divorce courts, where the war between men and wives who are left for Jennifers is waged.

"Jennifers are very good psychologists," he said dryly. "They have the same touch Hitler had. They tell people what they want to hear: 'You're the master race, you lost the First World War because you were betrayed, the Jews did it.' So Jennifers tell these men, 'You've got the look of eagles.' They stroke the imaginary hairs on their bald heads, and the men go for it.

"I'm not knocking Jennifer," he explained. "She's OK if you accept her for what she is. But I think all the toys aren't in the attic if you get seriously involved with her. If you're screwed up and you have to have everyone see you with her on your arm, you're a schmuck. If you're intelligent, you can handle Jennifers."

I repressed a smile and tried to find out what that intelligent way was, but Raoul Felder had another thought. "There's a line in an old movie in which a man says if he had his choice between having a woman in private and nobody knowing, and not having her but everyone thinking he had her, he would pick the latter. A man who leaves his wife for a youth injection is a schmuck. There has to be a narrowness of intellect there, some tunnel vision."

Jennifers and ex-Jennifers might not appreciate Felder's tough assessment of them, but those I talked to agreed that adoration played a key role in their love affairs with older men.

Sally Bressack, now forty-seven, met her lover, who is twenty-five years her senior, at a multinational corporate office in San Francisco twenty years ago. And for twenty years she's waited for him to leave his wife. Their relationship is less intense than it was, and Sally looked back to the beginning with a certain degree of disappointment and detachment. "You grow up and you have many men in your life, so I knew he wasn't the greatest lover. But it didn't matter; we couldn't wait to be together. We had a chemistry that had nothing to do with anything, an electricity between two people. Intensity, a lot of it, pure chemistry. It was so strong we couldn't ignore it. People talked about us before anything had happened.

"I adored him, *adored* him," she recalled wistfully. "Everybody needs a positive adoring person. Everybody needs somebody other than his dog to absolutely worship him. I was the best mirror he ever had. I gave him unquestioning love and adoration."

"It goes without saying," said sixty-two-year-old Lee Kalder, "for a guy married to a woman haranguing him blah blah blah, and some pussycat comes along and says, 'You're wonderful; I've been out with all those callow boys, and you're just marvelous.' Does that look better? Boy, does that look better!"

Elizabeth Rinaldi at forty is a raging beauty, with thick black hair, perfect alabaster skin. She says she was involved for fifteen years with a married man twenty years older. "I did wonders for his ego," she said, with modesty rather than braggadocio. "I admired him so he became a spring lamb, he had this great renewed surge of energy. Even his business improved."

For John Gray, of Midland, Michigan, "It's a turbulent time for a man; you're facing emotions you've never faced before, feeling things you've never felt in your life. You feel clumsy with all these new things brewing inside you. A young woman is a safe place."

Far from finding safe haven, Greg Fox says, at first the adoring young woman in his office created storm signals of her own.

"Finally I called her psychiatrist and set up a date. I'd never been in therapy; it was the first time I'd ever talked to anybody like this—it was a little bit unnerving. I asked, 'What am I to do? You know this young woman better than I do. I don't want to hurt her, but this aberration she has for me is upsetting. I could find her another job or fire her. What do you suggest?'

"And the shrink said, 'Why are you here?'

"I said, 'I'm afraid this young woman is going to get hurt, and I don't want that to happen.'

"Then he asked this stupendous question," Greg Fox recalled with a pained expression. " 'Do you always hurt the one you love?'

"I didn't know how to handle that. I said no. Anyhow, that didn't help, and I began to respond to her. She was absolutely gorgeously compliant; she was my slave. It really was getting out of hand. I was losing control."

Women I spoke to who had been left by husbands or lovers for younger women were not unaware of the power of the almost mystical adoration a Jennifer offers a man.

Joanna Ansen's marriage of thirty-five years ended when her husband fell in love with a young woman who worked in his law firm. Unlike the majority of women, Joanna, a successful artist, was not faced with serious financial problems after the divorce. Observing her husband's remarriage to a woman the same age as their daughter, Joanna developed some sharp observations on men, Jennifers, and adoration.

"The greatest aphrodisiac is not oysters," Joanna said with a smile. "It is a worshiper. A worshiper is irresistible. Men do all their brilliance during the day. They want to come home and not have to deal with anything, not have to think. They want to have someone who is more pliant."

She pointed with long, graceful fingers to her paintings and sculptures, which were on display in her Denver studio, testimony to her considerable accomplishments, and continued, with a brittle laugh. "I used to think being talented, bright, and successful was an asset. Women of my generation are caught in the be-all mode: Be all the things you can. But it's really an eagle's nest. Men don't really want that—at least not American men. European men are different, I think. If you want your equal in a man, you're not what they want. If you're equal, they think you'll de-ball them.

"You hear the old chestnut that men leave their wives for someone who understands them. That's bullshit. They leave their wives because their wives understand them *too well.*" Then, with a wink and a sly smile, she concluded, "And understanding does not make anyone an adorer."

Jennifers are not always the pliant, unthinking creatures that many women, like Joanna, think they are. Bill Zabel is an attorney who specializes in premarital contracts. He meets a number of mid-life men and younger women, because prenuptial agreements are a realistic, however unromantic, part of Jennifer territory. He says a romantic prenuptial agreement is an oxymoron. His office in his large New York law firm offers a sweeping view of the city. A warm, soft-spoken man, he smiled when I asked why he thinks middle-aged men are drawn to Jennifers.

"Go find a thirty-five-year-old investment banker at Salomon Brothers and compare her to a fifty-five-year-old woman who has never worked and doesn't know what a leveraged buy-out is, or, often, even care what it might be. Older men can talk to these younger women. They're more interesting.

"The trouble is that many forty- and fifty-year-old women grew up in a generation where they didn't have the opportunities women have today," Bill Zabel explained, "except for a few aberrations. It's not their fault. They're not as independent and productive as so many young women are today; but they didn't have the chance to develop that way."

He paused, smiled, and then, shifting gears, supported to some extent Joanna Ansen's opinions. "But that's only part of the picture. Many of the men I see don't pick young professional women; they pick what my son's generation refers to as airheads—beautiful but airheads. The sexual and psychological reasons are beyond my expertise."

But the Jennifers aren't just ditzes or bimbos. Not just the blowsy blondes of black-and-white B movies of thirty years ago. Not anymore. Yes, some of them may not do anything. Sometimes the Jennifers as well as the Janets may be what songwriter Sammy Cahn calls "women of fortune." With all the gains of women's liberation, there are still Jennifers on the prowl, seeking an older man as a passport, a ticket to a fast lane, a richer life, social access, security, prestige.

But many Jennifers are on the prowl for something more—and so are Janets. Today they are doctors and lawyers, biologists and secretaries, who have their *own* passport, can afford their *own* ticket. The "something more" that women are seeking is drastically changing men's lives. And for men gripped by an acute case of Jennifer Fever, the justifications, the rationalizations, can all be explained in one word: Entitlement.

8

Now It's My Turn

Adultery and divorce are as old as the Bible. But I wondered about the new elements in the atmosphere that might create a fertile environment for Jennifer Fever to flourish.

What *is* new today is that the sexual liberation movements of the sixties and seventies, the struggle for economic parity of the eighties, and the "me-ism" of recent years have had an enormous effect on all of us, including the members of the Jennifer triangle.

Taboos are quickly disappearing, one after another. Yesterday's whispers, what once were private horrors, are now matters of public concern. Child abuse and incest, unacknowledged by parents of a generation ago, are now openly examined in the press, discussed in the classroom, the subject for television movies.

In this atmosphere of psychological freedom, we search for moral values and a personal ethic at a time when religion, for many of us, seems to have fewer and fewer answers. The dreadful specter of the Bomb reminds us daily of our fragility. We read about the horrors of a nuclear winter, and while it reads like science fiction, we are chilled to learn it is *our* planet, *our* future, the scientists are describing. Some of us seek warmth in drugs or money, in sex, acquisitions, or personal fulfillment.

Many of today's young working women maintain that an affair with a married, older lover is just the thing; it suits their needs, because such a relationship involves a minimal commitment of time and emotional energy. They say this kind of relationship doesn't drain their energies, doesn't interfere with their careers.

But many Jennifers believe that is a bloodless approach, a sad reflection of the exploitive way men have used women for years. While they may assume positions of power, taking on culturally defined masculine roles in their work, some young women claim that in their private lives they aren't interested in replicating the male model. Nor are they willing to be stashed away for once-a-week liaisons. Brandishing American Express cards and strong egos, if they don't insist on playing Jack and Jill with the men in their lives, they are also not content to play Back Street, in some hidden, furtive affair. They are demanding to have more time with their lovers, even demanding that the men leave their wives.

Men, too, are being driven by the winds of change. Based on my own interviews and the reports of psychologists and marriage counselors, men feel less of an obligation to stay in a marriage than they did ten or twenty years ago. If in the past many men were willing to settle for what Philip Roth calls "daily insurrections," stolen moments with another woman to lighten the tedium of their daily round, today many men are less inclined to do so. Settling is something their fathers and grandfathers did, back in those dark days before men had a choice, before "I want mine now" became the national mantra, before Christopher Lasch labeled our society the "Culture of Narcissism."

Some women attribute this to postliberation backlash, a sense of narcissistic entitlement, which says in effect, "You've had your liberation; now it's my turn." Since more and more wives are now working, their husbands, believing the wives are less economically dependent on them, feel less of a sense of financial responsibility or emotional obligation than men did ten or twenty years ago.

Iris Moldine, an editor on a women's magazine, described the male sense of entitlement this way: "They're getting even, that's all, that's the main reason you see all these older guys with younger women. We've made demands, we've frightened them, they're angry. It's retribution, plain and simple."

Mara Gleckel was most eager to talk about the external forces contributing to Jennifer Fever, as well as the internal, subconscious factors, which are her specialty.

We were having coffee during a short break between patients. She grabbed a copy of the *New York Times* and handed it to me, declaring, "It's in the air everywhere. We even have a President in a second marriage who has very strained and distant relationships with his children. It's been on television, in the papers, and no one thinks less of Reagan, no one castigates him for being a distant father and grandfather. Remember what happened to Adlai Stevenson, how shocking it was for a divorced man to even consider running for the presidency?"

"So you think Jennifer Fever has as much to do with sociology as psychology?" I asked.

"Of course," Dr. Gleckel replied. "In addition to all the psychological explanations, you have to recognize the external factors. There are young, attractive, potentially adoring women at the office, at the health club, everywhere. Many men looking at their own lives, and looking at the world around them, feel they're entitled to another chance too. Why work at a first marriage? Why not start over?"

If the Jennifers don't want to play the "other woman" in Back Street, the Janets don't want to play the unknowing wife, stashed away at home while their husbands, secretly or not so secretly, are out enjoying the pleasures of a Jennifer. They, too, are less interested in settling. In the past, many married women who suspected a Jennifer in their husbands' lives would have averted their eyes, not wanting to know. Today many more seem unwilling to stay locked in a marriage based on denial.

Molly Rothberg's husband was having an affair for fifteen years; and for fourteen years Molly knew. She never told her husband she was aware of his affair with a secretary until years later. At fifty-eight, Molly's face is drained of color, her eyes look sad, and when she smiles, it is a sad smile, as though part of her is always thinking of past regrets, desperate to find signs of hope in the future.

"When there is a divorce, there's always someone in the wings, but these men have made life so difficult, so miserable for their wives, the wives get the hell out. In my case, I was forced into wanting a divorce. There was no love, no affection, and finally I felt, 'What do I need you for? Go.'

"My husband was forty-seven, he was having a midlife crisis, and had been having it for ten years." Molly's attempt at a smile was weak and strained, then she recalled, "I knew about the affair, but I didn't want to know. I wasn't ready to do anything because I had small children. I waited for the youngest to be seventeen, then I acted."

Some men told me they were aware that their wives, like Molly Rothberg, were willing to look the other way. Rex Lawrence, now fifty-nine, is married to Lynn, a thirty-year-old woman he met while still married to his wife of eighteen years. A short, slender man, intense and driven, he bubbles with enthusiasm and energy—a perfect candidate for a Type A personality. I asked if when he met Lynn his marriage was in trouble.

"You'd have to define trouble. Neither of us wanted to see we weren't suited for each other. When we were in our early twenties, I was just back from overseas." He paused to light his pipe, and then, with a smile of contentment, continued his story. "After we were married, we were always together. I have to travel a great deal in my work, and she traveled with me. But after we had kids, she couldn't leave them. This was a time when you had to feed the child on demand. After the birth of our second child, I was unfaithful for the first time."

"Was it with a younger woman?" I asked.

"At that time, in the series of liaisons I had, the age of the woman didn't matter. I thought it was perfect then, but looking back, it was a disaster. I see there's an emotional arrested development when it comes to thinking about women like that, something stagnated."

He slouched back in his chair, drew on his pipe, and then recalled, "If I said I had to work late, she'd say, 'Don't come all the way home from the city; you'll be tired.' Unconsciously she was afraid she would discover that I was having an affair, or that I would leave her, or that we were growing apart. She encouraged me to stay away and never asked why.

"So many men tell me their wives know nothing about their other women, and I say they're full of it. My wife was so disbelieving, so hypnotized. You know the emperor's clothes," he said with a smile. "If you want to believe, you believe. She knew, but she didn't know. She was a perfect wife—she knew her husband wouldn't see other women."

But Molly Rothberg *did* know—who the other woman was, what was happening—yet for many years she chose not to act.

"She was twelve years younger, a secretary, not Jewish." She shook her head, frowning. "When they change wives, they want to change everything that reminds them of their first wives, anything that reminds them of their mothers. At the time, it was better to stay married. I had no place to go, I had four young children, no money of my own. But I'm a very strong person, I could take a lot; and I just wasn't ready to do anything. So for years we went our separate ways. It was OK for me too; I didn't demand much.

"After my youngest was old enough"—she shrugged—"I said, 'What's here for me? It can't be worse out there.' He said, 'I'm not going to give you a divorce, not a penny.' And I said, 'If I have to go out and scrub floors, I'm not going to stay with you.' I hated him by that time; he realized I meant business.

"I wish we could take a pill," Molly said with a sigh, "and stay in love, or in like, which I feel is more important sometimes. The passion goes, the love goes; there's got to be, underneath, a comfortableness that stays."

Rex Lawrence made this comment on the subject: "After twenty years, she finally asked me if there was someone else. There was a mutual unwritten law that each would tolerate things without the other minding. If she had had affairs and had pursued other interests, business or a lover, then the unwritten law works and the marriage lasts. But this law was incorrectly founded in our case, because in my wife's case it was based on illusion."

Molly Rothberg had also lived a life based on illusion, knowing of her husband's affair, denying its reality.

"The rules have changed," she said, blinking back her tears. "It's a sad statement. Many years ago, our mothers and grandmothers lived with their husbands and if they were not happy they made the best of it, because nobody was doing anything then. That's what I did for years, I made the best of it. But after a while there was no dignity left, there was nothing left; I had to ask for a divorce. Today

I think men have benefited most from the change. And you can blame the pill a bit too.

"We have to tell young couples the grass is not always greener," Molly observed, "try to make the best of it, short of laying yourself on the floor and having him walk all over you. Men have to know that too."

What many men know is that they want another chance at happiness and believe they are entitled to it. If they feel vindictive, and are leaving their wives because the wives emotionally left them when they stepped out of the shadows and demanded to be treated as peers, or embarked on careers of their own, the sentiment is veiled in words like these from Rex Lawrence: "I think the best marriages are when people know each other very well and know the boundaries and operate within the boundaries. If you can't, and you discover you can find happiness with someone else, then you have to go. You *are* entitled. You have one life; there is no other choice."

Molly Rothberg had been talking to me in my hotel room in Chicago. After buttoning her coat, she started slowly for the door; then, as she wrapped her scarf around her neck, she added this final note: "You know, it costs them a lot to do this. Financially, they have to pay a lot." She looked down at her hands and then heaved another sigh. "They're willing to pay a lot to have this feeling: It must be *some profound feeling.*"

9

Sometimes She Plays the Cello

It *must*, indeed, be a profound feeling. But what made it so profound? Now I realized that the wish to be adored was part of it. Basking in the glow of worshipful attention. Even Freud had said overvaluation was a key element of the attraction between men and women, regardless of their age.

Perhaps there was another glow: Men traveling in the same orbit, breathing the same air, sleeping in the same bed with a woman who radiates the glow of fertility. And then men feeling the quickening of their pulses, their spirits soaring at the very idea that in the middle of their lives, in what could be Dante's dark, savage woods of despair, they find themselves energized by a radiating glow of their own. So they themselves become worshipful of anyone who imparts this special feeling.

Stan Silverstone is in his mid-fifties, and for a psychoanalyst, he has a surprisingly buoyant, outgoing, almost jovial demeanor. "So tell me about Jennifer Fever," he said, ushering me into his office.

I told him I believed that while a woman's youth is important to a man, what a middle-aged man feels or thinks he feels with his Jennifer is a complicated business. "To say it's only because she makes him feel young," I remarked, "is as simplistic and reductionist as saying an alcoholic drinks because it feels good."

He nodded his agreement and settled into his chair, his expression one of bemused thoughtfulness. When he began to speak, it was in slow, measured phrases, as though he wanted to be precise, and possibly because he sensed I wasn't going to be very enthusiastic about what he was going to tell me.

"In addition to all the things you've mentioned—all the things you say men have told you, there's one thing you haven't mentioned. I know of a man who left his wife in the pattern you are talking about and wound up marrying a much younger woman. She was a cellist, and he loved classical music. She also shared his interest in hiking and the outdoors." Dr. Silverstone leaned forward and continued, "But the wife's version of the story, unfortunately, was simply that he married a younger woman. But youth is only one of many factors, and I have no reason to suspect in this case that it was even the dominant factor."

"You seem to find the wife's reaction strange, but I can understand how she feels," I replied.

"I'm sure that's true." He smiled, signaling his understanding. "I don't know why this is so, but in my experience many women, I understand, have become obsessed with certain kinds of categorical thinking. One category is the stereotype of the younger woman. It's a way of answering complex questions with simple answers on an automatic or undifferentiated level. The wife's first thought was that he's involved with a younger woman. *Not* a woman who's accomplished in her field."

"I agree, but the wife doesn't live in a vacuum," I replied. "She's forty-five, and she lives in a society that isn't so terrific in its treatment of older women. To her, it doesn't matter if the younger woman is a brain surgeon or a concert cellist. The way she processes it, she's a *younger* brain surgeon, a *younger* concert cellist."

With a slow smile and a barely perceptible nod of the head, Dr. Silverstone responded: "I know, but by the time we got to it clinically, the wife *only* thought of herself as displaced by a younger woman, *not* by a woman who had interests in common with her husband. Earlier you said that's because of the culture. I can say wherever she got this notion of the younger woman from, it's the chicken and the egg. Surely some men do break up and reestablish themselves with someone who happens to be younger; it's not always *because* she's younger."

He paused, checking to see if I had grasped his point, and then repeated, this time with a hint of irony, "It is a complicated feeling and, Barbara, sometimes she plays the cello."

A hundred interviews later, I discovered that most of the men I spoke with who were involved with Jennifers had devised unique ways of describing this complicated feeling. Unlike Lee Kalder, who emphasized the sexual, reproductive appeal of a Jennifer, most men preferred to talk about the *nonsexual* benefits.

Sixty-two-year-old advertising executive Tom Reilly was talking to me in his San Francisco office. Gray hair tousled, features chiseled, unyielding to the stress of time, he was, as I commented to him, in great physical shape.

"Two hours of racquetball a day," he explained.

Ending a marriage of thirty years, he had just married thirty-one-year-old Melissa. Settling the brownish gaze of his smiling eyes on me, he leaned back, crossed his arms behind him to cradle his head, and remarked:

"Middle-aged women are bleak, pessimistic. It's really a pessimism about life and not just the individual. It's an attitude, having a down feeling about everything. That's because a man, for most women, is the focus of everything. And if they're feeling bleak, then their focus of the world is bleak. Everything is bad—plays are bad, restaurants are bad, music is bad, newspapers are bad, food is bad. You can get killed in airports. It goes on and on.

"And if life is bad," he asked, "why does a man want to have a relationship with someone like that?" Not waiting for an answer, he went on, "His life is bad enough; why would he complicate it with someone who feels like that?"

As one of those middle-aged women Tom Reilly was referring to, I am admittedly prejudiced; still I felt it was an unfair assessment. Most women I know who are my age are far from bleak. As for pessimism, speaking for myself, I veer between pessimism and optimism, depending on the day. I once read that the optimist says, "This is the best of all possible worlds."

And the pessimist says, "Yes, I'm afraid you're right." I can identify with both.

But I was suddenly aware that an incipient nagging pessimism had been aroused in me by Tom Reilly's words, and when I finally responded to his question, I tried not to seem overly defensive. "Perhaps you are generalizing from a couple of sour experiences with middle-aged women," I suggested lightly.

"No, I'm quite sure." His retort was swift and full of confidence. "The best age for a mature man is a woman in her early thirties, because she will have been around long enough to become mature but not long enough to have been injured by life's experiences with men, which would make her cynical and hardened. Whereas if he has a relationship with a woman in her forties or fifties, then she has problems relating to men that have nothing to do with him, which spill over into their relationship."

"And *your* scarring?" I asked, trying to sound innocent. "Your not so wonderful experiences with women? Do they spill over onto her?"

"I may have the same amount of scarring, but *she* doesn't," he added, neatly avoiding my question.

Tom whipped out his wallet and showed me a picture. "It's not that I'm attracted to a younger woman," he said, as we both admired his new bride. "I'm attracted to a woman who is less injured. And yes, I'm attracted to her youthfulness, but it's not her body. It may be that most people are attracted to the most youthful in looks and clothes, but that isn't my reason. Many men I know are attracted to younger women because they are less of a problem. But the immature man is not attracted to maturity in a being; he's attracted to immaturity and is drawn to younger women out of immature needs." Shaking his head disapprovingly, he added, "That is the man's problem, and I feel sorry for him. That's not why I married Melissa."

Seattle architect Len Rogers saw an ad I ran soliciting interviews in a West Coast magazine. In a letter, he described the elements of what I began to call the "scarring factor" this way: "I find women ten years younger congenial, physically more attractive, less set in their ways. They haven't had embittering experiences of terrible marriages, or troublesome children. I like women with verve, gaiety, and love of life. Bad experiences with men don't add to that in a woman."

Tim Lowe, of Erie, Pennsylvania, is forty-five. After he was displaced from his job in a steel mill, he and his wife divorced. Today he is moonlighting as a cabdriver until he completes his studies in computer programming. As he drove me to the airport, he said:

"A woman is dessert, and women's liberation and the equal rights amendment if and when it happens won't change that fact. And who wants to have dessert with someone who's miserable? Time and life make people miserable: The house is too small, the kids have the chicken pox; life is a struggle. For me at the end of a grueling day, that's not what I want in a woman. Who needs it? Who wants it?"

While the "scarring factor" was mentioned by many men, Peter Albanese, a fifty-four-year-old labor negotiator from Muncie, Indiana, said he was interested in a younger woman for totally different reasons. We met through a mutual friend, and over coffee he talked about himself easily, and about his journey to meet the right woman with intensity.

"Since my divorce I have dated many women, ranging in age from twenty-three to fifty. I found that under thirty-five was too young for me in terms of what interested them, emotional maturity, and mental focus. At that age a woman is generally handling issues I'm already through with, and the ones that concern me aren't of much interest to her. But women my own age often suffer from the same disease my ex-wife and I suffered from—mutual dependency."

His bright, dark eyes glinted with light, his angular face, the cut of his jaw, all became animated as he talked. But I was confused. "I thought mutual dependency was what most people wanted," I said.

"I know." He grinned. "So did I. Look, men are emotionally underdeveloped, and they want women to 'handle' the emotional side of life for them; while women want their men to handle life's legitimate demands for them—everything from getting the car fixed to setting long-range goals for their life. I don't mind doing those things, I can really be quite good at it, but a subtle yet important psychological shift occurs when this dependency exists, and it's very damaging for both people.

"A true relationship based on equality, side-by-sideness, is hard to bring off when that manipulation is going on," he explained, "and I don't want that. I worked too hard, suffered too much in my first marriage and divorce to simply fall back in that pattern."

"And tell me about the woman who is in your life now."

"The twenty-six-year-old I'm seeing has never been married, by choice. She has a career. She won't permit a man to handle life for her, yet she is caring and compassionate. She's also interested in the world outside her personal world and pays attention to it."

The signs of his affection were written all over his face, but he was sensitive to the fact that he was talking to an older woman, and went on to explain gently: "I have not generally found this balance of masculine and feminine qualities in the older women I have dated. There was a time when this balance would have deeply threatened me. I began life with the condition that you know well— the macho, 'nothing hurts me,' 'I don't need,' kind of image. I'm Italian, and that was the model I had in my father. It's been a long struggle to beat that legacy," he said, his voice filled with emotion. "I don't ever want to be that kind of man, ever."

For a moment Peter busied himself lighting a cigarette, pouring cream in his coffee, trying to regain his composure. "Why do so many men pick younger women?" he asked suddenly, snapping his lighter. "Because most men are the emotional equal of women twenty years younger than themselves. Men are emotionally children in our culture and are taught to ignore their feelings. Women complain, but they want it that way; they can be threatened if it isn't that way. That's how they control men; it's the only power they have in the classic male-female relationship of your generation and mine."

I wasn't sure I agreed, and I told him, "Most women I know want men who *are* feeling; they have achieved enough control over their own lives, especially if they're in their forties or fifties, that they don't need or want to control the men in their lives."

On this point Peter Albanese was adamant, unbudging, and he answered as if he were stating some basic canon dictating the lives of men and women. "Women manipulate men through men's unconscious feeling nature. All women know it; few men do. Women often do it in the service of their legitimate needs—children, the relationship, home, and survival. If men become more whole, more feminine, this power will be lost. Women know that. If men get in touch with their deep fear of women and begin examining things, women know that can be tough for them.

"I prefer younger women because I prefer not to be manipulated, to be treated as an adult emotionally so I can continue to grow. My girlfriend is the first woman I've ever met who doesn't seem intent on this dependency game. She's twenty-six, but I wish she were thirty-six, because she wants children and I'm having a hard time with that."

The next day, on a plane to Florida, I thought to myself that it wasn't adoration Peter Albanese was after. And certainly not a desire for the woman in his life to be fertile. And for him, the scarring factor that so many men, like Tim Loeb and Tom Reilly, had described so disdainfully hadn't even come up. Nor did it seem that Peter needed a woman to be a tabula rasa on which he could etch a woman's personality of his own design.

Through the window I watched the plane burrowing its way through a mass of angry clouds. Middle-aged women, I thought, are traveling in the wake of more prejudice than I had ever imagined. If we aren't so damaged, so bleak, that we're sour on life, then we are power-hungry, manipulative Amazons who wish to cripple men emotionally, with an inordinate need to control them to hold on to our power. This was tougher to fight than wrinkles or cellulite.

Tony Collins, a former professional hockey player, now unemployed, is fifty-five. Gregarious, curious, he has a great number of friends, men and women. We met through mutual friends, and when he arrived at the hotel where I was staying in Miami, I wondered if he would live up to his advance billing.

After his marriage of fifteen years ended some time ago, he had become, I was told, a convert to chronic bachelorhood. He was invariably seen at the beach, at the discos, always sporting a new woman on his arm. Of medium height, he is stocky, built low to the ground, as I understand hockey players are, and he flashes a perpetual impish, sunny smile, as if he's listening to some inner signals of his own. He had his own way of saying "sometimes she plays the cello."

"You've got a guy of fifty-five—lots of them are having early retirement forced on them. Men whose lives have *been* their corporation are suddenly faced with 'What am I going to do?'

"There's a tremendous catharsis men go through. The women think: Oh, it's so wonderful; we're going to have retirement, travel; he's going to be around more. Wonderful."

"It doesn't sound so terrible," I said lightly.

"Yeah, but the man doesn't look at it that way. He hasn't prepared for retirement; neither has the woman. Suddenly he's there around the house, underfoot all the time. This is common whether you're a President or a senator or a guy working for IBM. Remember what Betty Ford said after Gerald Ford lost the election? 'I married you for better and for worse. But not for lunch.'

"Well, this woman who's forty or fifty suddenly has this man around, and that causes problems, and she doesn't handle it very well. I see a lot of these men starting to look for somebody to sympathize with their problems. The men get scared, they're getting older, and these young women say, 'Forget all that bullshit, let's go to the beach.' "

Tony moved toward the large picture window, which offered an almost corny view of the Atlantic. Pointing his finger at the window as if it were a slide show, he continued, "God, his wife never thought of saying to him, 'Let's go to the beach.'

"So he finds himself at the beach with this young gal and they've got a little picnic, and they're taking a walk and they've got a bottle of wine. And the guy says to himself, 'This is kind of fun.'

"These gals don't want to get into a heavy psychoanalytic thing; they make the man feel good. They say, 'Straighten up, you got your wings, come on, let's go out, let's knock off that weight, let's get yourself to the gym and I'll meet you.' And they're not into heavy things. He takes a good look at her and thinks: That's not a bad little number."

Tony did a little dance as he headed back to his chair. "All of a sudden he feels perky," he went on. "He doesn't have that perky feeling at home, and that's a lot of the reason. It's not that he doesn't love his wife, or respect her. She's raised their children, but your average man is probably bored. He says to himself, 'God, what am I going to do about it?' "

I nodded and asked, "What do you think they *do* do about it?"

Sinking into his chair, he smiled weakly. "Guys say, 'It's so comfortable at home, the wife entertains for me when we have to, she takes care of things, it's comfortable. It's being taken care of. But she's boring in a way, and maybe I'm boring too, but what am I going to do? Am I going to change all this?' They don't want to have to find an apartment and live by themselves. It's too lonely and too hard. So they find someone."

"A Jennifer?"

"Absolutely. It's the young girls' spontaneity that a man likes. Young gals will reschedule something. They'll fit it in. And older women? They're not rescheduling. They say, 'We're going to the theater' or 'We'll be late for dinner.' He says, 'Who the hell gives a damn?'

"He can call one of these young gals and say, 'I want to come over,' and she'll say, 'Fine.' He wants that, spontaneity—coming home and bending her over the kitchen table. And if his wife's not receptive? Then you know—the hell with her. It's not that he doesn't want to make love to his wife, but he wants a little fantasy, maybe with costumes, something frivolous. If his wife would just offer that. The fear of retirement is murder. What men wonder is: How can we get some frivolity, some fun, some goofiness, some fantasy?"

Artist Joanna Ansen's husband left her for a younger woman. Today she's reached her own conclusions about Jennifers and fantasy. "I think men are more romantic and fanciful than women. Since they can't express it, due to inhibitions, it stays in their heads. We're more practical, more pragmatic, yet we're allowed to express our romantic side. So men express it with Jennifers 'cause they can't do it with their wives, who criticize gifts they bring them and say, 'It's not what I really wanted.' That is the atrophy of marriage."

Still thinking of Joanna Ansen's obituary on marriage, I entered the office of my good friend Don Sloan. A gynecologist and obstetrician, he had in recent years also become interested in sex therapy. Working with hundreds of couples, he had thought a good deal about what makes marriages atrophy, what draws men and women

together, and why they grow apart. As I sat before him, I recalled
our twenty years of friendship. While he is in his mid-fifties, he still
looked like the young man just setting up a practice I had met many
years before. Fabulous looking, his dark hair lightly, perfectly
dusted with gray, he is a smiling, warm man—a man who likes
women, and understands men.

"Sure, men have a fantasy," he began. "It's a fantasy about
themselves, about the way they want to be, to produce, to create.
They want to be kept on the ball, to be novel, spontaneous.

"I remember courting my wife." He shook his head as if he
couldn't quite believe what he was about to say. "Our first date,
going out to Southampton, and the water was cold, freezing, yet I
dived in and I almost died. But I wasn't about to show her I wouldn't
do it. I had a hell of a time doing it, but I loved it. I had a great time.
Now, with this same woman, my wife of eight years," he said
through a self-deprecating laugh, "I'm not going to get in any cold
water; I need a heated pool."

I laughed too, although it was a strikingly new picture of himself
that he was presenting. I never thought of Don Sloan as needing to
perform some awesome physical feat to make himself more attractive to any woman.

"It's not that it was clandestine or exciting or illegal or illicit or
dishonest," he continued. "What was great about it was that I felt
so *alive,* compelled to be at my best. When you feel you have to
produce to win something, it's better for you. Men want to feel that
way, fresh, sharp, and new. Youth enhances this sense of newness."

"Aren't you speaking just about novelty? Does it have to be
young novelty?" I wondered out loud.

"When you first meet someone, you have to woo them," he
replied. "Words become acute, important; you even want to use
better grammar." He laughed. "Later, one of the things that stops
you is you know there's a tomorrow. If you're out to woo and win
a Jennifer, you have to do something to make that tomorrow happen. That's what turns you on. Reggie Jackson gets turned on
watching his home runs on television, thinking: Who knows, I may
not hit one tomorrow. It may be the last one I'll ever hit.

"You like to be exciting; it's great to be put on the spot. Successful marriages work at that; you demand it of each other. When it doesn't happen, when the marriage is not progressing, it's dying. A dying marriage is not always terminal, but it takes work, real work. Many men turn to a Jennifer because she keeps a man acute, at his best, his best fantasy of himself."

"And erect?" I asked.

"That's the same thing," he said, grinning. "And there's one other thing. You *know* women are allowed the latitude to feel more, be more sensitive, to express themselves. Sometimes men feel a Jennifer is an outlet to express themselves more than they can with their wives."

I knew other men had said the same thing, yet I also knew from my talks with women and from my friends how eager women are to be with men who can feel more, who are more sensitive. "But things are changing," I protested. "Men are being allowed to express themselves, women want them to, many men want to. Aren't you talking about what used to be, rather than what's happening today?"

"Not at all." He stood up and sat on the edge of his desk, facing me. Underneath his white hospital jacket he was wearing a blue shirt, rep tie—standard gear. Then, almost as though he was reading my mind, he said, "Look, a man and a woman are going to a gorgeous, elegant gala. What does a woman do? What she does is go out and buy a gorgeous dress, has her hair and makeup done. And what does a man do? He takes off a suit and puts on a black jacket and wears what every other man wears. That's the amount of expression he is allowed.

"Of course sex is important, and no, sometimes Jennifers don't play the cello, they just somehow impart this desire for a man to be sharp, at his best. And an older guy with a Jennifer? That really puts him on his best behavior, and wow, that's seduction! And when a man who can't or won't work on a marriage that's in trouble discovers he can express his greatest fantasy about himself with a younger woman, that's powerful stuff."

Not only do men have fantasies about Jennifers; they also have very specific sexual expectations of what will and what won't happen, when the fantasies become real.

10

. . . And Sometimes She Doesn't

The image of Don Sloan diving into the freezing water was hard to shake; so was his description of the powerful seduction of being at his peak, all his senses sharpened, in every way.

Was that what it was for most men? I still didn't understand. Not that I thought you can ever perform a biopsy of an emotion, but men who became afflicted with Jennifer Fever did things in its name, to serve the affliction that profoundly disrupted their wives' and children's lives, as well as their own. Certainly sex played a part, a big part. But when I asked men about the sexual aspects of their relationships with Jennifers, it evoked a curious response.

Some men, fearful of being perceived as chasing around after young girls like a cartoon character in a burlesque show, deliberately avoided any mention of sex. Preferring to talk about anything but, they'd emphasize cooking, joie de vivre, love of travel, kindness to animals—anything but sex.

But it wasn't joie de vivre that seventeenth-century poet John Wilmot, the Earl of Rochester, was writing about in his poem "Song of a Young Lady to Her Ancient Lover":

> Thy nobler parts which but to name,
> In our sex would be counted shame,
> By Age's frozen grasp possest,
> From their ice shall be releast;
> And sooth'd by my reviving hand
> In former warmth and vigour stand
> All a lover's wish can reach
> For thy Joy my love shall teach . . .

Yet still I love thee without Art,
Ancient Person of My Heart.

Echoing the Earl of Rochester, some contemporary men were eager to talk about the sexual side of their relationships with Jennifers, whom they saw as a kind of trophy, attesting to their sexual prowess. They talked easily about the frequency and satisfaction of their sexual encounters—as signs of their own sexual vitality.

The most interesting comments came from men who thought that younger women bring something into bed that is just as important as supple skin or a sleek body. It can be described as a mind-set, and while men differ on exactly what the nature of that mind-set is, they believe it is unique to a Jennifer and, in terms of their own sexual performance, an asset.

It was surprising to discover that when men talk about Jennifers and sex, they not only corroborate some traditionally held beliefs but also shatter other pieces of conventional wisdom.

Don Sloan had this to say on the subject of sex: "There is only one aphrodisiac, and that is a sexual partner, *your* sex partner. The rest is a myth. Sexual response is involuntary, unknown, secretive, and uncontrollable. You're turned on, not because, per se, de facto, some Jennifer did it. It's what you wanted to do for Jennifer, how you felt about yourself with her. An aphrodisiac can be an oyster if you yourself want to be turned on by an oyster."

Cary Rogers, a fifty-five-year-old stockbroker, met me at a small restaurant near his office on a broad Chicago thoroughfare. He is a burly, self-assured man with a florid complexion, yet he made it clear that self-confidence is not a permanent fixture of his personality. For him, Jennifers must be avoided, and for sexual reasons.

"Sex with a younger woman is too hazardous," he remarked. "The whole time you're making love, you're wondering how you measure up to some twenty-eight-year-old surfer who has nothing on his body but muscles. Even if you're in good shape, you feel your potbelly is enormous. Besides, sexually those young girls know nothing about sex. They only know 'Harder, harder.' They are thumpers; they don't know the nuances that come naturally to most older women."

Curiously, former hockey player Tony Collins, who praised Jennifers for their spontaneity and joie de vivre, also believed there are times when an older woman is a marvelous sex partner. "I know men who love to take an older woman who's attractive, maybe matronly-looking, but a wonderful woman, and please her. It's almost like he's a gift from the gods. There is something about making love to a woman who has a mature look about her, in full blossom. You get satisfaction out of the appreciation you get from the woman. It's almost a confirmation of your abilities. Not just sexual," he said with a broad grin, "but a beautiful message to your soul.

"It makes you feel good, you can dally, you can take your time. Younger women tend to be a little more athletic. It's wonderful sometimes to be with an older woman, where that gymnastic aspect isn't so important as it is with younger girls. But it's being able to do for them what nobody else has done; it's incredible."

The idea of women of any age being in need of a sexual handout, a United Way for sexual charity, was a bit unnerving. But upon reflection, I realized that many men were only echoing variations on a popular theme regarding the sexuality, or lack of it, in an older woman's life. In fiction, rarely do we read about vital, sexually alive, fifty-year-old women living lusty sexual lives with husbands or lovers their own age.

Instead there is Colette, with her vision of a bountiful, generous, midlife woman, Léa, who gave as good as she got, gave as much as she took, sharing her sensual wisdom with an eager and hungry young man. Or the less attractive portrait of the sexually starved middle-aged female, voracious, grasping, willing to compromise, to endure humiliation—a woman who will pay any price, emotional or financial, to satisfy her sexual desires. Ironically, if a midlife woman is suffering sexual deprivation, it may often be the direct result of her diminished sexual status.

In 1745, Benjamin Franklin, in an essay, "Advice to a Young Man," suggested eight reasons why men should choose an older woman. He said that sex with an older woman was at least equal to sex with a younger woman, and often superior, as practice leads to improvement. And he concluded, "they are so grateful."

Perhaps men today aren't interested in winning a woman's gratitude. And who can blame them? They might prefer dating younger women because they are more pliable. Or, as author Noel Perrin described it, "For the young, sexual attraction serves as a kind of handy glue, keeping a couple together until other and more durable bonds take hold."

Even though his relationship with a Jennifer is now "kaput, an unmitigated disaster," Lee Kalder believes it was held together by the kind of sexual glue Noel Perrin described. Kalder stated the matter simply: "Making love to a juicy young woman who adores you? Why, it's almost more than the frame can bear."

When Dick Rosen, a fifty-eight-year-old insurance salesman from Chicago, talked about his new twenty-four-year-old wife, he eagerly, enthusiastically, described the sexual enhancements she had brought to his life. According to Rosen, the last ten years of his twenty-year marriage were clouded by sexual problems between him and his wife, and they stayed together as long as they did for the same reason we have heard more times than we care to remember: "for the sake of the children."

"My wife came from my generation, and I'm afraid that for that generation of women, sexual repression, sexual denial, was more the rule than the exception. She wouldn't experiment or play. Of course, this is also the generation for whom it was taboo to sleep together before you married. So I learned about her sexual prudishness only after we were married. I kept thinking it would change, but it didn't."

"And your new young wife?"

"I feel younger, there is no pressure; pressure makes you feel depressed. I'm more alive sexually. It's easy to feel sexual when you're not depressed. It's not her youth; it's her outlook, her positiveness."

There is another reason why men are drawn to Jennifers that has a sexual connection but spills over into many other areas as well. That is what I will call the "trophy factor."

Not one man told me he enjoyed being with a younger woman because he thought that by having a young, attractive woman on his arm, he would be enhanced in other people's eyes. Not one man said it mattered a whit that people seeing him arrive in a restaurant or at a party would murmur, "Out of the whole world she picked him! He really must be something!"

But while unspoken by the men, it is a syndrome not ignored by sociologists. Harold Sigal and David Landy, of the University of Rochester, conducted a study on the subject and in a paper, "Radiating Beauty," they concluded: "We have demonstrated that onlookers do, in fact, enhance those with pretty girlfriends . . . when an individual is associated with an attractive partner, others will view him more favorably and such an association also leads the individual to believe others will perceive him positively."

They admit these findings don't prove that when a man chooses an attractive young woman, he does so *because* he believes others will regard him with admiration, or even envy. But they conclude: "It is very tempting to regard these processes as part of the overall picture."

For Landy and Sigal, the trophy factor exists. But Tony Collins, who won his share of trophies on the hockey rink, and who never mentioned the trophy factor in the world of sexual relations, had his own ideas about the sexual benefits of a Jennifer.

We left my air-conditioned hotel room in Miami and were taking a stroll on the beach. It wasn't exactly the lighthearted, buoyant romp he said men enjoyed with Jennifers. Rather, because we were nearly at the end of the interview, we had decided to conclude our talk and enjoy the last dying rays of a late-afternoon sun.

"If a man has a sexual problem," Tony began, "he has an even bigger one with an older woman. Because of their own insecurities in this area, older women take a man's sexual problem as a slap in their face. They are so starved, if a man can't get it up, they feel deprived, take it personally, and you can't be yourself.

"A lot of men, when they get older, for whatever reason get into problems like premature ejaculation, and the women tend to be critical of them and angry, or they're sarcastic, saying things like, 'What's happened, are you over the hill?' They'll say mean things. What they don't know is the more they say those sort of things, the more they're digging their own grave, because the man is going to retreat more and more into his own shell. A woman can be very cruel when this happens."

"And how do you think younger women would handle the same situation?" I asked.

"Young women are more sexually adventuresome and flexible, willing to try all kinds of things, more than women of our generation," was his reply. "A younger woman has an understanding. That's one of the reasons men go to hookers; hookers are very understanding. And they know how to arouse a man, if they're good. Maybe their wives have forgotten how to arouse them."

"And a Jennifer?" I asked. "Some men have told me she doesn't know the nuances, isn't as sexually adept as an older woman."

"Sometimes that's true," he said, flashing his best impish smile. "But Jennifers take it as a challenge to restore impotent men to sexual vigor. She feels like a miracle worker, she becomes a 'special woman,' to herself and of course to him."

Ah, the old miracle worker from the Bible had reappeared in her twentieth-century disguise.

But it isn't Abishag, the bracing tonic of a virgin, that Harry Starr is seeking when he is with a Jennifer. A sportswriter, Harry Starr is rumpled, craggy, and, at fifty-four, effortlessly attractive. Separated for several years, he dates many women, among them several Jennifers. Because he has been a close friend for many years, I can add that he is a man who likes women as a species, and who has never in our countless conversations mentioned the age of the various women in his life.

Over two decades of lunches, we have talked about our respective love lives, about men, women, sex, mothers, and fathers. Yet as we sat in the back of a deserted Italian restaurant, sipping espresso, just the two of us and my tape recorder, I was surprised by what he had to say; also by the intensity in his voice, and the pain in his eyes that occasionally interrupted his usually chronic air of irony.

For him, the problem with older women is that they are *too understanding*. As for younger women? Far from seeing them as the miracle workers that Collins describes, Harry Starr says the advantage for a middle-aged man's going to bed with Jennifers is quite the opposite.

"You can bluff your way out," he said dryly, "and avoid the compassion and knowingness of the older woman trying to help you through it.

"I do think with a Jennifer there's a lack of judgment; you can fail safely. You read in magazines and hear that middle-aged women go through a whole lot of changes sexually, and you're afraid you may do damage, you're not sure. I obviously don't believe it, but that myth, it's in the back of men's minds. You know a twenty-five-year-old is going to be sexual, and the question is, is a forty-five- or fifty-five-year-old going to be or not?

"If this woman is menopausal," he went on, "you've got all those crazy things that you think could hurt her—that she's all dried up. It's crazy. Now, with a ninety-year-old, you could hurt her, but how that transfers to a forty-five-year-old woman, I don't know, but it does."

Over the rim of my coffee cup, I studied my old friend, and while we both can get passionate about food, movies, books, and politics, I had never seen him quite this animated on the subject of sex. Maybe throughout those decades of lunches we hadn't talked about it; certainly not like this.

"Remember," Harry continued, "a man *has* to perform, *has* to get it up and keep it up. Even if you fail, you don't fail as badly with a young woman, you can lie and get away with it. A forty-five-year-old may really care," he said, chuckling, "may want to work with you on it, may say, 'Don't worry, it's happened to me many times.' She has the experience the twenty-five-year-old hasn't. You can tell the young girl you're ill, pretend you've got a cold, a virus, or you're drunk, and you can get away with it.

"The forty-five-year-old will see right through it and may, God forbid, want to help you, which will make it only worse. The consistent vulnerability, it's the biggest fear of all men, from the time they're very young."

I sensed there was something Harry wasn't saying, so as we walked out of the restaurant into the suddenly blinding light of a late July afternoon, I asked gently, "Is there something more that a man thinks about Jennifers and sex, even if he doesn't have a young woman in his life?"

A sheepish smile was followed by a terse "Yeah." A few more moments of silence and then the admission: "I think the biggest thing, and it's a little sick to say it, but what makes sex so terrific with a younger woman is there's something almost forbidden and a turn-on about making love to a younger body; it's a private taboo; it's licensed incest.

"What's a fifty-four-year-old doing with a twenty-four-year-old? It has a taboo quality that is always a turn-on for anybody. You're afraid to approach the forbidden with a woman your own age; she's liable to judge you. There's something about the lack of judgment in a young person that allows the forbidden to take place.

"Who wants to be judged sexually? Oh, God! Men have a tougher time than women. I will never know if a night is good for you or not good for you except by my perception of your emotional response, but you can absolutely know whether I'm having trouble or not. I'm always on line for rejection."

We walked in silence for a few blocks until we approached his apartment, a slightly battered yet stately building on West End Avenue, and I was about to thank him for lunch, for our talk, when he said, "There's one more thing. You know there's got to be a reason you would go out with a younger girl on a consistent level, because you're afraid of someone of your own generation; but the advantages of someone your own generation are so much more powerful—friends, conversation—but . . ."

"But what, Harry?" I asked softly.

"All that doesn't seem important when you can hold off being judged. Being judged, Barbara, that's hell."

As I started back to my apartment, I watched the sunset as it flared over the Hudson across the twilight sky and reflected off the windows of the tall buildings along Riverside Drive. I remembered the haunted look in Harry's eyes when he told me of the horror of being judged.

I also thought of those "durable bonds" Noel Perrin had written about. Too often those durable bonds snap. When they break, whether out of a sense of narcissistic entitlement or a need to be adored, or out of security that a man's wife will be financially or emotionally able to handle it, or out of anger and resentment that she has been insensitive to his needs at this thorny time of life—whether for all or only some of these reasons, a man filled with that profound feeling is compelled to leave home and begin a new life with a Jennifer.

And what of the wives, left with their painful, ego-shattering feelings of loss—and who must somehow piece together the fragments of their own lives and their children's lives, before they can even think of starting over themselves, with new lovers? As I glided to my apartment on the sixteenth floor, I knew it was time to talk to the Janets.

11

It's Moonlight Madness

This has not happened to me. I have had my share of loves, star-crossed affairs of the heart, and have known the accumulation of hurts that comes when a love affair ends when I least want it to; and I have stayed too long at the fair with a man when it was not in my best interest. But the particular hurt of losing a man I had loved and lived with for some time to someone whose youth was notable among her many virtues—no, it has not happened to me.

When a married man becomes involved with a Jennifer, it generally remains a private ordeal—for him and his wife. Last year, several private episodes of Jennifer Fever became public, and men in high places made headlines when the press demanded that they account for their activities. With cameras flashing and microphones poked in their faces, their wives, at least publicly, stood by their husbands' side. Gary Hart was forced to resign from the presidential sweepstakes after the press reported that while his wife was home in Denver, he had spent time with a Jennifer named Donna. But when Hart announced his withdrawal from the race, Lee Hart flew across the country to be with her husband.

And Jim Bakker, reigning monarch of television's pack of evangelical ministers, host of the "Praise the Lord" TV show, would discover that it was not his wife but the Lord who wasn't on his side when his night with a twenty-one-year-old Jennifer named Jessica was revealed. Confessing his sins of commission, Bakker surrendered his exalted position, if not the millions of dollars the faithful had donated so he could continue doing the Lord's work. Wife Tammy bravely faced the press along with her husband, both convinced he would be forgiven by both the Lord and his flock for straying from the path of righteousness.

For weeks the lip-smacking headlines continued, then, in the cooler light of retrospection, the press settled down to ruminate about the persistent lure Jennifers offer men, and the chronic dangers they represent to men's wives.

In discussing the public's reaction to these highly publicized cases of Jennifer Fever, the media speculated on what drove the men. Was it merely recklessness, lust, arrogance? Or was it something darker, perhaps some subconscious self-sabotaging death wish? Were the Jennifers responding to the scent of power, motivated by a desire for money, instant fame, social access? Or, as others suggested, were they just young girls out for a romp and a good time? And the Janets who were described as "plucky," "loyal," and "spunky"—what were they really feeling? Were their brave faces masks of painted smiles, concealing their hurt and anger? Or were they less inclined to feel cheated or vengeful because the desire to travel in the heady circles their high-powered husbands offered them obscured their feelings of betrayal? Or were they doubly betrayed—first by their husbands' infidelities, and then when their husbands' power or ambitions were thwarted by public exposure of these indiscretions?

After hounding the men, their wives, and the Jennifers for weeks, and suspecting that the public was now bloated with juicy details, the press began asking more cosmic questions. What did all this say about our society? Was it a sign of moral decay, "a crisis in ethical values"? Or only the side effects of a vigilant press in a democratic society? Or wasn't it really another example of a scandal-hungry public needful of titillation, being fed its daily dose of gossip by a hyperactive, pandering, vicious press?

Hadn't Franklin Roosevelt, John Kennedy, and Dwight Eisenhower all had their Jennifers, and the press dutifully ignored it? Many suggested that if either Hart or Bakker had been involved with older, plainer women, the titillation factor and sense of outrage would have been less. But on one issue there was general agreement: The fear of losing a husband to a younger, prettier woman is one of the deepest psychic fears experienced by all women.

The problems, pleasures, and sometimes perils facing men who succumb to the attractions of younger women have provided fodder for writers through the years. Recently the press has questioned the sanity of enormously wealthy and once-powerful men like Huntington Hartford and Rudolf Bing, who appear to be living eccentric and reclusive lives, with Jennifers very much in attendance.

Pundits and political writers had a field day following the sexual career of Nelson Rockefeller, whose political aspirations dimmed after he left his wife to marry a younger woman. When he died in the arms of another, even younger woman, it provided grist for the mill of writers *off* the obituary page.

When J. Seward Johnson, heir to the Johnson & Johnson pharmaceutical fortune, married his third wife, Basia, he was seventy-six, she was thirty-four. According to writer Barbara Goldsmith, one friend observed, "He'd tell me, 'I can't believe my luck; someone like Basia—a beautiful young girl and she's in love with me. She's sexually attracted to me!' He couldn't get over it."

When their father began wearing turtlenecks and sped along in his Jaguar convertible "as if he were a race car driver," Goldsmith writes, some of his children worried about Basia's influence over their father. But when he died, and the terms of the will were revealed, hell broke loose.

Although Basia entered Johnson's life when she came to work as a chambermaid for his wife, when he died, at the age of eighty-seven, he left her almost all of his five-hundred-million-dollar fortune. One of his sons would write about his father: "as he became weaker and weaker, he totally gave in and became like moral mashed potatoes in her hands."

From Chaucer's fourteenth-century *Canterbury Tales* to Saul Bellow's latest best-selling tale, *More Die of Heartbreak,* writers have been aware that there is often a terrible price to be paid for lusting after a younger woman. The lure of a Jennifer for an older man has also stirred the imaginations of writers like Philip Roth, John Updike, and John Cheever. Some writers have rhapsodized about the joys of a Jennifer, while others have taken a gloomier view.

Woody Allen offered a lyrical view of a man and his Jennifer in his film *Manhattan,* but *The Blue Angel* is a classic cautionary tale depicting the darker side of this attraction—dramatizing how men can become "moral mashed potatoes" when they fall prey to young temptresses, losing their careers, wives, children, and finally their dignity and self-respect.

If life with a Jennifer is sometimes less than a blessing, and a man can wind up in a personal hell, for a woman to be left for another, younger woman is a terrible and unique kind of injury. Rather than deal with the awful reality, many wives who discover their husband's affair with a Jennifer may say, as Essie Johnson said when she learned of her husband's affair, "Oh, I just want to forget it all."

A woman may sense her husband's affair with nothing concrete to go on, when not even a whiff of adultery hangs in the air. When men become involved with other women, their behavior toward their wives is frequently more caring, more solicitous than usual. Sometimes that very air of concern, an overzealous attempt to please, can be worrisome to wives, who perceive it as an incriminating sign of guilt.

For others, the discovery occurs in a very prosaic fashion: the stale scent of an unfamiliar perfume, too many "working" dinners, inexplicably long hours spent performing the simplest tasks—or when a friend decides, for well-meaning or not so well-meaning motives, to inform the wife that her husband is involved with another woman. A woman, concerned she's no longer in her prime, monitoring the dreaded signs of aging in herself, may wonder if all those vital young women who are part of her husband's workaday landscape offer too much temptation.

While most of the women I interviewed had been apprehensive about problems in their marriage, few said they *knew* their husbands were involved with another, younger woman. Many divorce lawyers and psychotherapists are convinced that in most cases, wives know very well when their husbands are having an affair but refuse to admit it, preferring to cling, in the bittersweet words of the great lyricist Lorenz Hart, to "the self-deception that believes the lie."

Family law lawyer Harriet Pilpel sees a number of such women in her practice. "I have seen a number of women whose husbands, according to them, 'walked out on them without any warning.' When I talked further with them it turns out there were serious problems in the marriage. But the wife did not confront them herself, no less ask her husband to confront them with her."

Psychiatrist Anne E. Bernstein, M.D., agreed. "Most of the men who decide to leave a marriage after twenty or more years have already been involved with other women many years before that, and it was kept a secret. The wives, if you scratch the surface, have chosen not to know. But they knew. They still had children who needed care and attention, so everything remained unspoken.

"The threat comes most frequently when the kids are grown and go off to school. Then the men can leave without guilt; they feel their wives and their children are saying, 'Who needs you?' That's the last thing that frees them."

Whether by denial or avoidance, many women claim they *didn't* know.

Writer Sandy Green is fifty-five. Although her husband left her twenty-four years ago, Sandy, when asked how she traveled the rocky road from victim to survivor, doesn't have to search through the pages of her memory. As with other women, her recollections are not clouded by the passage of time. In the frighteningly lucid way that we all remember where we were on terrible days, days of assassinations or the deaths of loved ones, recalling each detail, however inconsequential—how the sky looked or what we wore— she remembered all that was said and all that wasn't, how she felt and how she coped, as clearly and sharply as if it happened a week ago.

With her short blond hair, wispy and fine, Sandy has a winsome, almost childlike demeanor that plays counterpoint to a more somber, grave expression which occasionally crosses her face. In her Boston apartment, curled up in a chair, elbows on raised knees, she began by saying that looking back to that day twenty-four years ago, her discovery shouldn't have been such a shock. Something was very wrong in her marriage, something she didn't want to examine.

"Our life-style required a lot of time in bed, not fucking, just hanging out in bed watching television. I certainly didn't pay attention to it, but he must have heard the song of low-grade depression singing out. I think I was moving in a state of semicomatose consciousness because I didn't want to see what was happening, just like I don't enjoy opening bills."

But it's easy *not* to see what's happening when there are conflicting messages.

"I didn't realize that for many years he had stopped loving me. I wouldn't admit it because the signs weren't there. Ten days before he left, I received an ardent love letter from him in our summer house. The signals were all mixed. There were silences and depressions, but there were long dreamy walks in the park, ardent kisses, too."

Sandy reminded me that Jennifer Fever can strike at any age. "I was thirty-one, my husband was the same age. We had been married twelve years, had a three-year-old daughter. It was at a writers conference where I understood I was in big trouble. I wandered downstairs and saw my husband, who was very drunk, in a corner with a very, very young girl. And he was fondling her breasts."

Sandy stood up and walked across the room, poured us each a glass of wine, and as she handed mine to me, said, "My heart sank, and I knew then the party was over. Because it wasn't that it was hidden away; he was doing it in a place where I could easily walk in and see him. So did half the world see him kissing this girl. As a writer groupie, she was very provocative. She called the next day, wanting to speak to him. I knew this meant trouble."

Sandy returned to her chair, closing her eyes for a moment as she recalled the rest of the story. "A few weeks later, at breakfast, I looked in his face and said, 'It's over, isn't it?' And he said, 'Yes.'

"It was a very Beckett kind of thing. I was a good sport, I thought. I was about to go out and get a divorce, but his lawyer said, 'This is moonlight madness; don't do anything, and it will pass.' So I did nothing for months. But it never passed."

Laura Rossen was a pale, fragile-looking woman who, when we spoke, was in the throes of adjusting to the fact that her husband, a consulting physician at a large Miami hospital, had left her two months before to live with a woman half his age and exactly the age of their daughter. Laura was forty-six, and for her it was a turbulent, awful time. Of all the women I met, Laura had the most difficult time readjusting. After spending a month in a private sanitarium in Florida, she came home. She had been Mrs. Bill Rossen for twenty-four years, and without him in her life, she was still searching for a new identity. Here is how she remembered her day of discovery:

"I was ironing his shirts. You see, there wasn't a lot of dough; financially we were in a bit of trouble. I saw something sort of red on his collar; it occurred to me he had cut himself shaving, so I finished ironing the shirt and made dinner. We hadn't been alone for quite a time. But the children were away. We had a drink and it was very stiff between us. We asked each other about our lives, but there was little rapport. I wasn't thinking of the shirt. It must have come from my unconscious, because it leapt out of me. 'Are you having an affair, seeing someone?'

"He turned ashen. 'What makes you think that?'

" 'Because I think I saw lipstick on your shirt.'

"And he blurted out, 'She doesn't wear lipstick,' or something to that effect. Then he said, 'Yes, there is someone I find very special.' "

Laura's pain was so recent, her memory so fresh, I didn't want to jump in and ask the question that offends so many of us when we witness television reporters asking the victims, the survivors of disasters, how they felt when the tornado struck, when the earthquake destroyed their home, when the fire took the lives of their children. So I said, as gently as I could, "It must have been awful; you must have felt wretched."

"At that moment I felt extremely numb," she replied instantly. "I didn't feel anything, but I wanted information, was *wild* for information, and I asked who she was.

"He said, 'She's a young resident I met in San Francisco.'

"I said, 'All those times you've been to California . . .'

"He said, 'Yes.'

"Later my cousin said, 'I hope you were Sicilian about it.' All I did was sit there, numb, for a few minutes. I don't know what happened to me.

"At some point I walked into the kitchen and threw the spatula at him. I said words I've never said before—you know, hell hath no fury like a woman scorned. I couldn't stop screaming, called her every name in the book. I watched myself doing it. He was very upset. I couldn't be in the same room with him, and I went to a woman in the building who had the same thing happen to her, spent an hour there, and when I came back, I found him asleep."

Georgina Ramonos, thirty-eight, has sparkling black eyes, curly black hair, and radiates Italian intensity and humor. She was thirty when her husband fell for a younger woman, reminding me, as Sandy Green had, that "younger" is truly a relative term.

Georgina has a full-time job and is raising a daughter; she asked if we could talk while she prepared dinner in her Chicago apartment. Her daughter, Karen, was with her father for the weekend, and Georgina had to be home when Joe dropped her off. She poured us both a glass of wine, and as she began to prepare dinner, she chatted matter-of-factly about what I knew were painful memories.

"It was Joe's annual company picnic and my thirtieth birthday, and I was feeling very old. There was this young girl throwing herself at him. She was about twenty-three. Attractive. Walking around in a T-shirt, braless, like a winner of a wet-T-shirt contest. And there I was toodling around with a baby, and every time Karen would get up and go off somewhere, I'd go after her, and this girl was still with him when I got back. I thought: My God, what is going on here?

"When I confronted him later he told me that he wasn't sleeping with her, but that she had made a pass at him."

Georgina handed me a knife, and we set about cutting up vegetables for the salad. "She made a concerted effort; she knew what she wanted," Georgina continued, examining a bruised tomato. "She worked for Joe in his office, and she was ambitious, ambitious to be married, a typical Jewish princess. Born getting her nails done. Spoiled brat. Her father's a doctor; she's always had everything she wanted. Joe started going out nights, and I began to realize he was fooling around. It was hard to believe, because he was the most family-oriented, conscientious man. You know, Italian, a wonderful father."

"You were only thirty," I said. "How long had you been married?"

"Seven years, and we had the kind of marriage where they photographed us for magazines, we were so adorably perfect." Georgina smiled a tight smile, but the expression in her eyes was rueful. "He was also extremely attractive," she continued. "We were good friends. I see now it was a boring marriage, but then I thought all marriages were like mine. Being as close as we were, and knowing him as well as I did, I knew in my heart I could take care of it really, make him behave as I wanted.

"But it got worse and worse; he was out more and more; and suddenly I found myself pregnant. Funny, because I was using a diaphragm, but I also happen to be the world's most fertile person. Subconsciously I must have caused the pregnancy because it was less threatening than being divorced."

Georgina had tossed the salad, and now, sitting on a kitchen stool, she became silent, sipped her wine. Then, with more than a touch of sarcasm, she added, "The night I told him I was pregnant was the night he told me he forgot to tell me he didn't want to be married anymore. Within a few days he moved out. Pregnant and with a small child, I didn't know what to do.

"Then one night Joe came over. There was no talk of the other woman. He said, 'I've been thinking, and I can't bear to have a child under these circumstances. It wouldn't be good for either of us. The only way to repair our marriage is for you to have an abortion.'

"I thought long and hard, and my mother said, 'No matter which way he goes, are you emotionally ready for a baby?' My mother would have supported me whatever I did."

"Your mother sounds terrific," I told Georgina. "Not all the women I interviewed received such support from their mothers."

"I would never have lived," she replied, "not been able to go through it without her. A few days later, he took me to the hospital, and they put me in obstetrics. The woman in my room thought I was there for a D and C. She thought we were newlyweds, thought he was such a loving husband. The loving husband stayed through the abortion, took me home, and said, 'I have to go; this is too emotionally draining for me,' and he left me at home with a three-year-old child, having just had an abortion. I hemorrhaged that night, and my mother got me to the hospital."

We both were silent for a time. Georgina's matter-of-fact style of chatter had vanished, replaced by a bittersweet, angry, sorrowful kind of attitude. The sound of the buzzer interrupted the silence. Her daughter was on her way up. Speaking rapidly so she could complete this part of the story before Karen arrived, she said, "He showed up five days later, and my mother asked him, 'Joe, what do you want? You have a beautiful wife and a beautiful little girl.' He said, 'But she's so young and so pretty.' And that was the only time he ever mentioned the other woman.

"After that he moved out; I think that's about as close as I'll ever come to having a nervous breakdown. Without my mother I'd never have survived."

Five years ago, Francesca Grayson celebrated her fiftieth birthday and four days later learned about her husband's affair with a younger woman. I knew her when her world fell apart—depressed, listless, she was convinced her life was over. As we sat in her rambling Greenwich Village loft, furnished with a bizarre combination of very conventional furniture and New Wave art, I remembered the suburban matron who couldn't drive through tunnels, couldn't travel because of her fear of flying. Amazed, as always, at her transformation, I listened carefully as she went back in time.

"I was married for twenty-four years," she began, "and I had seventeen good years. Some years before all this happened, my husband suddenly distanced himself. I felt rejected, not just sexually but on an everyday level as well. I absolutely felt it was my fault. I didn't know what was happening. When I asked Rod, he'd say, 'You're imagining things; it's all in your mind. You know you like to make things dramatic. Everything is fine.'

"He got more and more involved with business, and I was certain I was doing something that was turning him off. He was losing interest in me, but there was no question in my mind about another woman. I trusted him absolutely. I never opened a piece of mail that was addressed to him, not even a bill."

"After twenty-four years you knew Rod," I said, "what pleased him and what didn't. How did you respond to all this?"

"I tried to do things that would make him happy or interest him again, but he was unreceptive. He wasn't cruel; he was generous with money, getting me all the things he thought I wanted—a new car, a diamond bracelet. But they were unimportant to me.

"I became more aggressive sexually, but he was always tired or he had business. I asked him if he was interested in someone else. How could a man go without sex?

" 'That's crazy,' Rod said. 'Nobody but you—never was, never will be.' "

"Since you felt it was something *you* were doing," I asked, "did you try doing anything different, anything specific to help the marriage?"

"I had worked when we first married, but after he made some money he didn't want me to. He said he wanted to take care of me." Her tone was reflective and remarkably subdued as she went on. "But when it all began to turn sour, to make things more interesting I thought if I got a job in the city, I'd get away from the suburbs and the house and that would add a little spice. I'd have little stories to tell him again, and it wouldn't be so boring. But it didn't help."

"When did it all fall apart?"

"One night our friend Sam called and said, 'I want you to come to the house, right away. I have something to tell you.'

"When I got to his house he told me, 'Your husband has a mistress. I met her a few years ago.' "

She ran her hands through her short, stylish hair, as if she were remembering the Francesca of that night five years ago, Francesca with a long pageboy, dutifully sprayed and teased, and suddenly needed to remind herself who she was *today*.

"I went crazy, really," she blurted out. "I just became hysterical, ran out, and started driving crazy. Sam got scared and called my friend Jan. But I didn't know where to go. I came back and stayed with Jan and Sam for a while. I don't remember saying another word. We all just sat in the living room like somebody died. Finally Jan said I had to go home.

"'I can't,' I cried. 'How can I get into bed with this man?'

"Jan said, 'Don't. Sleep in another room, but go home.'

"I did and slept in the guest room. I don't remember the next day, except it was one horror after another. It turned out everyone had known about the girl, people I saw all the time. I learned it had been going on for six years; she lived five minutes away. And her name was Marie. Hearing the name was horrible.

"The more I found out," Francesca recalled, "the more it didn't seem real to me. We had gone from being so very poor to being comfortable, and then having a child together."

For an instant, an expression of confusion, bewilderment, flickered across her face, as she remembered the emotions that had plagued her when she discovered the truth.

"We had come such a long way, built so many things, done so many things. I thought I knew this man completely, and I didn't know him at all. When I finally asked, he tried to explain. 'It's not like you think,' he said. 'I don't love her. It's just something I got into.'"

Francesca's tone had been grave, but with a devilish laugh, she continued. "'OK,' I said, 'I will believe you if you'll call her now and tell her that you don't love her, with me sitting there.'

"I wanted to save it, really I did," she said quietly. "Twenty-four years, and I loved him. I didn't feel like starting over again. I don't know if I loved him, was used to him, or dependent on him, but I didn't want it to end. So I suggested that he tell me everything, tell her everything, expose it all. If we did that, maybe we had a chance. But if he couldn't, that was it. He said he couldn't discuss it, not with me, not with her.

"So I left."

Amy Whitten answered my advertisement, using a pseudonym, but even over the phone I could sense she was eager to tell her story.

"I would have been blind not to discover it," Amy began tentatively. "She lived in our building. She was pretty, not beautiful but very vivacious, and very young. I returned home once to see him helping her carry groceries out of her car. Honestly, I never thought about her again.

"But then things that I had accepted as normal things that happen in a marriage of twenty-five years seemed to get worse. He never made love to me; never. Said he was tired, said he didn't feel well. And the odd thing was he had gone on a diet, and he looked better than he had in years.

"The strangest thing happened. We have two teenagers, one seventeen, one fifteen. When we would sit down to dinner, there was a subtle change in alliances; I can't quite explain it. He would talk with them eagerly about music they listened to, music he usually couldn't stand. If I asked a question, the three of them looked at me as if I was strange. Then little phrases, slang words of theirs would crop up in his conversation."

I tried to picture Amy's expression, wondering if it matched the tone of confused anger I detected in her voice over the phone.

"Not only was I ignored, not only was I no longer sexual," she continued. "I became Mom to him too. Like those elderly couples you meet in little towns, where the old man calls his wife Mom. My husband didn't go that far, but it felt like it. You must understand, I was forty-eight, and you haven't met me, but I'm in good shape, not unattractive. But it didn't matter. I was Mom. They were this young, with-it trio at dinner. I couldn't believe it."

I could. Although Mom has taken her licks for being a shrew, a tyrant, and a manipulator, the neutering of Mom is almost totally unplanned, and quite unconscious. It happens again and again, and the effect is one of a highly choreographed dance, orchestrated by teenage children and Dad. Dad is with it, digging their music, even going to rock concerts, zipping around in a souped-up car or on a motorcycle. Mom, especially if she doesn't work outside the home, but even if she does, becomes the outsider—definitely not with it. Mom.

How and why it happens isn't clear. Possibly it's because of Dad's legacy, generations of men going out of the home, hunting, leaving, doing, earning, achieving, while generations of Moms were left tending the hearth. The Rolling Stones, Madonna, Bruce

Springsteen? Dad would understand. Biologically Dad is ever fertile, and Mom isn't. No eggs, no rock-and-roll. His sperm is entitlement for his with-it-ness. His need to feel he can, if called on, perform and *deliver* those sperm when he wants to requires him to appear and thus feel younger.

But it goes beyond biology. By now kindergarten children know women play more roles in our culture than men. Recognizing that her husband prefers it when she is an erotic mistress, Mom probably also knows that other roles she has to play in the family can get in the way. Even if she has a career of her own, her other job is to keep everyone's schedule, remember Dad's suit is at the cleaners, who has a dentist appointment, and who is allergic to strawberries. She is the taskmaster, the traffic cop, perceived as ordering around Dad and the kids.

With a wink of understanding, Dad bristles, signaling his children that he shares their displeasure with her in this role. Those are young, nubile children sitting with him at breakfast. His dewy daughter is dating handsome hunks; his son, another handsome hunk, is bringing home more dewy girls. Sexuality is pulsing in their loins, blossoming in front of his eyes. Joining their circle, he sees Mom in their eyes. Sexless. Neutered.

Some women told me they feel this ritual is an inexorable right of male passage, something men need to do. Others say it isn't subconscious but is used by men as a means of justifying their need for a Jennifer. Because it is so hurtful, so exclusionary, many women aren't aware of how this subtle game is played, even that it's going on, but Amy Whitten was.

"I tried to look more attractive," Amy explained, "and did everything I could not to be Mom. But he wasn't interested. Yet he was looking great, talking in a zippy teenage way, but too tired to make love. Sometimes I wondered if there was someone else. You read about it, you see it everywhere, but somehow I knew he would never do anything like that."

"How did you find out that he would?"

"One day I came home early from work and found them together in the apartment. I ran out. It was horrible." Even over the phone I could hear Amy's voice crackling with anger. "A few weeks later I insisted that he move out. I didn't want to live in the same building with that girl, and the kids still needed me around. Besides, he had done it; he deserved to be the one to move. I contacted a lawyer; I wanted a divorce."

Jill Brookner is an attractive, slender black woman who lives in a suburb of Boston. We met at a meeting of a women's support group, and when it ended, we chatted over coffee in her apartment.

"It's amazing," she began. "I was so busy raising our three girls, I didn't realize what was happening. Suddenly he started wearing bikini underwear, which was odd because he always wore boxer shorts. Suddenly he was on a diet. Suddenly I'd catch him posing in front of the mirror, changing his tie on the way out the door. Suddenly the drive to our home outside of Boston was too much, so he told me his company got a corporate apartment in town, which he began to use more and more."

Jill plugged in the percolator and then, taking a chair next to me at the kitchen table, kicked off her shoes and stretched her long legs before her. She scowled as she said, "Looking back, I don't know how I didn't see it. But I swear, I didn't. It came as a shock when I discovered he had a girl. How did I discover it? I had taken my daughters to visit my parents, and my husband told the maid not to come. When I returned I saw the towels were folded in a strange way in the linen closet. Not the way I fold them, not the way the maid folds them. And it couldn't have been him, because he *never* folds them," she concluded·with a chuckle.

I remember shaking my head incredulously. Observing her husband's bikini underpants hadn't told Jill Brookner anything. Nor had his sudden urge to diet, and a penchant for gazing in the mirror. Improperly folded towels had given it away?

"I know," she said with a self-mocking smile, and from her earthy laugh I knew she had read my expression accurately. "But you have to understand. He is a devout, religious man. Parochial schools, Jesuit college, the Catholic clubs. Proper. Moral. Almost holier than thou.

"Once I saw the towels, I saw everything. He had felt denied; he wanted to experience everything he hadn't because we married so young. Then it was just the usual thing," she went on wearily, ticking off the items on her finger. "American Express bills—I tracked them down and saw it all. The lingerie shops, the hotels, the wine bars. I confronted him; at first he said I was crazy, but I was persistent, and finally he admitted it."

Dory Previn's face is framed in a halo of curly hair, eyes hidden behind large tinted glasses. We had lunch in a quiet New York restaurant. The well-known composer and lyricist had made creative use of the bitter experience of losing her husband to a younger woman. She wanted me to understand from the outset that horrible as it was at the time, when her husband left her for a younger woman, it turned out to be "his terrible gift." But the way she learned about it was devastating.

"I heard about it on TV. I really see that this was too enormous for him to tell me himself. And people say to me, 'How could he go public with that?'

"It is worse when you're involved with people who are on the front pages. I saw it everywhere—on the cover of *Time* and in every paper. As my wonderful eighty-year-old ex-mother-in-law said, 'It's terrible when two people divorce, but when the world is in your bedroom!'

"I think that I created it too," she said with a slight smile. "I used a full fifty percent of my energies in bringing it about."

"How did you create it?" I asked.

"I wrote a screenplay six months before the breakup, which prefigured the whole thing. It was about a married couple and a younger woman who got pregnant. So I drew up the blueprints. I mean, I knew unconsciously; I didn't know consciously."

She paused to study the menu, and I took a moment to study her—the vulnerable smile, the strength of her gaze—and when we both had ordered and the waiter had moved away, I asked how she handled the emotions that followed the highly publicized breakup of her marriage.

Unsmiling now, she replied, "I worked it out, I wrote it out, I talked it out, I screamed it out, I attempted to suicide it out, I pilled it out, I no-pilled it out. But it just kept going. I had as much rage as anybody. Yes, I went quite bonkers. I went through a period of 'Shall I die?' Since I had the right to do either, I tried both, OK?''

Whether it is her husband's sudden liking for bikini underpants or a diet; his avoidance of sex or simply indifference—how a woman discovers her husband's affair with a Jennifer is only the beginning.

F. Scott Fitzgerald said there are no second acts in American lives. But it's in the second act that the Janets must deal with a flood of tempestuous emotions, and often those of their children.

For the wives, discovery can be either a shock or a final admission of reality. How they feel, and how they cope, is something else. As in the writing of a play, the major conflicts, the development of character, happens in the second act.

For the playwright, the second act frequently means trouble. And for the Janets, it's the hardest part.

12

A Whole World Lost

After discovering or finally admitting what she has long suspected and can no longer tolerate, the wife begins a roller coaster
ride of emotions, emotions she's never experienced before.

How women like Lee Hart and Tammy Bakker react when their
husbands become involved with a Jennifer is good copy for the
front page as well as the gossip columns. How less celebrated
women respond is a theme that informs the work of playwrights
and novelists.

Euripides' Medea is an unforgettable character, but Paddy
Chayefsky's Louise Schumacher is hardly a name remembered by
many. Unlike Medea's, Louise's moments in the script are few, but
they are memorable. Louise was portrayed by Beatrice Straight,
who won an Academy Award (best supporting actress) in 1976. So
did playwright Paddy Chayefsky, who wrote the script for *Network.*

In his film script, Chayefsky manages to crawl inside the head
and eavesdrop on the heart of both the man and the wife he's
leaving.

Max Schumacher, portrayed by William Holden, is struggling
with the agony of midlife terrors. He seeks refuge in the arms of a
beautiful young woman in his office, played by Faye Dunaway.
Louise, realizing something is wrong, finally asks Max about it.
Although she has been apprehensive, perhaps even suspicious,
when she hears Max say, "I love her," Louise explodes in anger:

"Get out. Go anywhere you want, but don't come back. After
twenty-five years of building a home and raising a family and all

the senseless pain we've inflicted on each other, if you can't work up a winter passion for me, then the least I require is respect and allegiance. . . . I'll be damned if I'll stand here and let you tell me you're in love with someone else. . . .

"This isn't some convention weekend with your secretary, is it? Or some broad you've picked up after three belts of booze. Your great winter romance, your last roar of passion before you settle into your emeritus years. Is that what's left for me, is that my share? She gets all the winter passion, I get the dotage? What am I supposed to do? Am I supposed to sit home knitting and purling while you slink around, sleep out like some penitent fuck?

"I'm your wife, dammit, and if you can't whip up some winter passion for me, the least I require is respect and allegiance. [She breaks into tears.] I'm hurt, don't you understand, I hurt badly. Say something, for God's sake. . . . You're in for a bad time, Max."

Louise is in for a bad time too. When *Network* ends, Louise is ill, so ill her daughter has flown in to help her through her depression. Jason married his young princess after he left Medea; but Max's affair has ended badly. He intends to ask his wife to take him back, but he doubts that she will agree.

Medea's responses are hardly those of the average Greek woman, still they are worth recalling here. Learning of Jason's betrayal, Medea rages, wishing she were dead. But the chorus reminds her:

> If your husband is won to a new love
> The thing is common; why let it anger you?

Medea lashes out at Jason, reminding him of all she did for him. She doesn't mean washing and ironing. She means the relatives she murdered to help gain his power. He brushes this off, telling her she is lucky to have been brought to Greece at all. If she hadn't married him, she'd still be an unknown eastern princess.

Medea pretends to agree, but then murders the princess and finally commits the act that history will always remember her for— she murders her own children. Jason asks why she did all this. Medea replies simply, "to break your heart"; it was "a fair price to pay to take away your smile."

JASON: You thought that reason enough to murder that I no longer slept with you?

MEDEA: And is that injury a slight one, do you imagine, to a woman?

JASON: Yes, to a modest woman, but to you the whole world lost.

At the end of the play, Medea is taken away in a sun chariot by one of the gods, because her cause is just. The gods don't punish Medea more than she has punished herself. Mercifully, we live in a society that does not treat murder as lightly as the gods of ancient Greece appear to have done. Modern women have no recourse, no tradition of revenge, no gods to carry them away in a chariot. When they are accused of acts of revenge, they will probably, like Jean Harris, land in jail.

As the women I interviewed described the pain they felt when their whole worlds were lost, their rage and sense of impotence, how naked they felt, stripped of their wifely identities, their financial and emotional abasement, how they coped—what helped them and what didn't—I frequently saw reflections of Medea and Louise.

Strangely, when women were *not* speaking of revenge at all but talking about how they coped with the sudden fury that had invaded them like an alien force, and ticked off the inevitable series of physical illnesses that accompanied their marital breakups, I understood another kind of revenge. A revenge of emotions with no place to go, of emotions so potent, so toxic, they had to be visited on the body.

In their specific voices we can best understand how contemporary women whose Jasons abandon them for young princesses cope with their anguish as they pick up the pieces of their lives, without surrendering to lives of victimhood, without becoming modern Medeas.

Sandy Green described it this way:

"I remember I felt this terrible thing, that the floor was falling away, that the earth I was standing on was giving way. I was in a terrible void. You suddenly feel absolutely terrified. I was jealous, obviously. I had no notion of how dependent I had become in this marriage, how connected, how attached I was to this man.

"I was invisible without him, or so I thought. Even though I was good at my own job, none of that seemed real or important; what was exciting was *his* work, *his* career. My job was like my putting on someone else's clothes to go to a grownup party. I never took it that seriously."

To me that seemed incredible. Lining the shelves in her living room were the books and journals Sandy had contributed to, good, readable articles on pop culture, which had been a sideline during her marriage and became a full-blown career when it ended. But other women had also felt that during their marriages their work was a sideline; and they had felt neither resentful nor cheated.

Sandy moved to the edge of the chair, leaning forward, eager to be understood. "I wasn't there," she said, her voice flat, as she tried to conceal her emotions. "I didn't exist except for the emotional pain. I was suicidal, but I couldn't do anything because I had a child. I looked haggard, lost weight; my menstrual period started coming every ten days. I assumed a stance, took on a role, a tough, survival kind of Barbara Stanwyck role, like in one of the movies of my youth," Sandy said, her voice raised in anger, "but I didn't feel it. I acted as if I wasn't hurting, but one had only to look in my eyes to see how hurtful it was. Even as we're talking, I realize I'm not telling you how tough it was."

"Did you experience other physical problems as well?"

"I suffered enormous stomach pain. But I know that a lot of women who invested their lives in men who left them for younger women got sick and died after this happened to them. Rage turned inward makes people sick."

After this spurt of anger her voice softened, and she said, almost in a whisper, "I was holding it in, couldn't get over this torch I was carrying. I didn't know how much in love with this guy I was. I mean, it wasn't perfect; it was inadequate; it wasn't sexually strong, but I was in love with him. He was my guy."

Laura Rossen remembered what happened the day after her discovery of her husband's affair.

"He had a trip to make. I lay in bed, weeping and carrying on. I remember his saying to me, 'How can you be so fragile?' I didn't know I was capable of doing this, but I did. I shut the doors, didn't talk on the phone; I stayed in the apartment for two days. It was like what people go through withdrawing from drugs. Hysteria. It was like waves. I wonder if other women tell you: You go through depths of despair and you rise up and get angry. And with the anger it's almost triumphant.

"There's a physical thing that happens, and it's like you can actually feel the knife in your heart. Later it's as though your heart has dropped, as though someone has stabbed you. That's how it feels."

"What did you do to relieve the pain, the immediacy of it?"

"I'd do a lot of physical things," Laura recalled, "washing up, cleaning, but then there would be a song on the radio, and I'd dissolve. A friend called and I told her; she was shocked and said I should call day or night."

Suddenly Laura's eyes were clouded with tears; battling them away, she lit a cigarette, and continued.

"We talked about it and he said, 'I will not give her up.' Ah, I saw it clearly—he wanted to stay married and still continue seeing this girl. He said, 'I'm in love with her; I'm fond of you.' Over and over, I kept hearing him say it, and I thought: Somehow this is not enough."

"Were your parents able to help, give you some support?"

"No, not then. My mother was ill, and my father was under a great deal of stress. And I decided to ask Bill if we could postpone telling the kids, so as not to ruin their graduation for them, the prom, all that. This meant from March till June I was living a lie. Couldn't tell the kids, couldn't tell my parents. Then in June he left."

In the silence that followed, I could see Laura struggling with herself. Her memories were so fresh, her hurt so recent; I hoped she knew that in time her pain would be less. She tossed her hair off her forehead, and continued. "She was half my age. The kids were in trouble. I felt old. I kept recreating happy times in my mind, but I kept picturing them together constantly. That was the most devastating. I just couldn't get this picture out of my mind."

Then—a flash of a smile, a new tilt to her head—Laura brightened, adding, "But there was an up side. Ironically, because I couldn't eat I began to get thin, actually better-looking. But it didn't matter how I looked; I didn't really care."

Francesca Grayson faced her crisis five years before, and the memory was still painfully fresh. "I would wake up behind the wheel of the car in a strange place," she recalled. "Hours, I would lose hours, finding myself in places. I didn't know how I got there. That was very frightening.

"We had been so close; he and the children were my life. Without him I felt as though my right arm fell off and was running around wildly, and there was nothing I could do to stick it back on."

Frowning, she hesitated, uncertain how to tell me the worst of it. "I took pills," she said finally. "I was scared to die, but I wanted to. I was humiliated, felt so ashamed in front of everybody I knew."

"Ashamed?"

"Ashamed that everybody else knew about it and I didn't. Ashamed of him, of the whole situation. I was so embarrassed, felt everyone was looking at me strangely, really kind of paranoid. I knew they were thinking I had screwed up. I had to have failed, or why would he leave?

"In time the pain got less, the humiliation got less once it turned to anger. It turned to anger and I was very vindictive. I was lucky that happened quickly."

I asked if her family had helped her through the difficult moments.

"No, and that was a shock. My mother's reaction was, 'You're having an affair with Sam.' Sam was a friend of the family, and because I was alone so much—Rod was off working or on business trips, or so I thought—I spent a lot of time with Sam. My husband had suggested it, encouraged it. But we weren't having an affair.

"We had a terrible argument. Even though I now knew about this girl, that it had been going on for years, my own mother was accusing *me* of being unfaithful. I was furious, and when she encouraged me *not* to get a divorce, to patch it up, I got more furious."

"Why do you think she reacted that way? The two of you always were so close," I said.

"We *were* close," she said, nodding, "but she adored Rod, and her logic was: Men are like that. You see, after my father died, my mother had been the other woman in relationships, so she identified with Marie. She was frightened. What would happen to her? So I had to get her an apartment too, and get her settled."

"And the rest of your family—how did they respond?"

Francesca was out of her chair, pacing back and forth with agitation. "I had my whole family encouraging me *not* to leave. My sisters felt, 'At your age, you're going to start all over? Who's going to want you? You're going to have to support yourself. How are you going to live? You've got to have a man take care of you.' I don't think they thought I would be a burden, but they felt a certain responsibility. I was going to be all alone. Someone had to watch out for me. Everyone was encouraging me to stay with him, except three friends."

"What would have helped?"

"It would have been easier if he had died." Francesca smiled ruefully as she sank back into her chair. "I know you think that's horrible, but in fact I thought about it at the time. I said, 'Why doesn't he die?' There wouldn't have been any divorce negotiations, everything would have been cleaner. I wouldn't have had to deal with him anymore, or the lawyers. If he dies, it's not of his choosing. You haven't been left by choice. It's the free will that kills you.

"And I would have been in a better position socially. Everyone's very sympathetic toward a widow who loses a beloved husband. They're not very sympathetic to a wife and a husband getting a divorce. I definitely thought it would have been much kinder, really much nicer, if he died."

"It's a worse tragedy than death," said psychiatrist Anne E. Bernstein. "For the woman who is left, there is less societal and family support. There's still a feeling that she's somehow at fault. Whereas if he's jogging and drops dead of a heart attack, everybody rallies around."

According to Dr. Mara Gleckel, "Death is much easier to cope with than Jennifer Fever. With death there's no sense of shame, no humiliation."

For Jane Spock, the separation came after forty-eight years of marriage to renowned pediatrician and activist Dr. Benjamin Spock. Jane Spock says that her former husband, who is now eighty-four, met his new wife after they separated. Jane had worked closely with him, helping him in the preparation of his popular book, *Baby and Child Care,* and joining him in his travels as a peace activist and presidential candidate. With children and grandchildren, so many years, so much history, between them, when Benjamin Spock asked for a divorce, in addition to profound emotional pain, Jane faced enormous problems of readjustment.

When they married, Benjamin Spock was many years away from the fame that would follow in later years. In fact, Jane says, he was a Republican and she was the socialist. She assisted him in all his efforts and believes she influenced his liberal political philosophy.

In her New York apartment, she spoke warmly about their early years. Today arthritis may make simple tasks difficult for her, but her eyes were shining, and her lively intellect and curiosity made our time together special.

"The first years of our marriage were pretty good," Jane recalled. "I mean, we had a lot of fun, a lot of friends. But he was very flirtatious with all women. It upset me; it made me feel the way you feel when you've almost been in an accident. I thought it would stop, but it didn't. I tried hard not to get those feelings, but they continued."

"Were you surprised that after all the years you and Ben shared, he would ask for a divorce?"

"It wasn't a total surprise," Jane answered softly. "I think I was getting signals that it might happen. The breakup came around 1975. At first he only wanted a separation, and then we'd see how things worked out. I felt badly, very badly, but I felt hope. A few months after we separated, he met his new wife—she's forty years younger—and they got married."

"Why do you think he remarried so quickly?"

"I think he needed a young woman. I thought he was always flirtatious," she said, echoing what she had said before, "and I think he wanted that satisfaction of appealing to a younger woman. I believe that unconsciously he thought it would make him feel younger; but consciously he didn't know that.

"You see, I wasn't sure of him at all. I think the trouble was I wasn't angry enough. I turned it inside and became depressed."

"What was the worst part?" I asked.

"The loneliness was awful," Jane replied instantly, "and not having enough to do. Really, my life was in threads; and I didn't have the guts to find what was good to help me. I was in more pain with my arthritis than now, so I couldn't take on a job, even though I wanted to. I think that's one of the first things a woman should do in my situation."

After their husbands left them, the wives I talked to traveled different paths in their journeys to create new lives. Still, almost all of them acknowledge that at the time, they experienced a sense of overwhelming *inevitability*. As if to say, "A younger woman? It had to happen. I could have handled anything, anything but that."

Jane Spock observed, "We show our age; a wrinkled man is attractive. I tried dyeing my hair, and it was much worse; it made me look much older. When I was divorced ten years ago, I was much younger-looking than I am now." Jane sighed, and with a sad smile added, "I'm more wrinkled than I was."

Dory Previn agreed; the discovery of her first wrinkle was a killer. It is often a turning point in a woman's life.

"I remember seeing the first line that wasn't a laugh line," she recalled. "It was a tributary, and I went 'Ahhh.' I was devastated. Because if I was seeing that, and focusing on it, someone else was seeing it too. Do you understand?"

I understood. Just as people obsessed with money check the assets in their bank accounts daily, women of any age habitually seek confirmation of their self-worth in a looking glass. But the mirror can be a cruel barometer of a woman's net worth. She views herself through the eyes of her culture, remembering all that the ads and movies and magazines have told her about the necessity of being and staying young.

While she may still feel young, lead an active life, her face in the mirror may seem to mock her. Even if she feels she's looking pretty terrific for her age, there are reminders everywhere that she "ain't what she used to be."

In fiction as in life, the realization of the tantalizing lure of younger women is confirmed again and again when middle-aged women view themselves in a mirror.

The college campus is a fertile breeding ground for Jennifer Fever, populated as it is by adoring young women and aging professors ripe for a love affair with young girls who hang on their every word. In Alison Lurie's popular novel *The War Between the Tates,* a college professor becomes involved with a girl half his age. His wife, Erica Tate, sits before a mirror and is startled, can barely recognize herself. She wants to scream at the mirror, to weep, and she remembers a friend who remarked that "if Martians ever came to America they would conclude our religion to be the worship of pretty young women, for she or her image is everywhere: at political rallies and parades and sports events; on billboards and packages . . . For over twenty years she, Erica, was one of the incarnations of the goddess. Now the spirit has departed from her. . . . She must camouflage the loss, but is uncertain how to begin."

Georgina Ramonos was only thirty when she discovered that the worship of pretty young women was her husband's personal religion, and that the spirit of youth had obviously departed from her. "Maybe I lost it on my way to nursery school, or maybe in my sleep; but to my ex-husband, I was no longer young."

When it happened, her brother told her, "If you really want to fight it, you can fight it on your years together and on your brains. Although you're very pretty, to a man, especially at Joe's stage of the game, a twenty-three-year-old *is* Nirvana."

"I was insulted, but he was right. She *was* Nirvana. Still, as far as I can see, he's now back in the same thing; he's now with a thirty-year-old woman. I felt anger, still feel it, but it took six years to feel it, because for so long I honestly felt it was out of my control.

Because she was younger and prettier, there was nothing I could do about it."

Model Jody Winters belongs to LADIES (Life After Divorce Is Eventually Sane), a Los Angeles organization founded by a group of women who shared several things in common. Their husbands were celebrities, well-known figures in the entertainment business, and all the women had been left by their husbands, generally for younger women.

With her short-cropped hair, pixieish expression, and boundless energy, Jody travels across the country, appearing on television, working with displaced homemakers, helping other women through the troubled waters of midlife divorce. With the sense of perspective that comes only with time, Jody has decided that painful as it is, the desire for another, younger woman is an inevitable rite of male passage:

"The hard part of it is to accept the sociological fact that some men have to move on. It might have nothing to do with you. You're a very nice person. It might not even have to do with the fact you're older. It doesn't mean you're a terrible person. If anything, they feel a little badly for you.

"Their life—it's the only one they have," she continued, her voice earnest, her tone totally without condescension, "and if they're so impelled to be elsewhere, that's just the truth of it, and you can't hate them for it; it's just how it is. The difficult thing is to accept that, stop hating him and the next Mrs. Her. It had to be somebody; she had nothing to do with it. If your life was working out perfectly, there wouldn't be a new her."

Dory Previn also experienced a sense of doomy prescience when her husband left for a younger woman:

"Women who aren't just interested in shopping or family, or being a wife and mother, women who use their minds, who know they're smarter than a younger woman by virtue of experience or study—I think they know they could compete with anything *but* a younger woman. And knowing that you cannot compete with youth makes it more devastating."

"Were you one of those women who knew that?"

"Sure. I knew I couldn't compete with that. There is no way. At that point one either gives up or goes out and gets rejuvenated. You've seen these artificial sixty-year-old women who look twenty-five. Many years ago, I capitulated to it for a time."

Sandy Green had a sense of living through an unavoidable nightmare when her husband left. "There's something about me that is fundamentally a fatalist," she said. "I don't fight for a lot of things once they've happened, because I feel a kind of fatality about them. I don't know if you can win back someone after he stops loving you and wants to leave. I didn't realize that for many years he had stopped loving me. I wouldn't admit it because the signs weren't there.

"When I fight for someone, it doesn't work out for me," Sandy explained coolly. "I don't think I can change the tide. The die is cast. A black can't change his color; a woman can't change her age. You can only get philosophically detached and say, 'This is life and women *do* get older and smart women can deal with it, and some deal with it better than others.'"

If the die is cast and women believe it's inevitable for men to seek out younger women, that they are as helpless in stopping it as they are in stopping an earthquake, tornado, or other natural disaster, one might imagine they would also feel to a large degree blameless. But ironically, the other emotion that coexists with inevitability is self-recrimination.

This is different from self-exploration, self-scrutiny, or a willingness to assume responsibility. Soon after their separations, the wives blamed themselves. Feeling defective, they tore away at their already diminished sense of self-esteem. A looking glass confirmed that physical flaws and signs of aging had driven their husbands into the arms of a younger woman. Looking *inside,* they were able to level additional charges of culpability at themselves.

Some of their self-accusations were doubtlessly on the mark, and their failings may well have contributed to problems in their marriages, adding to their husbands' unhappiness. But that couldn't be the whole story.

Even if friends and mothers, lawyers and therapists, tried to tell them it takes two, that there are other responses to lapses and failings than a man's leaving for a younger woman, the women could not believe it. Even if their friends told them that their husbands' leaving might have more to do with the men's needs, perhaps the men's failings; told them about Darwin and Freud, about a man's terror of being sexually diminished, about his attending too many funerals; about men seeing their mothers in their wives, a shrinking future in their lives; experiencing a fear of dying, a sense of personal entitlement, a narcissistic "I want mine now" social climate—still all the women went through a period of self-recrimination for a time.

They were of a generation of women born to please; and obviously they were no longer pleasing. Blame was a reflex, the product of a virulent superego, the by-product of the way they were educated and socialized. At the time of their separations, the wives became prosecuting attorney, judge, and jury. Arriving at a unanimous verdict, they declared themselves guilty of being imperfect. The sense of self-blame felt rooted within them; it had a life of its own.

Sandy said, "Sometimes I think if I had put curtains up, been a better cook . . . Why didn't I do that? Where did I go wrong? Why couldn't I keep him?

"I should have made a better home. If a woman creates a warm domestic life, it's harder to leave. My mother did, but I rejected it, was indifferent to it, didn't know how. Women who do have a better chance of keeping their men. American women aren't terribly gifted at that."

Laura put it this way: "I had leaned tremendously on him, needing constant reassurance. I was bogged down with the children, who were always getting colds. Then I'd get colds. I must have been a terrible drag. I blame myself for having two babies and letting that be a reason for not working."

Jane described her sense of self-recrimination in these words: "After forty-eight years of marriage, you feel guilty because you're a failure. That's the hardest thing: the guilt and the sense of failure." She paused to take a sip of water, and continued with a frown. "If

I hadn't been so critical of him, for being impractical, and for being so busy that he didn't have time for me, we'd still be married now."

Georgina said, "I felt like the ugliest, fattest, most nonsexual person that ever lived. It never went away, that feeling. Even now I can walk in a room and be surprised if a man makes a pass. I blame myself for my inability to stay twenty-three, for my failure to stay young and beautiful."

Only Francesca seemed reasonably free of self-recrimination: "Occasionally I've gone back in time and said, 'At this point if I had done that, maybe this would have happened, and that would have happened.' But it's just a game, because I *had* kept changing, and there was nothing else I could have done."

But there is a difference between self-scrutiny and guilt-inducing, self-lacerating recrimination. Many women were fortunate enough to discover that their marriages had been laced with a kind of emotional bondage, and based on suffocating dependencies. These insights changed their lives. One painful realization many of them shared was the fact that they wouldn't merely be separated from their husbands, but from a whole network of friends and associations that had been an important part of their lives.

As Francesca said, "I lost a lot of friends that needed couples. I was a single woman, and all of a sudden, to people who had been my friends for years, I was a threat! I couldn't believe it. They don't tell you, but they become very unfriendly, very protective of their mates, as if I was going to come on to them."

Vexed by the memory of herself in this distasteful role, in which others had cast her, Francesca gave a brittle laugh when she continued. "I found that people who wanted to stay friendly with Rod and me felt some sort of ridiculous obligation to report to me what they knew about him, giving me a blow-by-blow. I felt they were doing the same with him as far as I was concerned. They'd tell me they had met the girl, how young she was, and 'You're much nicer,' and 'How could he make a mistake like that?' It became very unpleasant. Some friends gave me up; others I gave up."

Jody Winters explained. "There is the umbrella of embarrassment," she said. " 'There's So-and-so, who's a failure in her life.'

There's no social script for divorce; people don't know where they stand in their friendships. That's because people are too embarrassed to call the embarrassed person. Then, because so much time goes by, they're embarrassed to call at all, then they forget, don't call at all, and they've lost a friend."

Jane Spock discovered that creating bonds of friendship throughout forty-eight years of marriage was no guarantee she'd keep them. "The interesting thing is that many people who saw you as couples drop you. If you can't come with a man, they don't ask you to dinner; you see them for lunch. So you lose your friends."

Laura Rossen agreed. "It did surprise me; none of his friends—not the wives, not the husbands, not one—has called or written, tried to reach me in any way. I don't have couples anymore as friends. I can't believe how few people I see, how terribly lonely I am."

New friends?

"I didn't like being around some women friends; I had to stop seeing two women I used to go to the movies with. They were so bitter, too grim. Who wants to spend an entire evening trashing men: 'This terrible thing happened to me; men are awful'? One wants to be with people who have started over and made it."

Losing friends was one thing that didn't happen to Georgina Ramonos. "I think that's something that people *think* happens. My friends stayed my friends. They know I'm not a threat." Georgina's eyes narrowed, and a sour expression flickered across her face. "That teenage T-shirted princess was the threat; she was the cancer walking around, not me."

But Dr. Mara Gleckel believes losing friends often comes with the territory. "Her friends become scared of her. She will lose a number of them, and this adds salt to the wound."

"Why do they become scared?" I asked.

"Let's say a married couple has a friend whose husband has left her for a Jennifer," she answered. "The wife is threatened because her husband might do the same thing. If the woman has gotten a divorce and is now single, she becomes just another sexual threat to this woman's marriage. The husband is threatened too, because it puts him in touch with feelings that make him examine his own life; and he doesn't want to do that."

"What if the woman who was left is handling it well, developing a life of her own?"

"In that case, her friend's husband *definitely* doesn't want his wife connected with her." Dr. Gleckel grinned at my puzzled expression. "Because his wife *needs* him, *depends* on him, and he wants to keep it that way. And if, by chance, he's having an affair with a Jennifer, he doesn't want this suddenly divorced woman around reminding his wife of all the possibilities available to him. Any way you look at it, even if that friendship is maintained, it's never the same."

Losing friends is a natural by-product of divorce, but for the woman who experiences the particular sting of losing her husband to a Jennifer, the loss of friends is especially traumatic.

Women were confronted with a startling discovery. A house that had recently been filled with chatter and the ordinary sounds of a family going through the daily round was suddenly filled with a shrieking silence.

Loneliness was only part of their battle. Whether their children were away or at home, the women had to help *them* through the crisis as well. Sometimes a child could add to the problem; for others, having a child kept them going, provided the life force, the will to survive.

Sandy Green said, "I had to stay alive for my son. But it was tough on him. He was the first one in his class whose parents divorced. He felt like an outsider."

Georgina Ramonos's daughter was quite young when her father left. I wondered how the child had been affected by his leaving.

"I thought she was fine, but about a year after he left, she decided one day she wouldn't go out of the house. At four years old, she just stayed inside. I tried to talk to her, but she said, 'I won't go, because when I come back you won't be here. Daddy left, and I know you're going to go too.'

"I told her again and again that mommies and daddies get divorced but children never get divorced." Georgina smiled weakly, saying, "That's hard to understand when you're three years old. Joe and I took her to a doctor. The therapist just played blocks and chatted with her. When she came out of the office, we were both waiting. And it worked. We went two times; that's all it took. She got the message: We'd both always be there for her. She never wanted to stay home again."

Laura Rossen's children were much older and had a different set of problems.

"The kids were absolutely in shock," she said. "My daughter was just the same age as the girl he was having the affair with. For her it was hell; she collapsed. When she found out, she lay in bed, and I felt I had to be a physical healer; there was nothing I could say. There was no rational thing I could do."

Laura wrapped her arms around a pillow, saying, "I held her like this, trying to reinforce in her that she was still a girl, a desirable, young, pretty girl. You're connected to your father; there's a bit of that. She was kind of jealous; she was being rejected too."

As Laura remembered her daughter's ordeal, her face was pinched with pain. "What I did was literally touch her all over and massage her and hold her," Laura explained tenderly. "It was all I could do. She has gotten over most of it, though there is still upset."

"And your son?"

"My son is more passive; and he's having real problems. He's doing badly in school, but I know he's just acting out, getting back at his father. He was attending his father's prep school; I had to keep explaining to the school that family problems were creating trouble for him, that it was essential for him to graduate. Everyone was yelling at him to do better," she said thoughtfully. "I think in some ways he was more hit than my daughter."

Francesca Grayson's children were older, and she had a rough time with her daughter:

"At first Rod told her that I left for no reason. She was away at school, and he called and told her I had walked out on him. So she didn't talk to me for six months."

"Didn't you tell her the truth?"

"She wouldn't listen. If I called, she would hang up on me. Or say, 'He told me you left him for no reason, and I'll never forgive you. I hate you.'

"It was driving me crazy, and I told Rod he had to tell her the truth, and finally he did. Then she stopped talking to him." Francesca laughed, delighted by the irony. "She called and said her father told her the truth, but she never said 'I'm sorry' about what happened."

Psychoanalyst Harvey Greenberg believes that for adolescent daughters, a father's leaving for a younger woman creates special problems. "Long before he leaves for a Jennifer—and even if he doesn't have another lover—his daughter's adolescence may have stirred up unconscious erotic feelings in a father. He may become rejecting towards her, in order to distance himself from these feelings. When such a man leaves his wife for a younger girl, the daughter often feels doubly rejected. Like her mother, she has been abandoned for another woman."

I asked, "How do they express their feelings of rejection?"

"Often they may develop a callous, promiscuous attitude towards relationships with men—what one patient of mine called a 'fuck around, fuck you' life-style. They may go into a shell, have no sexual relationships at all. Or they may get into a relationship that centers around money and material goods. They can become increasingly self-involved, more vain and narcissistic, with little interest in love, empathy, social concerns."

"And the sons?"

"The son may feel he has won the Oedipal battle. He's taken over the father's role; now he's the one who will watch out for Mom. He may become estranged from his father, while still secretly hoping for his love. These kids always seem to be walking on a tightrope, strung across the morass created by the father's involvement with the younger woman."

"How does a therapist help a family going through these difficult experiences?"

"You have to help kids appreciate both their parents. When the son goes to visit Dad, his feelings are often stirred by the young woman, who may be closer to his own interests, his own peer group, than either his father or mother. This can cause problems for everyone.

"I tell parents to be discreet, not to flaunt their sexuality. No walking around in underwear. The older child sees his father being a better father with his new baby, and it's not just perceptual. He probably is a better father, with more experience, time, attention, and money to spend on a new baby. That's a real problem for the kids from the first marriage."

After Jody Winters's husband left her, he immediately remarried and had a new baby. She described the specific issues facing the former wife and children of a public figure. "People think that what you miss are the parties and limos. They don't understand that isn't what your life was. It was your family, ongoing, continuing. Most of us married when we were young, and the fame accumulated, and the truth is the evolution happened and somehow the marriage didn't work out, or the men just *had* to move on.

"Our problems are exactly the same as other human beings'." Jody closed her eyes, pursed her lips, and inhaled, reminding me of a little girl preparing to swallow some awful-tasting medicine. "Plus when you turn on the TV, you can see your ex-husband with his new wife, having a good time. It's a public aspect. Sure, other women suffer through this in their own communities, but it's different in Hollywood. They may see it in their society pages, but this is on TV, it's on *Entertainment Tonight,* it's at the market newsstand, splashed in big headlines, with pictures of your ex-husband with his new young wife, holding up a little baby and saying, 'Happy at Last.'

"Happy at last," Jody repeated. "They've got other children, who wonder why they don't hear from them. That's not very caring for their first set of children. The mother hurts for herself, but she dies for her kids." Jody hesitated; for a moment she seemed locked in her own thoughts. Then she said softly, "You're wondering what they're thinking, and usually they're thinking: I'm nothing."

Dr. Greenberg says it doesn't have to be that way. "I work with parents to incorporate the older children into the new children's life so they don't feel dispossessed. If the father is really happy and healthy, he will treat his older kids as well as he treats the new one—that is, with time and help."

With time and help, the children and their mothers generally do recover. But undeniably it is a struggle. Berkeley psychologist Lillian Rubin has studied the attitudes of midlife women, and she gave a graphic explanation of why a man's succumbing to Jennifer Fever can make solid, stable women come unglued.

For the one who is left, man or woman, it is a body blow. But ironically, when their husbands leave them at midlife, that is the time when the Janets experience themselves as being better than they've ever been.

"They are sexually mature; they're free; and the kids are gone," Dr. Rubin explained. "Her sexuality is flourishing, and if his is waning, it's generally not because of her aging flesh but because of biology.

"But he *needs* to feel sexual." Dr. Rubin emphasized the point. "His sexuality is intimately connected to his estimation of his manhood. A young girl boosts his aging sexual drive. But for a wife who's been feeling good about herself, when he leaves for a younger woman, it creates a real disjunction between her internal notion of herself and his vision. She asks herself, 'I thought I was in my prime, and now he's leaving for a younger woman. Have I been crazy all these years?' "

Lillian Rubin had touched a nerve. Many of the Janets expressed a similar feeling, as do many of my friends. At midlife, we don't feel unattractive; and we *are* freer than we've ever been. Not just free of our children and their constant needs, but free of old tapes spinning out problems and anxieties, free of nagging insecurities and doubts that haunted us for years. To be told at this sweet time of life—sweet in spite of its implicit threats of mortality—that we are irrelevant, that our services are no longer needed, is indeed a body blow.

"I understand," I told Dr. Rubin. "So this woman who was feeling terrific buys into his view of her. And then she goes out in the world and shazam! Society's vision of her confirms his vision of her, a vision that says she's finished, bankrupt, kaput. And she comes unglued. Right?"

"Right," Dr. Rubin replied. "How could she not lose her moorings?"

Unlike Medea, many women endure the loss of their husbands without the desire for revenge. But when revenge *is* played out, it's not with a dagger or a pistol, but with a checkbook and a credit card, often out of a need to survive, and sometimes out of a desire to punish the man for his betrayal.

Or it may be seen in a painful tug-of-war to win the hearts and minds of their children. Most of the women emphasized that they were determined not to allow their children to become emotional pawns, foot soldiers in the war that had erupted between the parents; and that they hadn't willfully, purposefully inflicted their own violent emotions on their children.

Most of them didn't feel homicidal rage, or admit they felt it only for a fleeting horrible moment. Still, many report they had to battle a bout of depression, the length and severity of which differed from woman to woman. For some, it was a couple of rocky months; for others, a sadness too deep to be expressed in tears.

More than a few of them could say, albeit with twenty-twenty hindsight, and two to fifteen years after the event, that for all the pain, their lives were changed for the better. Frequently the woman who managed to turn loss into personal advantage and growth had been through the experience in her early thirties. Fewer of the women I spoke to who lost their husbands to Jennifers when they were in their forties or fifties indicate it was the positive, seminal event it was for some of the younger women.

Of all the women I sought to interview, the most difficult to find was one who had discovered her husband's affair with a Jennifer, perhaps separated for a while, and then, somehow, both she and her husband had agreed on a reconciliation. Certainly I knew such women existed, and in considerable numbers. Frequently I encountered them and they would agree to be interviewed, only to back away at the last moment. Embarrassment? Injured pride? Fear of being judged? Not wishing to seem an anachronism in a climate of female independence?

I never knew. I did know that not only would such a woman have to transcend wounded pride, anger, and embarrassment, but her husband would also wish to return, presumably giving up the affair with his Jennifer.

I would from time to time, in an advice column, happen on an anonymous letter from a woman who had done just that. Not so incidentally, the letter writer would generally be congratulated for being refreshingly unvindictive, a woman who had come to her senses.

Of the women discussed in this chapter, two decided that they would indeed forgive, and try to forget. I thought I would follow the women along the emotional journey they traveled to reach their decisions, before I disclosed which of them decided against divorce.

How do women find their moorings? I would discover they consult different maps and travel very different paths as they struggle to make their way to the proverbial other side.

13

Survival

As they traveled along the bumpy road from being victims to becoming survivors, the Janets told me that a pivotal moment occurs when they begin to see realistically how they may have contributed to the failure of their marriages. Without self-accusation, they are able to reflect and, possibly for the first time, develop insights into why their husbands needed younger women.

The popular perception is that a man becomes attracted to a younger woman when he's about fifty and a constellation of events—all replete with intimations of mortality—merge into a "now or never" frame of mind. Sandy Green knows that's not always the case. Her husband was only thirty-one when he left for a younger woman. More than twenty years have passed, and finally Sandy was able to talk about what fueled his need for a Jennifer:

"I think he simply *had* to have a young woman, and not just to feel younger or in that trophy way that many older men have, so they can be admired by others. I think he simply had to have a young girl."

"Why 'simply'?" I asked. "I don't think it's simple at all, Sandy."

"Look, he never had a youth of his own."

I was amazed at the change in her tone. She had changed from reliving the pain of being a victim, to this almost detached, omniscient narrator.

"He was ambitious since he was a little boy," she went on. "He never had time for youth, and never had much going for him in the way of girls. Now he's got plenty of fame, and a lot of women love that. He's an international celebrity, and he wants the youth he never had.

"Today he can play house with this new wife and baby the way he couldn't with me. He's not as driven. If he has a best-seller or a flop, the world will not stop. When we were married, a hit or a flop and the world simply stopped turning."

Sandy reached for a book and waved it in front of me. Like a lawyer arguing before a jury, she was pleading her case, the case of her hard-fought and belated comprehension of all that had happened.

"When he met this girl, he'd had his first financial coup, the best-seller, the movie deal; he'd won the grand sweepstakes. And here was his old life-style," she said, her eyes searching the room, looking for vestiges of her former life. "Suddenly he was around glamorous people, and he'd come home to this apartment, the baby crying, me depressed. How grim our life must have seemed.

"It was simply a case of a man who felt if he didn't take chances and make changes in his life now, he'd never do it," Sandy explained coolly. "He had it all, and now he could have girls. It was always clear to me that he was going to be famous."

Not bad. I was impressed by what Sandy *didn't* say. She'd never asked why she couldn't be part of that glamour package. Dry-eyed, in an even voice, and with not a trace of self-pity, she didn't ask, as women for whom the hurt is more recent might ask, why she had to be abandoned. After the years of working, the nineteen-hour days, the wooing of the "right" people to help his career, the endless networking, the childbearing, the scrimping, why couldn't she share in a part of the golden egg? Or why, like the faded, peeling wallpaper in their dingy apartment, she, too, had to be removed? What about "in good times and in bad, for better or worse"?

Perhaps Sandy thought those kinds of thoughts when it happened, but I discovered that even in women whose husbands had left them only a short time before we met, while self-pity had to have been there, it was vestigial, not a large part of their emotional arsenal.

Laura Rossen, whose experience is fairly recent, has, despite the rawness of her wound, developed an understanding of her husband's actions:

"My children told me the girl he left me for wasn't glamorous or sexy-looking. That's strange, because I had imagined her as a kind of sexpot; I felt so sexually neutered myself when he left.

"They told me she was very young, very thin, wore little makeup, and had a short, boyish haircut. Jung wrote about middle-aged men who are drawn to idealized mirror images of themselves as young boys, adolescents." Laura nodded, as if she were talking to herself, convincing herself. "Unconsciously they are trying to cling to their own youth, avoiding death by being in love with a boyish, unwomanly-looking woman. I've met other women who were equally surprised by the kind of girl their husbands left them for.

"Also, after some tight financial years, he was beginning to make it; he was getting the right referrals from the right doctors. More secure in his work, he could entertain these notions of a young wife, and he liked the way it made him feel."

For Dory Previn, painful as it was, her growth as a woman began after her husband left her for another, younger woman. "Oh, I mean he was the king and I was the subject." Dory shook her head, frowning as if she were leafing through a picture album, seeing an unflattering picture of herself that made her unhappy.

"That's an enormous responsibility, being king in a one-subject country. I only got to know me after my divorce; therefore how could others know me before? I was the shadow of another person, so I didn't exist. I once wrote about Marilyn Monroe; I call people like her 'shadowless beings.' You either have no shadow or become a shadow, OK? What did she become? She became one of the greatest shadows on screen, one that was so large that it ultimately enveloped her."

"How does it happen?" I asked.

"At first it's like a terrific game. You become him; you say his words and you smile his smile. Then he says something like, 'Isn't that wonderful?' And you say, 'Isn't that wonderful?' Then he says, 'I don't want you to do that anymore; will you stop?' And you say, 'Will you stop?' He goes, and you're left there, because of a game."

"That's horrible," I remarked.

"It *is* horrible to have someone reflecting you all the time. I can see now what it does to the partner. I know two women who are married to very famous men, and when you say how are you, they say, 'John is doing well; he just got a movie.'

"You say, 'Yes, but how are *you?*' Who are you? That's got to wear down the partner; the person who depends is a terrible burden on the person being depended upon."

That clinging dependency of women living only through their husbands would be the subject of one of Dory Previn's most poignant lyrics:

> i smiled your smile
> till my mouth
> was set.
> it was wrong
> i was you baby
> i was you too long

"I tried anything that was thrown at me," Dory said. "I have kinky, curly red hair, and so I dyed my hair dark and straightened it in order to look like him. I thought I'd do anything that would give me equality and life. When he left I did things that I had earlier thought would give me death. That is to say, I had an affair with a fellow who was twenty years younger."

Similar to other women of our generation, Dory had a belated discovery of the nurturing, sustaining value of her women friends. "The best relationship I had during that period was with a woman. It was marvelous; it began my love and respect for women, and commiseration with women. I would recommend to any woman who's in trouble to form a deep relationship with a woman; it doesn't have to be sexual: You know, what in Victorian times they called loving friends."

One of her songs has become a classic. To some women, it addresses an unspeakable reality, and for others, gives voice to their deepest and darkest psychic fears:

> Beware
> of young girls
> who come to the door.
> too often they crave
> to cry
> at a wedding
> and dance on a grave

Although most women don't have Dory Previn's unique creative talent, others also found self-expression the route to self-discovery. Francesca Grayson said, "I wrote till four in the morning, and it was a wonderful release. I'd say after reading it, 'Wow! Oh, so *that's* how it was; *that's* how I felt.' I nurtured the idea it would be published, and I tried sending it to agents and publishers, but nothing came of it. Still it helped me as much as anything to see things I never saw before."

In addition to pouring her thoughts into a word processor, Francesca tried other things: ". . . keeping busy and for the first time in my life being really alone and discovering you don't die from it. Take a walk, buy a dog, go to the Lighthouse and read for the blind. It's getting out of yourself and getting into somebody else, being helpful to someone, feeling useful somewhere.

"It does help to feel desirable, and soon after leaving my husband, I did have a great romantic affair with a sexy man, a beautiful man, so attractive and so much fun. It was brief, and there was never any serious intention on either of our parts; it was lovely. It helps make you feel like a woman again. It didn't help with the global picture, but it helped with the moments."

Laura Rossen said, "I went back to school. Getting focused in my studies helped a lot. And I had people to the apartment even though I had no money. People brought food and wine, and talk and laughter filled the rooms. It helped, although I couldn't believe I was functioning."

When Jane Spock reached out to help others, she found a lifeline for herself. She created a support group for older and midlife women confronting the problems of divorce. As Jane talked, I wondered how those women felt meeting a woman who had been married to such a famous man—and there was Jane Spock saying she had been in *their* predicament, felt *their* pain.

"I think the group, the Gray Divorcees, helped the most," Jane told me. "I went on TV and radio and talked about it, took out an ad, and I was amazed—over three hundred women called after they heard me. We met for two years, every week for two hours.

"I solved things for myself, but it was very painful for me. I'd come out exhausted, because I had relived my life with each person in the group that I had tried to help. But it helped in the long run. I got better when I stopped being depressed and got angry."

"And for the women in the group you worked with, what helped them most?" I asked.

"If they couldn't get a paid job—and most of them couldn't find work at their age—volunteer work helped many of them. So did keeping busy, getting out of the house every day. And you have to face what I faced." Jane's eyes widened and she pointed her finger at me, as if I were a member of her group. "You're not going to get him back. Women spend so much time trying to figure out how to win him back. I did too; then I stopped. The most help I got came at the moment when I realized: I don't want him back.

"Get in a group." Jane's voice rang with deep-felt emotion. "And there should be more groups. Our problems are special. It's different for widows—there's no guilt. Oh, there may be survivor guilt, but then there are lovely memories. Women who are left need a special kind of professional care and support."

"What about self-pity? Did you discover most women go through a time of blaming themselves?"

"I think they have to feel both for a while. If they have the money they should go to a therapist; that will help them gradually get over it. Many women in my group couldn't afford any help, yet therapy helped me so much."

Sandy Green could afford help, but for her it wasn't a positive experience.

"If I'd had a good shrink it would have helped, but I had an inadequate shrink. I had simply stopped growing at one point. I don't know why I was stuck for so long. Why it took me all this time. Why I was so dependent on this man. To nurse a wound for that many years!" Frowning, she shook her head and said, "Good shrinks can probably deal with it; the two I went to didn't help."

"Why didn't it work?" I asked.

"They didn't help me solve the basic problems: Why I do the things I do. Why the mourning process was so long. Why romantic natures like me invest so much in illusion. I could give you claptrap answers, but if you invest so much in another human being, you get stuck."

For Francesca, psychotherapy was a mixed blessing. "It helps, but not nearly as much as a few intense, good friends," she said. "Therapy felt like a crutch to me, not something I wanted in my life for an extended period of time. I pay a therapist to listen to me, and at the end of forty-five minutes he says, 'That's all the time we have; we'll continue next week.' A friend, on the other hand, you can call any hour and say, 'I need to talk to you.' They're there, and they really love you and want to help. I had three good friends and one son I could talk to."

If women develop an understanding of their own flaws, and what pieces of their husbands' psyches drove them to younger women; if they can muster a sense of irony to replace their outrage, they are taking important steps on the road to emotional recovery. But in the matter of money, for many neither insight nor irony can help.

Thousands of divorced women each year find themselves becoming a statistic in what sociologists call "the feminization of poverty," slipping from a middle-class to a lower-class standard of living.

A principal reason for this is that judges interpreting the new equitable-distribution divorce laws frequently assume that a fifty-year-old woman who has been married for twenty-five years will be self-supporting immediately after the divorce. But if she has no experience or has been away from her work to raise a family, that, combined with the fact of ageism in hiring, can make job hunting for the midlife divorced woman a struggle.

Women like Laura Rossen, who don't have a career of their own, money of their own, must tackle thorny financial problems, frequently for the first time in their lives. When gut issues—food, shelter, clothing—get heaped upon their emotional problems, the result can be devastating.

Laura and I had been talking for hours, but we hadn't discussed her financial problems, which I knew were enormous. She crushed another cigarette into the ashtray balanced on her knee, fixed her eyes on a distant spot somewhere outside the large picture window, and said, "I can't live here anymore. I have to find a smaller apartment I can afford. Bill wants to sell it; he needs the money for a new place with the girl. My lawyer says I have to do it. I hate leaving, so much of my life happened here, but it's his apartment and I have no choice." With a slight smile, she added, "Maybe living in a different place will be helpful.

"The other night I felt suddenly 'I don't know if I can cope': The money in my bank account was cleared out."

Laura turned to face me, and it was as if it were a sudden and unbelievable realization when she said, "I have to move; I don't even have money to go to a movie; the kids are strung out. I just sat on the edge of the bed and cried."

For a few moments neither of us said a word, then haltingly, her voice barely a whisper, she tried to continue. "My son saw me, but I don't want him to see me like this. I don't want to turn him into a husband surrogate or sour his relationship with his father. But I couldn't help it.

"I am outraged at the financial thing, outraged." Laura stood up, crossed the room, and then, standing before me, she continued, her voice trembling with anger. "I kept saying to myself, 'I can't believe it; why doesn't he care about me financially, just as a friend? How can anybody decide just not to?' But he was always lax paying bills, and if he doesn't pay the dentist, what makes me think he's going to help me?

"You think: Every other woman knows how much the schooling was, the insurance was. You feel like an idiot; you don't know anything. You can't imagine what it feels like when the lawyers ask you these questions. It will take two years to find out all these things."

Sitting down, she lit a cigarette, watched the smoke circle above her head, and said, "I'm the only one of my friends who didn't have a job. It was a mistake not to have a career, some money tucked away, a talent, a trade, something I could do to make money."

Divorce lawyer Betty Levinson described the reactions of women who arrive in her office. "When I see older women who don't have a clue as to what their marital assets are, who haven't balanced the proverbial checkbook, they don't know what I'm talking about. So when I say, 'This is your choice,' they can't make those choices at that time. It's shell shock, and your heart goes out to them. When the music stops and there's not a chair for you to sit in, you collapse. That's what it's like for them."

For Sandy, money wasn't a problem. But she has enormous empathy for women like Laura, who faced economic hardship in addition to the emotional issues of rejection and abandonment. "Whatever my life is, it's my life," Sandy told me. "Women who suffer financial hardship because of divorce, who aren't qualified to get a job and make a living, are up shit's creek."

"You went through your own version of hell, Sandy," I said to her.

"You can't equate that to emotional pain," she shot back in an instant. "I was an independent woman; with or without him, I could pay the rent. I'd rather have my own kind of heartache than be poor. When he left, I was in pain, but that's fixable. To be poor and to have no place to live? It's just not equatable."

Sometimes the problems of children and money combine, leading to financial crises for the wives, crises that provoke memories of the old injury, rekindling old rages that the women thought had been extinguished years before.

Georgina Ramonos and I met for coffee five months after our first interview, because, as she told me over the phone, she had news. "So it's seven years later, right? My daughter's doing great, I've got a job, a decent job, I'm not in love, but I'm alive." Georgina grinned as she admitted, "I'm even used to the fact that Joe and his T-shirted princess are married, have their own kid, and my daughter spends every other weekend with them."

"Not so terrible," I quipped.

"Wait!" she said firmly. "Now Joe says he can't afford to pay for private school. I don't live in the best neighborhood, and the schools are a disaster. When we divorced, Joe insisted that she should go to private school. I get no alimony, just two hundred a month in child support. I work, but I can't pay eight thousand dollars a year for private school."

"Why can't he pay it?" I asked.

"Was he fired?" Georgina said angrily. "No. He says his new kid has lots of expenses, and they just moved into a new house. Why doesn't his wife work? She has to take care of their baby, who is five. I reminded him I was working when Karen was seven months old."

"So what will you do?" I asked as we left the coffee shop and headed for the bus stop.

"I'll have to get a loan, or take him to court to enforce the agreement," she said, flagging the bus, "but that will cost money I don't have. I heard there was a law that says first families first, but I spoke to a lawyer and he said, 'No way.' "

It's not a law, but according to divorce lawyer Ralph M. Brozan there are some cases in which judges have ruled in favor of the first family. Brozan is not optimistic about the prospects for women like Georgina to achieve a legal remedy for their financial problems. "A woman has to have the 'stomach and money' to pursue a legal action to force her former husband to live up to the agreement he signed when the couple divorced."

In *The Divorce Revolution,* Lenore Weitzman reported startling statistics which revealed that divorced women and children suffer an immediate 73 percent drop in their standard of living, while their ex-husbands enjoy a 42 percent rise in theirs.

For mothers like Georgina, the news is worse. Child support is often "inadequate, unpaid, and uncollectable." The current laws reward men by making post-divorce fatherhood "optional," and penalize women like Laura, who "choose family over or even together with a career of their own.

"Economically, older and longer married women suffer the most after divorce. . . . When the courts project the post-divorce prospects for women after shorter marriages . . . they reason that a woman in her twenties or early thirties is young enough to acquire education or training and thus has the potential to find a satisfactory and well-paid job.

"But what about the woman in her forties or fifties or even sixties at the point of divorce? . . . Is it reasonable for judges to expect her to become self-sufficient? . . . The group of divorced women who report the most distress with their financial loss and who express the strongest feelings of outrage and injustice are the longer married middle and upper middle class women we interviewed."

In addition to facing the greatest downward mobility and contending with their children's confusion and anger at the sudden changes in *their* lives, Weitzman states, divorced older women must often move to smaller houses and poorer neighborhoods, and face the loss of neighborhood and friends. "She becomes increasingly isolated . . . finds herself on the outside looking in."

Weitzman describes Laura Rossen's predicament when she writes: "The woman who lived under one set of rules—gave priority to motherhood with no other marketable skills—is unfairly expected to live under a new set of rules that changed in the middle of the game. How can the courts suddenly force them to find work and support themselves?"

The fact is the courts do, and somehow, despite the odds and the obstacles they encountered, many of the women I interviewed came through and are living productive, self-supporting, and happy lives. Surviving the economic hardships, and their feelings of betrayal and anger, many were able to forge new careers and healthy relationships, and even Lenore Weitzman was optimistic on one count. The divorced midlife women said they were "personally better off than they were during marriage. They are proud of the skills they used to deal with the crisis, to marshal a support network, to manage their finances and to take control of their lives. They also report improved self-esteem, more pride in their appearance and greater competence in all aspects of their lives."

Sandy Green agreed to talk six months after her original interview. She looked wonderful, and is working on a new book. Sandy looked back on her hard-fought battle for self-esteem. "I can't emphasize enough when you finally shut the door on the past and go on about your life, how sweet it is," she commented. "It's just a regenerative thing that happens; it's healing. New things grow, new feelings happen, you get in new, fresh trouble." She laughed. "Then you begin to have some self-awareness. Maybe it's the law of compensation; you're older, you're not as pretty, you're stronger.

"My life is more enjoyable to me; that's partly age. I simply savor my place in this big universe." Her smile broadened, and while it was still the same little-girl smile I had noticed before, now it was brushed with a riper, deeper, maturing smile of understanding. "I have a much greater respect for life than I did. I've even become more religious; it's not something I can really be specific about."

"Happy at last?" I asked.

"I could use that word," she answered. "I'm simply much happier every day of my life, because I stop every day of my life to be happy and I didn't used to. Now I know it's important."

For many years the feelings of betrayal and rejection haunted her, but now Sandy was ready to speculate about the possibility of enjoying a new relationship with a man. "I do fear that it will happen again. Why it happens I don't really know, but I fear that finally I will be left. It's hard to accept that, but perhaps there's something in me that does not inspire loyalty."

"Sandy, I can't believe after all this time you can say that!" I exclaimed.

"It's true. My affairs always end because of another woman. I've come to the conclusion that I can have a longer relationship when it's a part-time relationship."

"Why?" I asked.

"I wouldn't permit another man to get that far. Since my divorce, I have taken chances on other men because I like men and I'm not about to give men up. I'm a middle-aged woman and I'll take a chance on men for as long as I can—until my looks give out completely," she said with a laugh, "or till my soul gives out completely. But you are taking a chance, because they *are* very untrustworthy. But I made the decision to take the chance."

"What do you want for yourself now?"

"I see where I victimize myself with men who have authority in my life. I want fun now; the stakes are different. I don't want a child; I'm not interested in living with someone, picking up his socks, making his dinner. I don't want to be judged. I want a little love affair. I want romance, moonglow."

Pieced together, with time and work, many of the women are ready to take the plunge again: if not into matrimony, at least into romance. But just when they're ready for romance, the Janets have to face some rather dispiriting 1980s sociological facts.

In 1986, a *Newsweek* headline shouted: "The Marriage Crunch, Too Late for Prince Charming," and *People* magazine proclaimed: "Harvard-Yale study says that most single women over thirty-five can forget about marriage."

Though later challenged and qualified, the new study only acknowledged what women had long known in their hearts; still, many of them were surprised to see cold, stark figures trumpeting the news that now both biology and demographics were against them. The specifics of the study were few but chilling. For the Janets, it was not wonderful to read that for a woman over forty, the chances of meeting a man and getting married are so slim that, as *Newsweek* put it, she is more likely to be killed by a terrorist.

The chief reason for these dreary statistics is that when men divorce, they choose to remarry women considerably younger than themselves. Add a gay population of 13 percent and you have Mandrought: an ever-increasing number of available women in the population and an ever-decreasing number of men. Of course, when they divorce, men and women appear in equal numbers in the population. But it's only for a moment in time. Because men remarry faster, and often choose a Jennifer, to midlife women it may seem as if available men appear as frequently as Halley's Comet, and when they do, are about as accessible as the Rosetta Stone.

Word of the study's findings created a cacophony of response. Like the bad news it was, the story ripped across the land, seizing headlines, providing grist for the mill of television and radio talk shows. While some reporters treated the story as a sidebar, others reported it as if they had discovered the wheel.

There are few things worse than having your darkest fears confirmed in shouting headlines or reported dispassionately by television newscasters for all the world to know. Apparently women who knew from experience that each passing year lowered their sexual status harbored a secret hope that they were wrong.

The tempo of the male-female duet intensified. Some Janets raised their voices in a chorus of disdain, steadfastly refusing to be characterized as yet another species of female walking wounded. Pointing to the new realities of the 1980s, they argued that because of increased economic power and greater employment opportunities, women no longer marry for the musty old reasons of the past. They reminded the doomsday forecasters that today there is far less stigma for a woman remaining unmarried; living with a lover is as acceptable as marriage, and for a variety of reasons many women actually opt out of the marriage game.

The study was based only on census figures; but if it had considered the views of single women who were living with men without benefit of matrimony, those who lived alone by *choice,* and lesbians, writer Katha Pollitt says, the results of the study would be cause for rejoicing rather than despair. "If large numbers of women have enough economic independence to reject the traditional hierarchical marriage, in which women barter domestic servitude and emotional submission for economic support and social recognition, in favor of a marriage that promises intimacy and equality," Pollitt maintains, that's good news.

The bad news is that for women who don't want to live alone, or who aren't gay, the fact remains it gets harder and harder to find a man to have all that intimacy and equality with.

Darker voices in a minor key (including a significant number of men and, I believe, only a minority of women) greeted the news as if, after so many years of liberation, it was a deserved comeuppance for women. It wasn't the liberation they objected to; it was merely the style with which it had been attained. Uncompromising, unyielding, unattractive, unrealistic in their expectations, angry, strident—these women and their unceasing demands were too much. Battle-weary men could do no more. Younger women were less demanding, less angry, less strident. Why can't women understand? Why are they surprised? They bring this on themselves.

And the beat goes on.

From many women on the front lines, who find themselves at midlife searching to meet a man, the response was more temperate.

My own reaction was strange. There was comfort in learning that despite a growing suspicion among some women, American parents had not been engaged in the systematic murder of male babies at birth and only now had the Harvard-Yale team of sociologists unearthed a domestic My Lai. Yes, there were men out there. But the reasons for midlife Mandrought left me less sanguine, and stirred some memories out of the dusty recesses of my mind.

An earlier generation of American women faced greater odds and confronted worse myths when headlines were even more prejudiced against them. Sociologist Carroll Smith-Rosenberg writes that "in the nineteenth century midlife women were told by physicians to resign from life for their own good." One doctor of the period warned, "My experience teaches me that a marked increase of sexual impulse at the change of life is a morbid impulse."

As for Prince Charming, it was improper and risky for a midlife woman even to be looking for him. In the words of a nineteenth-century physician, "It therefore is most imprudent for women to marry at this epoch without having obtained the sanction of a medical man."

But similar to today, there were women on the barricades, chipping away at the conventions of society, refusing to allow the gloomy forecasts of the doctors to become a self-fulfilling prophecy. Social reformer Eliza Farnham took on the doctors, saying that "menopause could become woman's golden age, when she was freed from the physical and emotional demands of childbirth and childcaring, and her spiritual nature could develop to its fullest."

America began its love affair with young women long before the nineteenth century. Sociologist Lois Banner maintains: "Since the days of . . . Hawthorne and Poe, American writers had used young women as symbols of the American character, as representing the conflicts between . . . traditional society and the future." Years after the settlement of the new land, the mystique of the young female persisted for Americans as "an essential part of the American imagination and spirit."

According to Banner there was a period after the Civil War, which she calls "The Renaissance of the Middle Aged." It wasn't that the "physical attributes of old age—white hair, wrinkles, sagging muscles—were suddenly seen as beautiful," Banner observes. It was just that women were allowed to do whatever they could to "attempt to *appear* young."

The beauty business, which would cash in on this feverish attempt by midlife women to emulate youthful style and appearance, was coming into its own. Banner says it played its own "powerful role in standardizing the connection between beauty and youth. To have conceded that older women were intrinsically beautiful would have been to destroy a potentially immense market before the exploitation of it had ever begun."

It isn't necessary for a Janet to know of her country's long infatuation with Jennifers. All she knows is that her husband has been involved with one. Of the women I interviewed, two did not seek a divorce, nor did their husbands.

Although separated, Jill Brookner remains married for religious reasons. Both she and her husband are Catholics.

"I confronted him," she explained, "and he said I was crazy. But I was persistent, and finally he admitted it. He stopped seeing her. A few years later there was another. Now, I understand, there's another." She shrugged, adding, "I don't mind; he's paying the rent and school for the girls, but I know he's in financial trouble. IRS."

"And what would that do to your financial situation?" I asked.

"I'm working in a boutique, but it would hardly be enough to live on, if he runs out of money. And I know he's paying his young girl's rent plus his own."

"Yet you stay married," I said. "Don't many Catholics today manage to divorce and get remarried?"

Without a flicker of annoyance, Jill answered, "Not and be a good Catholic. Sure, they can get a legal divorce, but in the eyes of the Church they are sinners. That's why I couldn't understand how he could do it—sinning, adultery. He had been an altar boy, never missed mass. He said, 'I'm not sinning. I love her.'

"That was a good enough answer for him; it's not for me. I believe in my Church. Besides, I guess I'm not angry enough. I was a good mother, a good wife, but sex was never my thing. He was always bigger on sex than I was. I mean, in the beginning it was great, but I got bored.

"I'm dating someone else, but I don't know how I would ever in my own mind be able to remarry. But I'm happy. I'm on my own, working, busy; I'm really fine."

It's not just her religion but the realities of demographics that Jill Brookner is facing. She is a middle-class, middle-aged black woman, and her prospects for marrying again are not sunny. According to Robert Staples's study "The World of Black Singles," a basic problem for middle-class black women is that the men who have a similar status are married, and the largest number of black men in the eligible pool are those who have a much lower status.

There is an estimated excess of one million women in the black population, resulting in the ratio of ninety males per one hundred females. This imbalance is due to a number of sociological factors. Young black men have a comparatively high mortality rate, and many are confined to prisons, mental hospitals, and military bases.

As with the studies of white men, statistics on remarriage show a much higher remarriage rate for middle-class black men than women. And when these men remarry, their new wives are typically much younger than their former wives. Black women who remain divorced have a higher education level than those who decide to remarry.

As for those women who appear willing to forgive and forget, even if they are not familiar with the intricacies of the new divorce laws, statistics, or demographics, some of the Janets had a general idea that if they gave in to their rage and got a divorce, it would cost them.

Amy Whitten, who had answered my advertisement under a pseudonym and agreed to be interviewed by phone, told me her reasons for continuing in her marriage are not religious, but to her they are equally compelling.

"It was awful," she admitted. "Even though we're back together, it's still awful sometimes. But for me, only for me, I know it was the best thing to do."

"What convinced you it *was* the best thing to do?"

"I was a member of a women's group at the church, thirty-five women who had their husbands leave them for young girls. Incredible as it sounds, I was the only one who, when her husband asked for another chance, took her husband back.

"Why did I? Oh, many reasons. I heard the women talking week after week, complaining about the loneliness, how hard it is to meet a man, having to move out of their apartments, scrounging to find a job, no money, the hell it was for the kids.

"Twenty-five years is a long time, and I hated being alone." For a moment, her words hung in the air; neither of us said anything to break the silence. I didn't know her real name or what she looked like, and she was protected by the anonymity of the phone. Still I knew she was wrestling with herself, questioning whether she should have been so candid. Finally she broke the silence, saying, "The separation and the threat of divorce was disrupting all our lives. The kids were angry at me for breaking things up, and told me these things happen. We never had much money; my husband works in a dry cleaners. I knew if we divorced, neither of us would have enough to live decently."

Money was a primary concern to Amy Whitten. It is interesting to note that the common perception is that age-discrepant relationships are most prevalent among the upper-middle and upper classes. The most recent studies do not corroborate the conventional wisdom. One of the latest studies concluded that "contrary to expectations, age-discrepant unions are clearly more prevalent among lower-class groupings."

I asked Amy how the reconciliation had come about.

"He came to me and said the girl was a mistake; he was sorry. He said it wasn't love, just something that happened. Could I forgive him? After a while you ask yourself: What's more important?

Your pride or your family? Your ego or twenty-five years?"

"Has it worked out?" I asked after a few moments.

"We're both working at it," Amy replied, "but it's not easy. I'm embarrassed with some of our friends, who know what happened."

Again she was silent for a moment, but I was sure she had wanted to say something more. I asked what was the biggest problem she faced in her marriage today.

Amy hesitated, then began softly, and even over the phone I could imagine her back stiffening as she spoke:

"My biggest problem is trust. I'm never quite sure he's telling me the truth. But it's OK. I can handle it. I can handle that better than being divorced at fifty."

Whether she was actively striving for it or not, Dory Previn's books and songs transformed her as a woman.

"You really did it, Dory," I said admiringly. "You were able to turn your pain into art, something like turning a sow's ear into a silk . . ."

"You can't make a decision to do that," Dory interrupted. "You can't say, 'Now I'm going to turn all this pain into my work.' You have to let it breathe, and then it will come alive. If you smother it and say, 'I'm now going to be *this*, or be *that*,' it will die, and you'll probably die with it."

Today Dory Previn is happy, busy, successful in love and work. Her career as a writer and performer is flourishing, and the rage that both tormented her soul and informed her music has been transformed into something else: acceptance.

"When you accept a condition which is irreversible, you can find victory. Liberation is a better word. I have no rage now. We're friends," she said, speaking of her former husband. "Yet I had as much rage as anybody. But I will always love those I loved. Always. If for twelve years I was with a human being, and felt all the rage, then do I continue to be angry, sad, and furious for the rest of my life?"

Behind her tinted glasses I could see her eyes shining, and her face was flushed with emotion. "So do I stay enraged and sad? If I do, then I'm negating those twelve years. Then what were they? What was that person I loved and who loved me? It's got to have been. You cannot deny it."

She is also remarried to a man who happens to be considerably younger. She didn't have to tell me about her happiness; it was written all over her face. She suggested I talk with her husband, Joby Baker. That, she believed, would explain her happiness as much as anything she could say.

Joby Baker is a man who combines tenderness and strength, and exudes quiet confidence without bravado. He also happens to be marvelous-looking, tall, with dark hair and wonderful, searching, hazel eyes. We talked at the art gallery where some of his paintings were being hung for a show. I asked about being in love with an older woman, and how he and Dory have managed to stay so happy for so long.

"A woman like Dory creates variety, like painting or drama, she has tension, and she's never predictable," he said, his enthusiasm increasing with each thought. "But midlife men who need a younger woman need predictability, they equate 'doing it,' having sex with young girls, with life.

"I gave all that up, but giving up that kind of running around doesn't mean giving in, right?" he said, smiling. "Look, some years back there was a period when I was unhappy about my career. Dory heard me telling a lie to a guy, kind of inflating how well I was doing. She said, 'What's all that bullshit? You don't have to do that.' And I never did it again.

"I love Dory. She is not a victim. How could I not have loved her?" he said, shaking his head. "We have an ideal love; she is my lover and also my intelligent sister."

"And Jennifers?"

"I don't want some Jennifer draped on my couch," he declared nonchalantly, casting his hand to one side in a dismissive gesture. "I don't want some girl with no tension, no drama. If you're an artist you want to be with someone who has style and taste. With a Jennifer you have to face the 'And then what?' factor. I never get from Dory, about a painting or a restaurant, 'So what do I think?'

I'm married to a woman who knows, who understands. How could I view that as a threat? I'm married to a national treasure."

Georgina Ramonos is working for a public relations firm, but finding work was never her problem. She has been less successful in her efforts to meet the right man.

"It's like putting your finger in a dike," she said with a sigh. "You get the divorce, you learn he's got a young girlfriend, who quickly becomes his wife. Miraculously, you find a job, raise your kid, and reach a point where you are making a living, actually enjoying your work. You're moving, going, reading, doing, a long way from being that woman who sat in the park and thought she had nothing to say to people over three feet tall.

"You've developed into the kind of woman they write about— whole, intact. *Then* you discover you've turned into exactly the kind of woman men don't want. But I refuse to get depressed, and I won't believe that from now on my major satisfaction in life will be my job or the day when my daughter makes me a grandmother."

Francesca Grayson is thriving. After twenty years in suburbia, she moved back to the city and made a number of different stabs at different jobs. Finally she got a license and has become a real estate agent. Recently we were having dinner and she was eager to reflect on her former life, looking back to the other Francesca. About her ex-husband, she spoke with bemusement and a curious kind of empathy.

"He called last year, saying, 'Help me, help me.' Want to know what he needed?" she asked, unable to control her laughter. "He was about to get married and wanted me to stop him."

"To Marie?"

"Of course. And I didn't stop him. I know Rod, and I feel sorry for him. He needs to be married; men do, you know. Needs someone to take care of him. Let his young chick have the pleasure." Francesca laughed. "When he hung up, he said I had failed him. Isn't that delicious?"

For two years Francesca has been having her own love affair with youth, a relationship with a man twenty years younger. "You remember me, Barbara—I was this dependable nice person, good hostess, good mother, but in these two years with Larry . . . I've never known such spontaneity, such tenderness.

"I enjoy doing things for myself as well as others. I've become more accepting of myself, less judgmental of others. Larry and I appreciate each other."

"One of the problems experienced by women who were left for Jennifers is the inability to trust, a fear of getting hurt again. Did you go through that?"

"How can you not trust a man who becomes your best friend and for six months doesn't make a move and when he does, asks you to think about it before responding. How can you not trust a man who is generous, who brings out the best in you?

"Barbara, five years ago, when I found out about my husband's affair, I thought I'd die, and when he finally admitted it, I wanted to die. Remember?"

"I remember," I said softly.

"You won't believe it!" she exclaimed. "Guess what I just gave Larry as a present?"

"I give up," I said with a laugh.

"Two weeks in Europe, that's what I gave him. Just him and his camera. And he gave me a week at a marvelous spa to rejuvenate myself. It's been so hectic at work.

"Can you believe it?" she said, her voice slightly incredulous, but with a radiant smile. "We give each other freedom. Me, Francesca, who couldn't be alone. Me, Francesca, who couldn't drive through tunnels. Me, Francesca, who wanted to die."

None of them died, although most of them wanted to. Many of them are today flourishing, having developed skills and discovered resources of strength and coping they never dreamed they possessed. If today they view their husbands' need for a Jennifer as an inevitable rite of passage, many of them could say they had gone through their own. And like most rites of passage, they must be endured, without blinding bolts of light, sudden moments of illumination, or dramatic epiphanies.

Unlike Hollywood movies, which show growth as a blinding

realization, the metaphoric hand of God reaching out, swooping down, and touching you with a cure, the Janets learned there was no Lourdes to cure the pain of abandonment and rejection.

But was it only Hollywood that had turned survival into a cliché? Was it only America that had trivialized the words "victim" and "survivor"? Did Janets in other countries want to die as Francesca did?

As early as the nineteenth century, Lois Banner says, "literate American women . . . were aware that French people found older women more attractive than younger ones and held that a woman did not reach her peak of attractiveness until the age of forty."

I wondered if the French feel that way today. And if Frenchmen feel the need for a Jennifer as American men do, as a flight from Mom, or as a trophy on their arm, or as a miracle worker in bed, or as a twenty-four-hour-a-day adoration factory?

As a relatively young country, the United States has always worshiped youth. I decided I had to go to France. Perhaps her name was Nicole, or Geneviève, or Agnes, but France had its Jennifers. The question was, did it have many cases of Jennifer Fever as well.

14

"La Vie Est Courte, Il Faut Suivre la Magique"

Time and again I heard the comment that Jennifer Fever is a uniquely American phenomenon, and inevitably France was held up as the model of a society where women remain sexually alive and well far longer than in America. Whether from novels, films, or travels in France, for many that country has earned the reputation of being a bastion of high regard for "women of a certain age."

As proof Americans point to actresses like Anouk Aimée, Catherine Deneuve, and Jeanne Moreau, who play romantic leads in movies long after the time when American actresses are limited to nonsexual cameos, playing doctors, lawyers, mothers, everything except objects of desire. They endure, outlasting the film star whose career was the incarnation of youth worship, the sex kitten of all time, Brigitte Bardot, who according to many reports is having problems reconciling herself to the passage of time.

Was this mystique of the older woman true, or just a myth that holds as much attraction for the French as Aphrodite and Apollo do for the Greeks? Was it a self-deception, a product of cultural arrogance, one the French were happy to export along with Beaujolais and Camembert?

Fact or fiction, myth or reality, the idea had a strong following, and I wondered how it had originated. I called universities and French institutes, combed the library looking for a clue, and for months I came up with nothing. Then I found an article, "The New Older Woman," in which the novelist Francine du Plessix Gray examined how older women are viewed in literature. Using the example of older woman and younger men as a literary theme, she wondered why that subject, which permeates French literature, is treated so rarely in English and American novels.

Gray's article focused on sexual relationships between older women and younger men (which will be the subject of a later chapter), but her observations provided the first glimmer of an answer to my question. "Only a deeply feminized society such as France, where the prestigious civilizing power of older women has been deeply rooted since the sixteenth century in the tradition of the salons, could nurture a creative vision of this particular form of bonding," she wrote.

The salons! Of course. Armed with a clue to the mystery and thrilled with my discovery, I called Francine du Plessix Gray and told her of my interest. She said that unquestionably the women of the French salons had nurtured a positive image of older women that had endured for centuries, leaving a powerful legacy in the minds of French men and women. So had the medieval tradition of courtly love. Doubtlessly Catholicism, with the adoration of the Virgin Mary at its very core, had contributed to a positive view of older women in France.

To most of us, Colette and Simone de Beauvoir are legends, but according to writer Germaine Bree, from the Middle Ages through the Renaissance, a long line of courageous and gifted French women—women like Christine de Pisan and Marguerite d'Angoulême, who later became queen of Navarre, Ninon de Lenclos and Anne de Noailles—"won from French society the right to conduct themselves sexually according to the rules applied to men without forfeiting their rank in society."

Flouting convention, they carved out literary careers and gathered into their social circles the best and brightest minds of their day. Breaking the double sexual standard, they flourished in middle age, and were courted and admired, some even having highly publicized love affairs in their fifties and sixties. Because Paris was the symbolic capital of Europe, the pacesetter of fashion and social affairs, the women of the French salons dictated fashion and social mores throughout Europe, where for generations midlife women were viewed as desirable, worldly, and sexually appealing.

So it wasn't all a myth? No, Gray didn't think so, but she hadn't lived in France for some time, and she suspected that the side effects of rock-and-roll culture had global implications, and it was likely the youth-cult mania had made inroads in France, forever altering that country's traditional esteem for older women.

It is in the work of Colette that we see intimately the writer's understanding and her country's unique appreciation of sensuality in a middle-aged woman's life. In *Chéri,* Colette's heroine, Léa, must deal with the fact that her young lover, Chéri, has married a younger woman. Léa stands in front of a mirror, smiling at her own image, and realizing she is still Léa, she tells herself:

> Surely a woman like that doesn't end up in the arms of an old man. A woman like that who's had the luck never to soil her hands or her mouth on a withered stick . . . always she had escaped elderly lechers, so she felt pure and proud of thirty years devoted to radiant youths and fragile adolescents.
> . . . This youthful flesh of theirs certainly owes me a great debt. How many of them have me to thank for their good health, their good looks, the harmlessness of their sorrows . . . and the habit of making love unselfishly and always refreshingly.

How could Jennifer Fever be an issue in the land of Colette? Impossible.

As I prepared for a trip to France, I reflected on Madame de Staël and Madame de Sévigné, who were renowned for their beauty as well as their intelligence, for a sensuality that went hand in hand with their skills at royal networking, which they displayed at their salons; women who guided the fortunes of kings and nurtured the creative spirit of aspiring novelists—and accomplished all this at an age that in other cultures would have doomed them to sexual oblivion. Could such a culture also contain an American-like obsession with youth?

Once I had arrived in France, a series of interviews with sociologists and lawyers, Janets and Jennifers, revealed that while the legacy of the sixteenth-century salons still finds expression, there are also countervailing trends.

If the French have exported a cultural myth along with their wine, so America, in addition to jeans, *Dallas,* and rock-and-roll, has exported the notion that for women, youth is the quintessential standard of beauty. Everyone I spoke to—shopkeepers, beauty editors, plastic surgeons, and journalists—was aware of the infiltration of this notion into French life.

It is true that the traditions of French culture may make some French women less obsessed with aging than American women. Jacqueline de Mornex, a beautiful woman in her forties who works for a cosmetic company and writes about women's issues, told me: "In France we have models to help us age; there were famous mistresses of kings, equally renowned courtesans of prominent men, who were not so young. I am in my mid-forties, and it's the best time of my life. But I take care of myself, and I am busy, involved. For the woman who is bored, who doesn't work or isn't involved with life, who stares in the mirror every day looking for signs of aging, I think it must be difficult. Then all the history and the culture will not help her."

For forty-one-year-old plastic surgeon Gérard Pullenc, the legacy is real.

"It's part of the air a French schoolboy breathes," he told me. "It is in the textbooks, and even when it isn't, it's in the atmosphere." He paused and, with a small smile, added, "I live with a woman who is nine years older, and I hope you won't take offense, but we have a saying in France: 'From the oldest pots you make the best stews.'"

But for others, an old pot is merely an old pot. One of France's most gifted playwrights, Françoise Doran, is a woman of fifty. She looks marvelous, has a gaminelike face, laughing eyes, a natural sense of style, and wit. Divorced, she says marriage is not for her. A lover? Of course. What about the idea that French women have it made, that aging is less of a problem in France than in America?

She threw her head back and laughed. "Nonsense! That's a piece of cultural hypocrisy, one the French cling to with particular relish." But the laughter disappeared when she added, "I have never met a woman, never, who wasn't in terror of getting older."

Another French woman stated the matter this way: "I thought one day when I was forty, 'Deep in that looking glass, old age is watching and waiting for me: and it's inevitable, one day she'll get me.'

"She's got me now. I often stop flabbergasted at the sight of this incredible thing that serves me as a face. I had the impression once of caring very little what sort of figure I cut. In much the same way, people who enjoy good health and always have enough to eat never give their stomachs a thought. While I was able to look at my face without displeasure, I gave it no thought; it would look after itself. The wheel eventually stops. I loathe my appearance now: the eyebrows slipping down toward the eyes, the bags underneath, the excessive fullness of the cheeks, and that air of sadness around the mouth that wrinkles always bring. Perhaps the people I pass in the street see merely a woman in her fifties who simply looks her age. No more, no less. But when I look, I see my face as it was, attacked by the pox of time, for which there is no cure."

Obviously these are not the words of an ordinary woman. They come from Simone de Beauvoir. When she wrote them she was an attractive, beautiful woman, but even de Beauvoir, whose books became the Bible of modern feminism, was not immune to the anguish of aging.

At other times de Beauvoir would write about women in a less personal voice, but with no less passion: "I have never come across one single woman either in life or in books who has looked upon her old age cheerfully."

And about men she noted that since he "is not a quarry, neither bloom, gentleness, nor grace are required of him, but rather the strength and intelligence of the conquering subject—white hair and wrinkles are not in conflict with this manly idea."

I was stunned by de Beauvoir's comments on aging. If the myth of the older woman wasn't felt by all French women, certainly de Beauvoir, because of her ardent feminism, the force of her intellectual life, and the body of her work, would be more insulated from the pain of losing her youthful attractiveness. But women's feelings about aging are rarely related to intelligence, feminism, or professional pursuits.

Many women in France agree with de Beauvoir, and share

Doran's view that the image of women of forty or fifty living in some kind of unique paradise in twentieth-century France is "a big lie." They hate, as Simone de Beauvoir said she hated, every trace of aging in themselves. Françoise Doran concluded, "It is a human problem, not a cultural one."

Everyone I spoke to, male and female, Jennifer or Janet, regardless of where they stood on the matter of "cultural insulation," agreed on one thing: Jennifer Fever is doing very well in France. Everyone mentioned it, referring to it by its Gallic name, *le démon de midi*. "The devil of midlife" generally strikes a man between the ages of forty and fifty who has lived a very traditional life. He has pursued a career, been a dutiful husband, loving father, often the pillar of his community.

Without warning, he falls in love with another woman (usually very young) and leaves his wife and family to marry her. Generally this happens to a man who hadn't enjoyed a great deal of sexual experimentation before he married, or who married very young. Finding himself in the middle of his life, he feels suddenly trapped, deprived. This gnawing sense of deprivation becomes an incessant ache, and he reaches for a cure, a last chance at experiencing something he feels he has missed.

The frequent occurrence of *le démon de midi* conflicts with another piece of cultural mythology: the notion that Europeans, particularly the French, have historically demonstrated a pragmatic attitude about a married man's need for sexual experimentation. Infidelity is not thought to be as noxious—hardly suitable grounds for breaking up a marriage—as it is in more puritanical America. The French woman, according to the conventional wisdom, knows her husband's infidelity has nothing to do with *her*, or her husband's loving or not loving her, and is quite prepared to look the other way.

When people spoke of this Gallic pragmatism, they reminded me of an old Arabian fable. A scorpion, desperate to get to the other side of the river, spots a tortoise paddling about near the shore. He asks the tortoise to carry him across the river.

The tortoise, staring at the scorpion's poisonous tail, says, "I'd like to, but you're a scorpion, and you'll sting me and I'll drown."

The scorpion promises not to sting him, and the tortoise agrees to carry him across. The scorpion hops aboard the tortoise's back, but midway across the river he reaches out with his tail and stings the tortoise. Shocked and struggling to stay afloat, even as he knows he's dying, the tortoise cries, "Why did you do that? You *promised* not to! Now we'll both drown."

"I know," says the scorpion, "but I *had* to."

"Oh? Why?" cries the tortoise.

As they begin to sink beneath the water, the scorpion replies, "Because it is my nature."

So the average French wife has repeatedly been neither surprised nor outraged by her husband's affair with a Jennifer. And if she was, she told herself, as generations of women before her told themselves, "He can't help it. It is his nature."

If her husband was as helpless as the scorpion, the French wife often saw herself as powerless and accepted her fate, sometimes embarking on love affairs of her own. And the woman who couldn't or wouldn't accept her husband's infidelities frequently found *she* was the target of outrage. In a chorus of disapproval, her husband, her friends, even her children could scarcely believe her puritanical behavior.

That piece of cultural mythology, I discovered, has until recent years had great relevance for French women. However, a variety of forces are eroding the notion. As divorce lawyer Michel Alexandre told me:

"A French woman doesn't have to look the other way anymore. In the last ten years the laws have been greatly liberalized, making divorce easier for women. But the alimony and child-support payments she can be awarded are very small compared to America. In France a woman can leave, but she can't leave *well.*"

Other factors are impinging on the old cultural stereotypes. When Jeanne Dunaud discovered her husband's affair, she shocked her friends and family when she demanded a divorce.

"He wanted to stay in the marriage and see his young girl a couple of times a week." She raised her hands in the air in that typical French gesture, and said, *"Merde.* I knew he would take care of me financially. And I also knew I could get a job. I didn't want him if I had to share him. My husband was amazed that I would not accept this small affair. So were my friends when they heard I wanted a divorce."

"How has it worked out for you?" I asked.

"Times are changing. Fifty isn't as old as it used to be, right? I have a lot of life ahead of me," she said with a smile. "I knew I could get a job. And I did. Now I own my own travel agency. Since I have remarried, money is not a problem at all."

Michel Alexandre told me that in one respect, economics, French women face the same problem as women in other countries.

"If a woman doesn't have money of her own, or if she will have a hard time finding a job or a new husband, it's still necessary for a French wife to blind herself to her husband's infidelities."

In some ways Jennifer Fever transcends cultural distinctions. In the words of Françoise Doran, it's a "human problem," which has nothing to do with geography. When Jeanne Dunaud talked about discovering her husband's affair, at first she didn't sound different from many American women:

"I was forty-four when I figured out he was having an affair. I was devastated physically and mentally. So I went to the doctor."

"A psychiatrist?" I asked.

Jeanne stared at me as if I had said something bizarre. "Of course not; my family doctor. He gave me pills, but I threw them away and went skiing."

As it turned out in her case, that was a good idea; for it was there on the slopes of Saint Moritz that she met the man she would marry after her divorce. Now in her late forties, she has quiet good looks and haunting green eyes that seem to register her every emotion. With a puzzled expression, she added, "He always laughed at men who left their wives for young girls, said it was stupid, he'd never do that. But he *did* it.

"It hurt when it happened, but I don't dwell on it. You do look in the mirror and ask, 'What's wrong with me? Am I old?' I lost five kilos; I couldn't sleep. What made it worse was that everyone assumed it was my fault, I had done something that caused my husband to find another woman."

"And today, years later, do you have a better understanding of why it happened?"

"My ex-husband was a driven, consuming man; he used up all the oxygen in the room. I didn't know how tough it was to live with him till it was over. Now I'm all right."

"How did the divorce affect your children?"

"They were seven and nine, and after he moved out we continued to meet, the four of us, at dinner. Not to make us separate parents. As hard as it was for me, I did it for the children. Though it was awful to be with him, knowing about that girl."

That girl.

While many wives may have a burning curiosity about "that girl," they somehow never meet her. One therapist I spoke to believes women want very much to see the Jennifer. The unknown, the Jennifer of their imagination, is such a horrifying image, they believe that if they manage to see her with their own eyes, see how young she is or isn't, they will somehow feel better, reassured. I asked Jeanne what it was like to meet her ex-husband's new young wife.

"She is so insulting. When she came to pick him up one night, my mother was with us." As she mentioned her mother, Jeanne's green eyes seemed to deepen in color, her smile envelop her face. "My mother was wearing jeans and sneakers; at eighty, she's terrific. And this young woman says, 'A woman that age shouldn't dress like that. It's horrible.' I watched the way she is with him; she hangs on his every word. He wanted someone to make him feel secure and important. Now he's got it."

The needs of a Jennifer, the reactions of a Janet—in many ways, both are universal. Danielle Mignon is thirty-five, her husband of seven years is sixty-four, a twenty-nine-year age difference between them. Born in Paris, today she lives in a large country home not far from the heart of the city. She echoes themes I heard from Jennifers on the other side of the Atlantic, but in one respect she was more candid than many of her American counterparts:

"I loved that Gabriel introduced me to things. When I was a little girl I had an uncle like that. He introduced me to the world, taught me things. I love when Gabriel teaches me things, explains finance, science, good wines. I love it!"

We were having coffee at a café on the Left Bank. I spotted her instantly as she got out of a taxi and headed for Deux Magots. She walked with the unstudied ease that is the essense of French style. As she approached my table, I noticed her makeup was subtle and her clothes were perfectly smashing. Everything about her was chic, buoyant, while still reflecting the natural style of many French women, which was, I had to admit, sexier than the more studied, harsher, overly made up look of some American women.

Her English was far better than my French, and we managed to have a delightful talk. I asked how she met Gabriel.

"We met in his office when I was twenty-one, he forty-nine," Danielle began, her voice bright and a bit wistful as she recalled the beginnings of their affair. "At first he thought I was a silly young girl. Immediately I was impressed with his looks, his experience. And I must confess I was dreaming of having a certain standard of living in my life. You see, our family was very poor.

"I wanted to go to America and learn English, so I could become a stewardess, but he didn't want me to go. He said he was attracted to me. I was still a virgin, and we began a love affair. He was like a charming, handsome prince, but I told myself, 'It's a fairy tale, ridiculous. It will lead to nowhere.' "

The waiter brought our coffees, and Danielle hesitated, waiting for him to leave before continuing.

"I told my mother the truth, and she was happy I lost my virginity to someone I cared for, someone who deserved it. But he was married, and it went on and on. I decided to go to New York, where I worked in a shop. Gabriel called and asked me to come home."

"Did you return to Paris?"

"I was lonely in America, so I went back to France. He helped me find a job. He comes from a very traditional family, so I knew he would never leave his wife and family until his father died. For five years this went on; it was very wonderful and very hard.

"After his father died, he arrived at my house at 3 A.M. and told me he had left. He said his wife was very upset when she learned our affair had been going on for years. About the years of betrayal."

For a moment neither of us said a word, then she looked up at me expectantly, as if she was saying it was all right to continue. "Do you have children?" I asked.

"I'd like to, but he's retired, and it would be difficult for him now. After all, he's a grandfather. But it's all right; we have such a comfortable life—golf, tennis, travel."

"Danielle, do you ever think about the fact that you will probably outlive your husband, that he will grow old when you are still a quite young woman?"

She nodded. "My father is Gabriel's age, and he adores Gabriel. And again and again my father tells me, 'You must never leave him for a younger man. He needs you; it would kill him.'

"Sometimes I worry about being a young widow," she went on. "But Gabriel's so full of energy, has good health; he's always willing to go and do things. He puts me high in the sky and says that because of me he gains ten years." Her words had been accompanied by a radiant smile, but now the smile vanished and her expression became pensive. "I can see that he's still attractive to women. Does that worry me? I'd worry if it was the contrary. I'm pleased he's attractive to other women. But if he has affairs, I don't want to know about it."

"Do you have any fears about your future?" I asked.

"I fear more living alone than being older; being older is not that frightening, but I have friends who are very worried about getting older."

"And the biggest problem in your marriage?"

"We're married seven years and his sons don't speak to me. I don't ever see them or his grandchildren. This causes me much pain. Also I have money worries. When he dies will his children take the house from me? What will happen to me?"

For a moment the confident, radiant woman had become little-girl lost, and I was touched by her vulnerability, didn't know what to say. Then she continued: "We quarrel most about his sons. I say, 'By not coming to our house, by not accepting me after all this time, they don't respect your life.' He says there is nothing he can do. It makes me angry for him."

Annette Denis is fifty-five. Her husband left her eight years ago for a younger woman. A short, thin woman, Annette wore pants and a sweater tossed casually over her shoulders; no makeup, no effort at style or being in fashion. She appeared uneager to make an impression of youth, disinterested in winning approval from anyone. At first, what she had to say supported the myth of French pragmatism regarding men and Jennifers.

"Yes, it is very French to say, as many people said to me, 'Why did he leave? He could have had you both.' I was devastated. I had a young baby, no money; I had to get a job." Given her nonchalant attitude about her appearance, I was surprised when she added, "After looking in the mirror, the first thing I did was get a face-lift. I knew I'd have a better chance getting a job if I looked better."

Jean Michele, an investment banker, fifty-three, has gray curly hair, a pudgy, doughy face, deep circles under tired brown eyes. His dark-paneled office was filled with a soft pinkish glow of late-afternoon October sunlight, which streamed through the shuttered windows. His wife was a good partner in the marriage, he conceded, but things got bad when she came to work for him.

"She came to be better in my office than in the marriage. I don't know quite what happened; I didn't like my life. I felt trapped in my marriage.

"It's a question of personal desire, what in life is *my* business. It's no one's fault. Life is short; you must follow the magic."

"The magic?"

"It's a connection, a sexual connection; you know it in an instant. And while it can happen with any woman, I think it does happen to a man more with a younger woman, what you call a Jennifer and the French would call Agnes or Nicole."

"Were you troubled by guilt, leaving your wife and children because of a love affair with a young girl?"

"No guilt. Because I didn't destroy my life or my wife's or my children's. My children have no problem with my girlfriend. The children love equally the mother and the father."

"Now that you've followed the magic," I asked, "how do you feel?"

"It's wonderful how I feel with this girl; older women think it's awful. My work is so important to me, I will sacrifice time now for my work and that is all. Perhaps I am an egoist; if so, that's it. But with this young girl I don't have to answer questions about where I am. Tonight I have a dinner to go to. I could take my girlfriend, but I don't want to. Married, that would be impossible. Now I don't have to run home after work. I love being free."

The room had grown dark; Jean turned on an antique brass floor lamp, which cast an eerie amber light, creating strange shadows on his face, odd patterns on the dark wood floors. His secretary tapped lightly on the door; my cab had arrived. As he escorted me to the rickety old elevator, he said, slipping his arm around my waist, "Other men masturbate the mind. They ask, 'Is it good? Is it wrong? Do I love her?' I don't do that. I follow the magic."

Even though Annette Denis lost her husband to a younger woman, she sees a distinction between French and American attitudes:

"My husband was with an international pharmaceutical company, and we lived for a time in Princeton. I was amazed at how few beauty salons there were. In France a girl is brought up with the idea that it's important to keep herself looking beautiful. It's not that she's brought up to try to look young, but to take care of herself. Keeping herself beautiful is taken seriously; it's part of the culture. I think beauty is less equated with youth than in America."

In France, where the care and feeding of the body is a high art form, it is unsettling for an American woman to hear people speak disparagingly of her country's obsession with youth and beauty. Walking through Paris streets, not just the main thoroughfares but residential areas far from the hordes of tourists picking up bargains from Orlane and Lancôme, or in suburban enclaves, you see that salons and shops dedicated to the business of making women beautiful are everywhere.

American women, the French believe, have adopted a concern with beauty rather late in the game, and when they did, it was because their own cultural imperatives transformed it into a hybrid in which *youth* became the sine qua non of beauty. It is only in recent years that this "taking care of" business has become synonymous in France with looking *young.* That, they believe, is a decidedly American characteristic. Not surprising for a young country, not surprising in a society that tears down fifty-year-old buildings, but a strange notion in a culture where two-hundred-year-old buildings and cobblestone streets coexist with modern towers of steel and glass.

As if to draw a parallel between the beauty of the ancient architecture and the admiration, bordering on reverence, he had for maturity in a woman, one Parisian businessman, scowling at a new skyscraper that had crept into his beloved skyline, exclaimed, "We are a culture that goes back hundreds of years. We treasure our antiquity. Look at the leaded windows, the iron grillwork, look at Notre-Dame and Sacré-Coeur. Beautiful, no? And not young."

But plastic surgeon Fabrice Juilliard said that the Frenchman's love of the old may well be limited to his country's architecture.

"Many fifty-year-old men come for face-lifts so they can look young for their twenty-year-old girlfriends," he told me. "And many women who haven't grown along with their husbands come to me and say their children are gone and they feel completely alone. They think they look old, but I tell them, 'Looking younger will not fill that vacuum. The reason your husband has someone else is not because you don't look young.'"

It was the magic hour in Paris, *l'heure bleue,* when the stars wake up and blink in an unreal slate sky. A time for lovers, a time of promise, romance. I was with Julie Meadows, an American who works for a fashion house in Paris. At forty-six, her skin is unlined and she looks like the slightly older sister of her twenty-year-old son. We were having an aperitif at an outdoor café when she told me the following story:

"A forty-nine-year-old man, an officer of an international bank, has been living with a twenty-one-year-old woman named Martine. The members of his bank were meeting for dinner and the opera. He asked me to do him a favor and go with him. 'But what about Martine?' I asked.

"'My colleagues wouldn't understand,' he said. 'It wouldn't be good for my career.'"

Ah, I thought, the mystique lives; his bosses wouldn't understand his Jennifer.

"And me?" Julie asked him.

"You're not young, but you don't look your age," he answered. "You're beautiful and worldly. Come, it will be a great help to me."

Julie's face colored as she admitted she did go with him, feeling every moment like the aging foil for a Jennifer. Throughout the evening she felt lines and wrinkles that hadn't yet emerged, even buried her hands under her handbag, for fear they would betray her age.

"But the worst, the absolute worst moment came at dinner." Julie frowned. "He took my hand in his and for a moment I thought that he had been kidding all along. But he pinched my hand, then let it go. 'You see, *ma chérie,*' he said, 'your skin does not go back fast. It's soft but it's not supple.'"

Wordless for a moment, finally she sighed and said wearily, "So much for your French mystique. It's there and it's not. I'm the right age for dinner and the opera with his bank cronies, but too old for his bed."

Julie lit a cigarette, crushed it out, and continued, her voice trembling with anger: "What if I looked forty, whatever that means? And how did Martine feel? What the hell difference does it make what his boss thinks about the age of his girlfriend? What's he doing with a twenty-one-year-old he's embarrassed to be seen with anyway? And supple? My skin's not supple? What about the rest of me? My mind, my books, my heart? What about Colette? I'm forty-one and I'm sitting having dinner with a man who's testing the elasticity of my skin? It's awful. I hate it."

Exhausted from the battles of recent years, the French believe men and women must declare a truce. The return to traditional values we read about in America is even more blatantly apparent in France. If American women have trouble meeting men, in the eyes of the French it has nothing to do with demographics or ageism; it's feminist fallout. Their noisy feminism has made them hard, tough, and uncompromising. What man wants that?

Claudia Léon is a stockbroker. At forty-seven, she has a faded, serene kind of attractiveness—unchic, unstudied, and just a bit overweight. She spoke to me in her large high-tech office, reeking with all the accoutrements of corporate power; she was surrounded by files and batteries of phones. In the middle of our interview, she suddenly reached for the phone, and as she dialed, she said, "By day I can pick up the phone and call the most powerful people in France." She said something into the phone, speaking French so fast I couldn't understand, and then nodded at me knowingly. "You see, I'm making a date for dinner with Mitterrand. . . . *Ah, bien,*" Claudia said into the phone. *"Entendu, vendredi. Huit heures. Bon. Au revoir."*

Plopping the phone back into its cradle, she announced with obvious satisfaction, "You see, that was not difficult. Dinner with Mitterrand. All day I meet fascinating people, handle millions of francs, but when I go home, *I* pick up the bread for our dinner. I believe it's the right thing for me to do. I am not a feminist. To be a feminist is to be against men. I have a high-pressure job, so does my husband. But when I go home to him, I am a geisha."

Whether Claudia Léon was indeed making a dinner date with the president of France or whether she was speaking to a dial tone I'll never know. But her point was clear. In France today, "feminism" is a nasty word. Even women who by all definitions live "feminist" lives, being self-defined, not living through a man, depending on one for their identities or income, see American feminists as being more "against men" than *for* their own emancipation or economic equality.

Simone de Beauvoir has compared American and French men's attitudes about Jennifers and Janets. The American man, she says, "feels a certain antipathy to the 'real woman.' He regards her as an antagonist . . . a tyrant. He abandons himself eagerly to the charms of the nymph in whom the formidable figure of the wife and the 'mom' is not yet apparent. In France many women are accomplices of this feeling of superiority in which men persist."

Philippe Sollers, author of the best-selling book *Femmes,* is a well-known French commentator on male-female relations. A tall, attractive man, he has chiseled features and exudes a steady stream of airy self-confidence. For Sollers, feminism is the culprit. "French women are clever," he observed wryly. "They know when an ideology no longer works *for* them. And they give it up when it's bad for business."

Sollers reflected the thinking of many of the French when he said, "If American women are lonely, they brought it on themselves."

With the pragmatism regarding sexual matters for which his countrymen are noted, Sollers added, with more than a hint of sarcasm, "Actually the perfect match is an older man and a younger girl. His sexual powers are waning and the young woman knows very little of her own sexuality.

"From my point of view, sex and love affairs are more of a commercial transaction in the States," he said. "Then Jennifer Fever makes sense. If you're going to spend money, wouldn't you rather have a new television set than an old one? I do think Americans view love affairs as just another piece of business."

I suggested his last observation was rather strange, considering the fact that his country was distinguished for its pragmatism about everything—politics, sex, and romance. He tried to change the subject, but ironically, he made my point when he said:

"I don't understand why American men have problems choosing between a wife and a Jennifer. Every man knows two women are hell. Better to have a thousand!"

Since I had invited him for cocktails, when the interview was over I reached for the check. Our talk, while amusing and provocative, had after all been business. Sollers shook his head disdainfully; I sensed what he was thinking. My paying the bill was a perfect example of all he had been saying—another pushy American woman clinging to an ideology, even when it was obviously, so obviously, "bad for business."

"You see, it is only one thing," he said as we stood outside the café, searching for a taxi in the late-afternoon traffic that clogged the broad boulevard. "The need for connection, that's what a man wants. And for some men it's easier to connect with a Jennifer."

Françoise Tournier, an editor of *Elle* magazine, also spoke of the need for connections. "Men see women all day at work, and because of this they are having to lose their macho. They are longing for tender moments with women."

In one last attempt to test the reality of the mystique of the older woman, I asked Madame Tournier if *Elle* in France uses older women in advertisements and fashion layouts more than in the American edition of the magazine.

"In our magazine, in articles we write about women as they are," she answered, "but old faces don't sell."

"Not even in France?" I asked.

"No, but you see older faces in *Elle.* In the articles just a few pages away from the ads with all the young faces, women can read the truth about themselves.

"There is in France a return to tradition. A few years ago I wouldn't believe that now we'd have articles on the family decorating the Christmas tree. I think the terrorism on the streets is forcing people to reexamine their lives, forcing them to make stronger human connections. I think the war between men and women is over. Today everyone looks for connections, but there are spaces"— she sighed—"chasms we must cross."

Whether it is Fiona, Sonya, Kiku, or Nicole, each country has a trendy name for its Jennifers. And each culture devises its unique way of handling the need for those connections between men and women.

Japan has its tradition of geishas and bar girls; the Arab world, its legacy of polygamy, which today has become more a state of mind than a state of matrimony.

Each country has different rules, customs, and traditions, which may make it difficult for the Janet who doesn't want to play by those rules. For example, the sweeping changes in the Arab world are quickly making the harem a cultural artifact. This is creating serious problems for the Janets of the Muslim world. They find themselves suddenly alone, divorced, no longer able to be part of a harem, no longer able to even enjoy the privilege, however nonsexual, of mothering a batch of young co-wives.

In Japan, the accepted ethos is that a wife must expect and accept her husband's affairs with other women. The Janet who doesn't want to play by those rules can't rush into divorce, because if she does, she will likely lose her children. In Japan, children are considered part of the husband's ancestral family.

The Soviet Union, as a result of wars, purges, and revolutions, has a disproportionate number of women in the population, compared to the number of men. The scarcity of men has radically affected Russian patterns of marriage and divorce, as well as the incidence of Jennifer Fever, as does the Marxist ideology ordaining that marriage should be based on the whole personality, not based on convenience, money, or property.

There are primitive cultures where men are allowed to experience their passive, non-macho, non-warrior selves with ease and aren't thrown into a panic about a sudden spasm of midlife passivity; they do not need a Jennifer to lessen their terrors.

But certainly it is France, with its legacy of the salon—even with an increasingly mythical regard for "women of a certain age"—that has most affected the attitudes of countries like Spain and Italy, and even England. And it is the French attitude, fact or fiction, that most Americans are aware of—sometimes with amazement, sometimes with envy.

But for all the cultural differences, all of these countries gobble up American movies and music, devour information about our fashions, face-lifts, and film stars. There is a hunger for things Western. And of course, especially, the youth culture.

I am convinced that Jennifer Fever has unique expressions in my young but powerful country, a country carved out of the wilderness, settled by trailblazing pioneers who vanquished the native inhabitants and created a new world.

America, the new land where, from its very beginnings, starting new lives and the quest for innovation, both technological and social—the love of the new, the lure of the quick fix, the fresh start, the last chance—have been as revered as Sacré-Coeur is by the French. America, where the words "American dream" are a promise, supposedly attainable one way or another by everyone.

America, where the pursuit of happiness is enshrined as a national code, as the written law of the land. America—where there were still some voices who needed to be heard.

15

Breaking the Rules

It was an Abstract Expressionist opening at the Metropolitan Museum, and I was attending it with my friend Ron Silbert. Ron owned a small gallery on Madison Avenue, was an ardent art lover, and adored big parties. And for this party a huge throng had gathered in the atrium of the Metropolitan.

Women of all ages sparkled with jewels and sequined dresses, but their glittery efforts were dwarfed by the majesty of the vast hall. Even with a hundred tables, dotted with candles, the flocks of waiters weaving through the crowd, and the hordes of people pouring through each entrance door, the space still seemed enormous.

People wrestled their way through the crowd to get a drink. Suddenly a stunning man appeared. He seemed more at home in his black tie than most joggers are in running suits. Hair tousled, black tie askew, he had a slightly rakish look. His expression was knowing, and if he appeared bored, it was, I thought, probably due to the depressing predictability of the crowd. He seemed to be alone, not part of a larger constellation; not linked to another, female, twinkling persona, he moved in his own orbit.

Effortlessly he found a place for himself at the bar, which only a moment before had been a sea of waiting outstretched hands. So fluid were his movements, so uneager, so casual his gestures, it was as if the vast atrium of the museum were *his* living room, the hordes of people *his* guests.

The sheer weight of my stare must have reached him, for he turned; with a small, enigmatic smile his eyes connected with Ron's, then, taking his drink, he wandered off and was swallowed up by the crowd. Ron murmured, "Wasn't he something!"

An expert in nineteenth-century Postimpressionism, Ron Silbert was quick to recognize the beauty of a late-twentieth-century objet d'art as well.

Later that night I remembered Joanna Ansen telling me about her ex-husband and his new wife, then asking, "Doesn't that tell you everything?"

I was beginning to realize nothing ever tells you everything. There's always a hidden text, a subplot, a back story. Observing my handsome, elegant companion and me prowling through the museum, who would have known that Ron Silbert was gay?

That night, the seed of an earlier consideration grew into a full-blown question: Did Jennifer Fever play a role in gay love affairs? If left for a young Jeffrey, would a middle-aged gay man feel the same sense of devastation as the Janets? And what about gay women? As they passed through their own Jenniferhood and entered middle age, how did lesbians view themselves and the women they desired? Did they worry about being abandoned and assuage their anxieties about aging by leaving one lover for another, younger woman?

According to Ed Mattlis, a thirty-eight-year-old stockbroker in New York, Jeffrey Fever is the norm in gay male relationships. Although almost forty, Ed, with his boyish crew cut and impish smile, looks younger. We were walking in the West Village, a neighborhood populated by many gay men, as he explained his dilemma:

"I'm in charge of an enormous department, with offices in Europe and Africa; I have forty people working under me. And at work I'm considered a young wizard. But," he said, scowling, "when I get home, back here to my neighborhood in the West Village, only fifteen blocks away from my office, among the men in the bars and restaurants, in the shops and on the street, I'm considered old business. Over the hill. It's very confusing and very crazy."

"Why do you think this discrepancy exists?" I asked.

"I have a theory. When gay men grow up, we have no models to shape our attitudes around. So we tell ourselves, 'Well, since I like men, I must feel and react like a woman. So just like many straight women, we get in a panic about every wrinkle and every pound. When it comes to aging and attractiveness, we respond the same way. How could we not?"

Forty-five-year-old Alan Willis lives in San Francisco. Of medium build, blond-haired, he was dressed conservatively—standard gray suit, blue tie—and toting his attaché case, he looked every bit the investment banker he has been for twenty years. Alan thought there was good news and bad news for gay men when it comes to Jeffrey Fever. He acknowledged that gay men mimic women's reactions to aging, panic about wrinkles and gray hair. Alan said there is good news too:

"Ask any gay man, and he'll tell you he was probably the last kid to get picked for any team for any sport in all his years of high school or college. He just isn't as competitive as straight men are. He is much more used to being vulnerable than a straight man. And friendship and intimacy require vulnerability."

We were having coffee at an outdoor coffeehouse, a spot favored by gay couples. We watched the men arrive, alone or in pairs. While I could think of gay men who are fiercely competitive in sports and business, the theater and law, I realized that for Alan and the gay men he knew, this competitiveness was probably not a dominant characteristic.

Alan continued: "Although it's beginning to change, straight men still cannot let down their guard to male friends, female friends, wives, or lovers. They have to prove themselves on all fronts—from bedroom to parlor to boardroom. Homosexual men *know* they are vulnerable. Their adolescent years were painful."

He paused, struggling to keep his voice even, dispassionate, struggling to stay in the third person. "They were different. They were always separated from the crowd. They don't long for victory, but for acceptance and affection. All this at least suggests that a gay man should be less needful of being competitive in a sexual way and having to attract a younger, more appealing partner."

"And the bad news?"

"The bad news is it doesn't usually work out that way," he said with a thin smile. "Often a gay man feels that by being gay he broke the rules, and he will continue to defy the rules. He feels exempt in an odd way, so he pushes beyond what's expected of others and believes that things that happen to others won't happen to him. Aging won't happen. Being left won't happen. And he wakes up one day and he *has* gotten older, he *has* been left for a younger lover, and he isn't prepared. If he is left for a younger man, it's just as devastating, if not more than it is for your Janets."

"Why?" I asked. "The Janets who played by one set of rules— stayed home, raised the children, ran the house—face enormous problems when they're left: money, jobs, identity."

"As horrible as it is for anyone to be left," Alan said, "for a gay man it's a nightmare." He hesitated, and discreetly pointed to a table of four young men close to ours. "Even if he has been with a partner for years, he has no legal recourse, no economic redress. He doesn't even have a right to a lease, alimony, nothing. Look at those young guys who say they lived with Rock Hudson and Liberace; they were left with nothing, and they were no longer young. If a gay man has been dependent on his lover for income, friends, social networks, even business associations, he'll probably lose them."

To me it sounded as if a gay man who is left for a younger lover finds himself in a position similar to that of the Janets who don't have any money of their own.

"Just as there are perpetual Jennifers, there are a lot of guys who only know how to be Jeffreys," Alan continued. "Many gay men wake up and discover all they have, all they know, is that they were great at being nineteen years old and adored. Suddenly they're thirty-five and they're not young and adorable, and older men don't court them anymore. Of course, I think a lot more of this leaving for younger Jeffreys went on pre-AIDS. A lot more of this 'I can defy the rules, it won't happen to me,' kind of thinking went on pre-AIDS too. It's all changing."

Finally Alan emphasized something I would hear from many gay men. "Most gay male relationships start with sex, even more so than the sleaziest male-female one-night stand. In many gay relationships there is *only* sex. Many of the problems gay men encounter, straight men face too. One of the most difficult ones is that they aren't prepared for what can happen in their relationships when any attempt is made at something more."

Paul Rienzi and Roger Rocheck are a perfect example of what can happen to gay men after the initial sexual rush, after years of living together. A forty-three-year-old designer, Paul has lived with forty-year-old Roger for six years. He described the issue facing many gay men this way:

"I love Roger dearly. We share a house, the same interests, friends. To me he is more attractive than when we met. But when he turned forty this year, suddenly our lovemaking stopped. He told me that he still loved me, but he felt the need for someone new, someone young, to admire him—not necessarily make love to him; just *want* him."

Paul took a deep breath, blinked his eyes to bat away a sudden rush of tears, and continued: "I understood, but I felt awful. I don't think he's acted on it. It's just a phase, I hope. He says it's also because of his fear of AIDS." Paul frowned, shook his head as if he were in a dialogue with himself, adding, "But we practice safe sex and I think we're both healthy, so I don't believe it's that. You've seen him; he's so attractive. Yet at forty he feels he's lost it."

Today many gay men are attempting to achieve that "something more" that Alan Willis talked about. Tom Donnelly is a short, dark-haired man with a slow smile, who speaks with a Midwestern twang. A specialist in genetics, he works at a large research institution in Dallas. For eight years Tom has lived with his lover, Evan, who is ten years younger. I asked Tom if he was concerned about Evan's becoming attracted to a younger man. After a few minutes of thoughtful consideration, Tom answered, choosing his words carefully: "If I learned Evan had an occasional fling with a young boy, you can be sure it wouldn't cause World War Three. Fidelity, or the lack of it, isn't the big deal it is in heterosexual relationships. Or at least it wasn't for many years. I can't think of a gay couple I know where occasional sex with a young guy altered a long-term relationship. Now there *would* be an issue.

"If fidelity isn't the issue, AIDS is. Today if your lover goes out and sleeps with a young boy, he isn't just courting young flesh; he can be courting death. He can bring something much worse than infidelity into your lives; he can bring disaster."

Today, for men and women, gay or straight, sexual relations present a new and terrible fear: the terror not of giving life but of receiving death.

The merging of death and desire is a familiar literary theme, but now it is a grim reality that pervades every day of our lives. Psychologists report that the fear of AIDS is significantly changing sexual relationships, suggesting that one-night stands, anonymous or casual sex, are quickly becoming artifacts of a bygone era, and monogamy or celibacy are fast becoming not only the safest but *the* sexual fashion of the day. It's too early to assess the number of men who because of AIDS are forgoing an extramarital fling with a Jennifer or a Jeffrey. Or how many are using the fear of AIDS to support other anxieties, assuage the guilt they might feel about leaving their relationships. Undoubtedly it is a factor and will remain one for years, until a cure and a vaccine are developed for this abominable disease.

Withal, none of the men I interviewed who were heterosexual reported that a fear of AIDS had affected their relations with a Jennifer. But for gay men it is a bitter reality. Each of the gay men I interviewed mentioned that in some way AIDS had affected not just his sexual behavior but his way of thinking about sex and his possible attraction to younger men.

But the dread of AIDS doesn't lessen gay men's concerns about aging. In many gay men's minds, youth is still equated with sexual attractiveness, fueling their own insecurities, troubling them even if they feel they cannot act on their deepest wishes.

Peter Gross has just turned forty. His lover, Alex, is fifty. The three of us had dinner in a quiet restaurant in Georgetown. Both men are supremely attractive, yet Peter voiced anxieties that to a casual observer would be difficult to believe.

"At forty, I feel I'm better than I've ever been," he said. "Yet I'm so aware I'm older. The goals I set for myself are not quite there. I look older, I feel older; my lover is older but has gotten more attractive through the years. I fear I haven't. I always went for older men, and we've been together thirteen years, yet he doesn't seem to age. I do."

Alex's affection for Peter was very apparent, as was his surprise at learning Peter believed that by turning forty he had suddenly diminished in attractiveness in his lover's eyes. When Alex spoke about his own salad days, he said with a laugh, "I know, when I first hit D.C. we were all the same age, yet I was always the young lover, drawn to older men because they were more interesting, more experienced. I wanted to be Paolo," Alex said, referring to the young lover of the aging Karen Stone in the only novel Tennessee Williams ever wrote, *The Roman Spring of Mrs. Stone.* "And now I'm Mrs. Stone."

"I worry, what if Alex got sick?" Peter interrupted. "I wouldn't know what to do. What if something happened? It's awful and it's depressing, but I have to admit it. I feel my aging has changed me in his eyes."

Peter Gross merely reflects how gay men have always felt—that aging wipes out sexual attractiveness.

"Not how *gay* men feel," my friend David Rothenberg corrected me, "how *men* feel about aging. Jennifer Fever isn't a straight or a gay issue. It's a *male* issue."

In his early fifties, David is a leader in the New York gay community. He ran for the New York City Council as, in his words, "a self-accepting homosexual," and has been a social and political activist in both New York and national politics. For eighteen years David was the director of the Fortune Society, a self-help organization for ex-convicts. He is host of a popular New York radio program and I have known his voice for years, and although we are friends, I am always impressed that when he talks it is with the same intimacy, the same humor, that I have enjoyed for so long on the radio.

We were chatting in his Greenwich Village apartment. A slight man of medium build, he has a knowing smile and a quick wit. David is also one of the shrewdest observers I know of the political scene, as well as of what's going on at the social battlefront.

"Barbara, you're not writing about straight or gay, you're writing about men," David explained. "A lot of things that are perceived as homosexual or heterosexual are really just maleness or femaleness. Gay men are no less or no more guilty of it than straight men. It manifests itself in the same way."

"Jeffrey Fever?" I suggested lightly.

"Right. Older men have the same self-delusion of feeling young or powerful with younger men.

"It's how men are socialized by the time they are fully mature. The social pressures that define what is desirable to them are exactly the same, straight or gay; it's a youth-oriented culture and youth is very prestigious."

"You're talking about the Jennifer or Jeffrey as trophy, people oohing and ahing when a man walks into a restaurant with someone younger on his arm? The drop-the-fork syndrome?"

"Of course. It's so immature to live a life and have a relationship based on the impression you're going to get from strangers. I don't understand it, but people do live that way. You know, when you see some old guy walk into Sardi's with a tootsie on his arm, it's prestigious."

"It isn't just Sardi's, David. You don't think it's just a class thing, something men with money feel the need to do, and can *afford* to do?"

"Not at all," David answered crisply. "I think I've become sensitive to this because when I worked with ex-cons at the Fortune Society I saw men who are the most exaggerated example of this. In prison, it's a feather in a guy's cap to get a younger kid, a chicken; it's an acquisition. Little girls grow up on the *same* streets, the *same* kind of homes as little boys, and they don't do that."

"Why?" I wondered.

"Because the peer pressure to perform to satisfy other women isn't there. Girls are socialized to perform for other boys. Boys perform not just to get the right girl but to please other men— whether it's a car, a Jennifer, or a Jeffrey. If people don't have access to money, they do other things to demonstrate their power to impress other men, including the women on their arms. Objects of conspicuous consumption."

"Even if they *do* have access to money," I replied. "And do you feel that need to impress?" I asked, suspecting I knew his answer.

Settling back in his chair, he shook his head, looking at me over the rim of his glass. "I can't do that," he said, "can't live my life to convey an illusion, or try to get a raised eyebrow from someone whose opinion doesn't matter to me in the first place. I'd rather be with someone who pleases and excites me on many levels than with someone who looks good.

"When I first came to New York, I was always more interested in older men, who were more interesting, more experienced, more challenging. I was a Jeffrey. As the years went by," he said with a laugh, "there's nobody alive who's older than me."

With a melancholy shrug of his shoulders, David continued. "Because men are more insistent, more demanding than women, about the physical appearance of whoever they're attracted to. Men want someone who is attractive in the traditional knockout sense of being attractive. With gay men, since it's only men involved, we've become our own fantasies of the body beautiful. We have gay men who have become overmasculinized with good looks.

"And we have more income. We're not spending money on dentists for children, and private schools. We can spend it at a gym or on clothes or travel. Besides, we're appealing to the sensuous needs of other men who are insisting on appearance, whereas you often see a very attractive Jennifer with a man who, while he may be interesting and provocative, has a face that could stop a clock." David laughed. "That's because women are socialized to be more exploratory; they are less willing to make a commitment based on a superficial appearance."

How men are socialized in a youth-oriented society is only part of it. A gay man in 1980s America carries a potent legacy, which over the course of thousands of years has seeped into his chromosomes and become part of his DNA, creating a genetic code of prejudice against aging homosexuals. And as he ages, a prejudice against himself.

Experts may differ about the genesis of homosexuality, but on one count there is no argument: It was the ancient Greeks who made the greatest contribution to the worship of young male flesh.

Professor Bernard Murstein, writing about homosexuality, observes: "The Athenian man had to marry a cloistered girl . . . less experienced in the ways of life and probably foisted on him by his father. What could he have in common with such a creature? . . . Homosexuality, in short, was in no small measure a direct consequence of the vilification of the Grecian wife."

It is in the world of homosexual attraction that we find exquisite examples of the high priority the Greeks placed on youth, female and male. We've already seen the contempt the Greeks had for aging females, and Dr. Amy Richlin writes that "the aging male is rarely described as diseased, foul or decaying as women were. The most biting critique of men, however, was reserved for the aging homosexual."

The beautiful boy is viewed in the same terms as an attractive young woman, but Dr. Richlin says there is one significant distinction: "The genital area of attractive women is never described until a woman ages, and then it is described as revolting. But the genitals of young boys are often described and praised. A young boy is to a hairy (older) boy as a rosebud is to a bramble, a fig is to a mushroom . . . or like cultured milk is to an ox."

A rosebud to a bramble. A fig to a mushroom. The bloom of youth is the prize. "Adult homosexuals are the male equivalent of old and/or repulsive women, and the anal orifice of such men is often attacked in terms similar to those used of repulsive female genitalia. It is clear that an orifice which is penetrated by the penis or which submits to the penis becomes disgusting when the one who submits is one who is normally barred by age from such submission—it is not proper for old women and adult males to do so, hence their orifices are perceived as overused and stained."

In our day the stereotypical image of the aging homosexual man continues to be gloomy. He is perceived, even by gay men themselves, like Aschenbach, the tragic hero of Thomas Mann's *Death in Venice*, a pathetic, lonely figure—rootless, loveless, a man who suffers inordinately from the ravages of time. Yet recent studies report this stereotype may be more myth than reality. They suggest that a majority of aging homosexuals make a better adaptation to the unique stresses of midlife than do straight men, and in some ways

Jeffrey Fever should be *less* of an issue than Jennifer Fever is for heterosexual men.

The most compelling argument goes something like this: In confronting and admitting their homosexuality, gay men have faced the greatest conflict in their lives, one that no midlife trauma can possibly match. In his book *Gay and Gray*, Raymond Berger contends that this "mastery of crisis" hypothesis plays a vital role in shattering the myth of the despondent lives led by aging gay men. Generally, heterosexuals experience their first crisis of independence in old age. As young boys they are integrated into their own family, and when they leave this family they move quickly into what Berger calls a "family of procreation." But the older gay man "typically faces the crisis of independence much earlier and he cannot usually look to a family of procreation for support. His need for concealment may distance him further from other family members. Because the crisis of independence must be resolved in young adulthood, his transition to old age and retirement is often less severe." Additionally Berger argues that the homosexual man is forced to face his isolation at an early age, and is possibly "more likely to have developed close friendships which he can turn to in crisis situations."

As men age they may become increasingly passive, both sexually and nonsexually. To compound the problem, with the natural biological diminution of sexual desire and performance that also comes with aging, straight men can experience a severe blow to their ego, threatening their masculine vision of themselves.

But for the aging homosexual, Berger offers a rosier prognosis. He claims that older male gays are less concerned with "maintaining a masculine self-image, and are therefore less likely to experience male menopause and a crisis related to physical prowess."

As David Rothenberg suggested, some gay men have more spendable income at midlife than do men who are burdened with the costs of children's education and supporting their households. Finally, as a rule these men are less physically ravaged by their advancing years because as a group they are more devoted to the idea of taking better care of themselves with exercise, dieting, health clubs, etc. The scourge of AIDS has driven gay men to an even greater concern with health and nutrition.

But despite the optimistic studies, the common perception persists, even among gay men themselves: The aging gay man is frequently an object of pathos, an object of scorn. The reality facing many gay men may be less positive than these studies indicate.

For some gay men the studies are merely intellectual theorizing and far from the bitter realities they encounter as they age. Therapists who specialize in treating gay men believe that they do experience a severe midlife panic, and like heterosexuals, they fear that each year diminishes their sexual attractiveness to their lovers.

This has as much to do with biology as with sociology. No matter what the values of a culture are, or how much it emphasizes the prestigious value of youth, no matter how fashions, advertising, and movies confirm the prejudice, one biological fact is immutable: A man's sexual organs are external, and men depend on externals, visual cues, to arouse their sexuality, including the visual cues they receive in the mirror to confirm or deny their own sexual attractiveness.

Add that biological fact to a cultural prejudice and it's not difficult to see why gay men, like heterosexual men and women, dread the signs of aging. And why, like straight men, they search for youthful sexual partners to assuage that dread.

Dr. Alfred Borne specializes in treating the psychological problems of gay men. He says one factor that contributes to the terrors of aging for gay men, which can lead to Jeffrey Fever, is that they tend to separate love and sex.

"At an early age, men have learned from all sources that sex is dirty, wrong, something you do in the bathroom," Dr. Borne explained. "As one doubts he can continue to be found sexy by his lover, he must find sex outside. Often roommates discover they can't always be lovers.

"Just as women may misinterpret what's going on with their husbands as being reflective of something wrong with them"—he paused, his eyes meeting mine—"nobody finds himself sexy alone, so a gay man feels my sense of me, my sense of attractiveness, is being rejected. A gay man goes to a young lover to prove his version of himself as attractive, because he needs someone to answer the question: 'Do you find me attractive? Do you find me sexy? Do you? Do you?' "

"But we all need someone to confirm our view of ourselves," I said. "Why is it so particularly onerous in gay men?"

"Because of the way they attempt to *solve* it," he answered. "The more you try to overcompensate by sexually performing with a stranger—the whole business of genital sex as a means of connection, of anonymity—the more you make it a prophecy."

Kay Prothro is a psychotherapist who treats men and women, straight and gay. She is a self-assured, high-energy woman. She has an earthy, breezy, open style; her clear green eyes connect with yours, and she exudes a no-nonsense, "this-is-how-it-is" attitude. We were having breakfast in a coffee shop near her office, and her reactions to my questions were fresh, unstudied, and unguarded.

I asked her how her gay male patients' problems with aging differed from gay women's.

"For gay men there's such a value on youth, their midlife crisis comes early; most of the gay men I see feel they don't attract men their own age, are convinced they've had it at thirty. There's such an emphasis on their physicality; for a gay man it's devastating."

"And gay women?"

"The whole thing of the sex being external in men, and our sex being internal. Women look for connection, closeness; and are concerned about what's inside. Gay men look for gratification more through a genital connection; they seek validation that way, by performance. As they age, they fear they cannot attract a young guy unless they can offer money or social access.

"Barbara," she continued, her expression serious, her tone firm, "a lot of women as they age lose power because of the emphasis on youth and pleasing the male. Straight men always gain power as they age, but gay men lose power, since they identify with straight women's emphasis on youth and beauty."

"And for lesbians?" I asked.

"Gay women don't lose power. A lesbian woman gains power—that is, if she has resolved issues of her sexuality and is satisfied by her career. And most gay women have had to resolve those issues by middle age. I don't think Jennifer Fever is a big issue for gay women. There are issues of equality and power; gay women tend to be more equal in relationships than others. Troubles arise if one is more successful, and an attempt is made to equalize."

Psychotherapist Rosanna Murray agrees. In her practice, specializing in treating gay men and women, she told me that in ten years she has never encountered one lesbian for whom Jennifer Fever was an issue. "I think that's because it probably doesn't exist as it does among gay males and heterosexuals."

"No Jennifer Fever?"

"No; I don't even have anecdotal information about gay women being left for a younger lover," she replied. "But one of the biggest issues gay women experience is facing the biological clock. More lesbians are having babies today, and they must deal with what it's like to have a child in a fluid environment, in a relationship not sanctioned by marriage." Resting her chin in the cup of her hand, she hesitated, gathering her thoughts. "And those who don't have children must confront the issues of what it means not to have a child. And they are all facing the issue we all face as we age—what they've achieved and what they haven't. Those seem to be the issues for gay women. Not cellulite or wrinkles."

"Really?" I was quite surprised.

"Most lesbians have rejected that." Rosanna Murray smiled, sensing my confusion. "Look, simply by virtue of being lesbians, they are saying, 'I won't play by those rules. Perhaps I don't know all the new rules, but I won't play by those rules.' Once you make the choice to be a lesbian, you have to connect with your own power. As a straight woman, you may get power by linking up with a powerful man. Even if her needs for nurturance and connection are the same as lesbian women's, she will see emblematic value in his money or other signs of his power and take those as signs of connection and nurturance."

Kay Prothro also talked about nurturance. "Gay women need and express tenderness and affection," she commented. "For some gay women, this leads to a de-emphasis of the strictly sexual and more emphasis on companionship. Gay women also tend to stay and fight it out more in the relationship rather than running to someone else. That isn't to say there aren't problems; some lesbians face enormous problems in separation which sometimes lead to self-destructive behavior.

"Gay women are very interested in sharing, connection, close-ness, but because of that desire to share, to be close, they can merge, fuse, and that can lead to violence. Having two women constantly taking on each other's feelings, absorbing each other all the time, can sometimes lead to violence when one wants to break away."

"Violence?" I was truly surprised.

I knew that in my close friendships with women, we do absorb each other—the pain as well as the happiness—but I had never considered how that merging, that closeness, could lead to problems in a sexual relationship between two women.

"To me, Jennifer Fever has to do with a dread of death," Kay continued. "It gives the illusion that it's farther away; it's an avoid-ance mechanism of coming to terms with your own mortality. That's not the way gay women deal with death. Gay women go through a creative process, if they're well-adjusted and productive; by virtue of surviving all they've had to survive to be gay, they enjoy the now."

There are a number of reasons why lesbians appear to be the only sexual group that seems to be immune to Jennifer Fever. Rosanna Murray, however, believes there is one transcendent rea-son why it isn't an issue; or as one lesbian lawyer put it, "Gay women are less interested in the packaging than gay or straight men."

"In heterosexuals the main difference between a Jennifer-proof man and one who isn't is not just narcissism," Rosanna Murray explained. "It is the difference between a man who gets his value of himself from the inside and one who gets it from the outside. A man who learns not to rely on outside accoutrements won't need a Jennifer as he ages. Of course, no one, man or woman, straight or gay, gets to that place without going through an internal struggle, in which he discovers 'I'm OK.' "

"Ah, the 'mastery of crisis' theory. Once you've confronted

your gayness, just admitting you're a lesbian, then aging isn't such a big deal."

"You've got it," Rosanna Murray replied, smiling. "Lesbians, at least most of them, have had to make that struggle, and for them the outside packaging just isn't the issue, just isn't where it's at."

During our interview, David Rothenberg said he has a number of lesbian friends. He related this story to explain why Jennifer Fever is a *male,* not a gay or straight, issue:

"I wrote an article called 'The Golden Fuck.' It was about the fact that gay men pick up somebody to go to bed with them and have a perfect orgasm. Then they hope the guy can finish a sentence afterward and they'll have something to talk about. Whereas for women, before the golden fuck happens, there has to be—women *insist* on—some socialization."

David paused. He had just made a sweeping generalization about my gender, and he was checking to see if he had ruffled my sensibilities. I nodded. "It's OK. This isn't a case for the feminist police."

With a slightly bemused expression, he went on. "I introduced one lesbian friend to another; I called the next day and she said, 'We made a lunch date for next Tuesday.' I said, 'Lunch?' So they had lunch six weeks in a row. Gay men, if they haven't been to bed three times that night, then by the sixth week they're considered golden oldies."

In his book *Homosexual Behavior,* Dr. Judd Marmor reports that some studies indicate that gay women are as concerned about aging as heterosexual women. But he also writes, citing the work of Elsa Gidlow, a lesbian poet, "The aging process is easier for lesbians than straight women, because 'the gay woman is insulated from what Gidlow described as the more feminine emphasis on remaining youthful and retaining one's physical attractiveness.' "

But for aging gay women, particularly those who grew up in the pre-feminist, pre-gay-liberation era, there are problems; maybe not the problem of having been abandoned for a Jennifer, but agonizing problems of discrimination and invisibility. Marcy Adelman studied the lives of older lesbians and asked them to write about their later years and lesbian life. She concludes that their reports break the stereotypes of older lesbians as invariably depressed and alone.

"What affects them is the level of homophobia in society and ourselves. In the end," she says, "the conditions of older lesbians are determined by the conditions of older women." She cites statistics which reveal that among all people aged sixty-five or older, twice as many women as men are below the poverty line, and 40 percent of women and 15 percent of men live alone. Adelman says, "Society's negative attitude toward lesbians can make challenges of aging harder for us. . . . What is unique is the stigma and discrimination we face and the repertoire of creative solutions that we devise to cope with it."

But about lesbians who grew up in the "supportive environment" of gay liberation and feminism, who had a lesbian community as an "alternative to invisibility and isolation," Adelman is more optimistic. For them she predicts that things will be different.

I was in Portland, Maine, talking with Gail Jacobs. At forty-seven, Gail is a short, slight woman who practices law in a small town north of Portland. She had been talking openly about being gay, and about her lover, who is the same age as she is. I asked her, "Do you ever feel a need for a Jennifer, or fear you'll be left by your lover for one?"

Rather than resenting the question or avoiding it, she tackled it head-on, her voice filled with emotion. "Speaking for myself as a midlife lesbian, I am so grateful to have survived my life in a city where I thought I was the only gay woman. How did I do this? Luckily, I was smart. I got a scholarship. At forty-seven, I'm so grateful. I am living in a world I felt oppressed in for so long. I don't feel oppressed anymore."

Her face was flushed with animation, her expression gleaming with the pride of self-acceptance, when she exclaimed, "Barbara, I have money, I have a career; I have a lover who happens to be close to my age, a terrific, exciting, successful woman. At my own menopause, I felt freedom. I said, 'Hallelujah. I can be me! I can be.' "

16

Pearl Harbor's Not an Actress

Is it all bliss?

For those who are left, straight or gay, it's common to imagine that their former lovers are dwelling with their younger lovers in a perpetual paradise. But aren't there downside risks for the men and their Jennifers . . . or Jeffreys?

Louis Richards, a forty-one-year-old gay man in San Francisco, recounted the following anecdote:

"I met a beautiful and fairly innocent young man. We had a wonderful sexual relationship, a gentle and tender time. One morning he noticed a print that hung over my bed and remarked, 'That's a pretty painting.' I told him it was a Van Gogh print I bought at a museum in Amsterdam. He said, 'Van who?'

"I sat up with a jolt. How could I have a relationship with a man who didn't know who Van Gogh was? That was the last ignorant statement he made, because I ended the relationship. I wasn't putting him down; I just realized I knew too much."

When the poet Elsa Gidlow was in her sixties, she experienced ambivalence about beginning a relationship with a much younger woman who was enamored of her:

"Like the ghost of the old moon behind the rising new moon the young woman's life with her mother, her mixed often ambivalent memories, her mother's continuing influence shadows the new relationship."

I wondered if any of the men or Jennifers wished they had exercised Elsa Gidlow's caution before embarking on their relationships. What were the shadows that clouded the lives of the Jennifers and their older lovers?

When I was a Jennifer, my older lover and I were probably nourished by the hidden, furtive, touched-with-angst aspect of our affair. While I was not an ignorant, malleable, fresh-off-the-farm young girl, like many Jennifers I was impressionable and adored the vast stores of knowledge, experience, anecdotes, and worldliness he shared with me. For some young women it may be their older lover's expertise in corporate takeovers, stock splits, or constitutional law. For me it was his knowledge of theater, books, writers, and a delicious sense of irony about the world, and an equally delicious ability to laugh at himself in that world.

Trouble arose in the paradise we had carved out for ourselves when I decided that in this survey course of life that he was offering and I was taking—an unspoken, implicit aspect of our affair—I didn't want to be a part-time student. Eager to be a full-time lover, I didn't just want to audit the course.

I wondered if other Jennifers or former Jennifers and their older men also discovered problems when the young women were no longer content to live in the margins of their older lovers' lives, or to remain with a man who was married to a woman who had a legitimate claim to his time and affections. What happened when a Jennifer found her voice and, when she did, sang out her own wishes, desires, and opinions? For men who had problems dealing with wives who assumed peerdom and in their eyes took on a maternal resonance, was it a shock to see their formerly pliant and adoring young lovers staking their own claim on their identities?

I knew there were many reasons why a man and his Jennifer might encounter some bumps as they traveled together along the yellow brick road. Shakespeare listed a few when he wrote the following:

> Crabbed age and youth cannot live together:
> Youth is full of pleasance, age is full of care;
> Youth like summer morn, age like winter weather;
> Youth like summer brave, age like winter bare.

> Youth is full of sport, age's breath is short;
> Youth is nimble, age is lame;
> Youth is hot and bold, age is weak and cold;
> Youth is wild, and age is tame.
> Age, I do abhor thee; youth, I do adore thee . . .

Shakespearean scholars disagree about whether this sonnet was written to lament a disappointing love affair with a young maiden or, as some suggest, a younger man. But they do agree that at thirty-five, Shakespeare was melancholy about the prospects for "crabbed age" and youth walking off into a blissful sunset.

Some older men and Jennifers are just as melancholy. Disillusioned, and with the clarity of hindsight, they say that in their relationships they were, in a sense, grasping at flaws.

Either they blinded themselves to a lover's hidden agenda, or a personality defect emerged, one that had remained undisclosed in their lovers or, more infrequently, in themselves. Whatever the reason, for some it doesn't work out, and statistics indicate no happier prospects for second marriages to a Jennifer than for first marriages to a Janet. If first marriages face a fifty-fifty chance of succeeding, recent statistics for second marriages range from fifty-fifty to sixty-forty odds against their success.

One reason these relationships run into trouble is that at their core lies a basic cynicism about the motives of the Jennifer. And because of his desperate need for her to support and fuel his inner vision of himself, an older man may blind himself to those motives. An often-told joke reflects this widespread cynical attitude:

A seventy-five-year-old man tells his friend, "I've met a wonderful girl and you won't believe it, but this twenty-five-year-old girl wants to marry me."

"What did you have to do," his friend asks caustically, "lie about your age?"

"Of course."

"So you told her you were only fifty-five?"

"No, I told her I was eighty-five."

Recently *Spy* magazine sardonically suggested that some young women are members of the Double or Nothing Club: They marry men twice their age and ten times their own net worth. But it isn't merely a suspicion that the Jennifer is plotting to become a rich widow. Often it's assumed she also wishes to inherit and partake of things other than money that a well-established, well-connected older man can offer.

Sixty-two-year-old Lee Kalder felt his Jennifer time of three years ago was a sour, bleak experience, and he's still recuperating. After a leisurely lunch, he was stacking the dishwasher and, refusing any help, insisted that I sit on a kitchen stool, with my tape recorder perched on the counter, while he sorted through some unhappy memories.

"I think she could see what the future held. She could see that I was sixty today, and I'd be seventy tomorrow, that kind of thing. She fell out of love when she realized she had given more than she got."

"What did she expect to get?" I asked.

"When we met, she was bored with her husband sexually, and with me she thought she could get her sex together. And because of my success in her field, she thought she could get her art career together.

"I was with a top gallery, one that could have helped her career." He hesitated for a moment, ill at ease with his memories, but then continued in a rush of words. "But when it didn't happen, it must have been disappointing to her."

"And today, three years later, how do you view that relationship?"

Lee slammed the dishwasher shut and sat on a stool next to mine.

"Disaster. My Jennifer experience has been a fucking disaster. I'm still putting myself together." He drained the wine from his glass and slouched on his stool, his expression gloomy. His tone was bitter when he continued. "I was really rocked. She was a cruel, ego-busting, ball-breaking woman. Certainly all of that can't be attributed to her age, but in a way it can. She was too hungry, too ambitious. At first I fit into her long-range plan. And when it turned out that I couldn't help her advance her career, she checked out.

"But by the time all that happened, we had gotten married. I'm still plowing through the shit with lawyers and property settlements."

At forty-one, Alex Walters is barely nudging middle age. A tall, lanky man, he has an infectious smile nestled in a ruggedly attractive beard. He said he wanted to talk about his Jennifer because while he was having a wonderful time, he was troubled by what his attraction to a twenty-three-year-old woman said about him, and was disturbed about the prospects for their future.

It was one of those incomparable late-September afternoons, and we had chosen to bring sandwiches and wine into Central Park. We settled beneath a sprawling maple and for a while merely enjoyed the passing parade of émigrés from corporate towers, young lovers, mothers, toddlers wielding pails and shovels, and two teenage boys who were guiding a shiny silver high-tech kite through the soft early-autumn wind.

"Alex, did you always go out with younger women?" I began, reluctantly breaking the magical spell of silence that had descended in this tiny sliver of the city.

"Up until I was thirty-five, I called men with younger girls perverts. And then all of a sudden I wasn't attracted to women my own age. My sexual fantasies started involving younger women."

"So what's the problem?"

"The problem is I have a sense of doom about my attraction to my Jennifer." His hand stroked the outlines of his beard as he searched for a way to explain this sense of doom in words I could understand.

"I mean, in 1955 I was a person, I watched the Army-McCarthy hearings, and she wasn't even born yet," he said through an enormous laugh.

"You mean it's unnerving when she thinks Pearl Harbor is an actress?" I suggested lightly.

"Pearl Harbor? Try Vietnam." He laughed again. "Eighteen years as a running head start is a lot. I don't like it; it bothers me that she doesn't know who Joseph Welch was.

"Contrary to the notion that a young woman keeps you young, my attraction to younger women makes me feel older. Compare, for example, the importance of the assassinations of Martin Luther

King and Robert Kennedy in 1968 to John Lennon's a few years ago. To this Jennifer, the Lennon assassination was more significant. Not just more significant; it was the seminal event of her life!"

"So?"

"So if I talk about 1968—you know, contemporary stuff—I have to remind myself, in '68 she was a child. It makes me very uncomfortable, reminds me of the chasm between us. I never see the rewards in that position."

For a moment his gaze was fixed on the shiny kite that was bobbing nervously in the sky. "Alex, why do you think it makes you so uneasy?" I asked.

"Possibly it's because I'm not an older man," he said with a sly grin. "At forty-one I'm not dealing with issues of mortality or impotence, which trouble older men. I think that explains why instead of feeling younger with my Jennifer, I feel the gaps. If you're obsessed with dying or worried about becoming a dried-up, sexless creature, then I guess the gaps can seem like a small price to pay if she makes you feel like you're young."

"Some men like the gaps, need the gaps," I observed. "The gaps allow them to play Henry Higgins."

His eyes returned to earth, and he looked at me, startled. "Henry Higgins?" he exclaimed. "The feeling of being Father Time? Some men may like it, but it only reminds me of the chasm, the gulf between us. No, I don't like it at all. I want a complete relationship. I don't want to play Henry Higgins with a woman.

"I have two daughters from my first marriage. Sometimes I catch my Jennifer talking with them about clothes and makeup. They have so much in common. It's a strange and horrible feeling."

"Yet for many men, it's not strange or horrible. They say they feel younger with younger women," I said.

"Maybe, but I feel older with my Jennifer," Alex insisted. "I was at the movies with her recently, and as we left the theater I said that an actor in the film reminded me of Eddie Cantor. She gave me a glazed look. That look makes you feel old."

There's another reason Alex Walters wasn't overly optimistic about his future with his Jennifer. "The whole Jennifer thing is based on non-peerdom," he said. "Everyone wants to be superior at some time in a relationship—the man being more powerful, more established financially. Well, it's easier for him to be more powerful with a Jennifer. I admit that.

"I guess I feel less threatened by a younger woman on a sub-conscious level, yet I am aware there are many danger signs in the relationship. One day she will feel she has to reject me, resent me. It's inevitable."

A note about Alex Walters. Since our interview, I learned he has somehow transcended his sense of doom and horrible feelings about the cultural chasm and married his Jennifer. From his latest reports, despite the glazed looks, the pleasure outweighs the pain. As he told me recently, "We're very happy. So far so good."

For Wendy Redfield, that inevitable rejection Alex Walters referred to *was* inevitable.

"There's something inherently unequal about the relationship that is built in. When you are that much younger, that person is a teacher, a father. When you have a disagreement, they win because they're older, just like your parents. There's probably a lot to be said for living with someone who's lived thirty years more than you. They probably know more about the world, but I don't know if you want to be told that every day. You want to grow with someone and learn those things together."

Wendy Redfield is a bronzed and blond advertisement for youth, burnished by a golden California aura of well-being. As she entered the garden in the back of a trendy Santa Barbara restaurant, she was airy, bubbling with life, the quintessential California beach goddess.

She quickly explained that a few years before, when she and her older husband separated, she was distraught. A bubble had burst, a dream gone astray, a dream she had nurtured since childhood. When they met, she was twenty-two, he was fifty-five.

"I was overwhelmed, smitten immediately, and I knew just what to do. Oh, they want some of the good stuff of older women—"

"For example?" I asked.

"The intelligence. They don't want you to be an idiot, though some clearly do. But I know what they really want, and I know how to be a little girl for older men, know what they like, do what they like."

"And what *do* they like?"

"It came naturally to me," Wendy answered, her voice full of self-deprecating sarcasm. "I fell into the pattern of being cute and charming in a way that's unlike who I am. I know how to dress for them: wear clothes that show your body—tight jeans, open shirts, little bathing suits. That's part of your whole appeal. After all, if they're going to be with you because you're young, I thought you should play the part.

"When we went out, people thought he was my father. I was uncomfortable with that. When I married Ted, I think money had a lot to do with my attraction to him. It's glamorous when you're young, and here comes this person and he buys you things, sends you flowers, and you tool around in fancy cars. It sweeps you off your feet."

"When did things begin to go wrong?"

"He was worried I would leave him, that he would get too old. He made it very secure for me, made this little world for me to live in, but he didn't want to let me out. He said my working was fine, but didn't mean it. He built a little prison for me: We lived on a huge, eighty-acre ranch outside L.A., with cars and clothes and stuff."

Wendy paused to glance at the menu, shoved it aside, and added, "But most men of his generation didn't have mothers who taught them to be warm and loving. He would look at me with that air of authority: 'Here I am, here's what I've done, I'm successful, I'm supporting you.' Go argue with success. He always gave me the feeling, even if he didn't say it: You're lucky to be here, kid; look who you've got.

"We were married for two years, and it was a disaster. He was too controlling and powerful. It took a long time for me to be miserable enough to get the nerve to leave. By the time I did, there was no ego left."

Some Jennifers bristled at the idea that perhaps they were searching for replicas of their fathers in their older lovers, but after we had ordered lunch, Wendy introduced the idea on her own.

"I guessed he would adore me the way my father adored me. I had the most wonderful father, truly remarkable. Bright, wonderful sense of humor, warm and affectionate. He worshiped the ground I walked on."

Wendy's smile was radiant, and her eyes filled with tears as she spoke of her father. "When I was eleven I got a horse for Christmas," she said. "When I woke up, it was there waiting for me in the driveway. How do I top that?"

"But you said Ted was generous as well," I offered.

"What was ultimate about my father was not the horse in the driveway. It was that he adored me. Ted didn't know that; he only knew how to put the horse in the driveway."

When Wendy realized that "the horse in the driveway" was not enough, it shocked her into the kind of rebellion Alex Walters fears in his own relationship. Unable to tolerate a marriage "based on non-peerdom," she bolted, and began a painful journey of self-discovery and, ultimately, a life of independence. Her eyes fixed on the swirls of cream in her coffee cup, she suddenly looked up at me, and when she spoke, her words were precise, decisive:

"It took a long time for me to make the decision to leave, and it's taken a long time to put myself back together. He made me believe I couldn't function or survive without him, that I needed him to exist. I was so dehumanized, but I allowed him to do it. It's amazing. We're divorced and he still sends me gifts, wants me back, wants to take care of me."

"And today?" I wondered.

"I don't need to be taken care of anymore." A rush of color filled her already bronze complexion, and she ticked off the current successes in her life with obvious satisfaction. "I have my own house, my own car, my own dog, my own business, I pay the bills. I remember he wouldn't even tell me the name of our medical insurance. I don't need a man for that; I don't *need*. I want someone to enhance my life. I can't be bought."

"Ted courted you, wooed you, wanted you," I said. "Why do you think he couldn't change his behavior when you married; why couldn't he see what was happening?"

"I think there is that sense of control at any age. If they can buy it, men think they control it; they'll support you as long as you're home for sex."

It was difficult to imagine Wendy Redfield, or at least this year's model of Wendy Redfield, being controlled by anyone. She continued, her voice confident, assured, and with perhaps a trace of the zeal of the newly converted. "Men in their thirties, who grew up with the women's movement, know they can't get away with that stuff. For years they've been told not to expect to be taken care of and waited on, and they can't be in control all the time, either. Sure, some of them still want it, but many also want women with their own lives and careers, who aren't dependent. They're more threatened by women who are 'clingy.'"

We were working our way through the cramped little garden, crowded with tables, when Wendy stopped suddenly and whispered, "I've grown into men my own age."

Discreetly pointing to four men in their thirties having lunch at a table on the other side of the garden, Wendy laughed at her belated discovery. "And guess what?" she added. "At thirty-six, they *know* how to send flowers, how to order in restaurants. They know it now; they didn't know it then. The women who had them when they were in their twenties taught them."

Shaking her head ruefully, and with a tinge of self-mockery, she quipped, "But I didn't want to do that; I wanted to be a princess."

If the Jennifers shared one central complaint, experienced one theme park of disillusion and discontent, it was that they were unhappy with their older husbands because the men were too controlling, and because they tried to exert too much power over the women's lives.

For a great artist, controlling all the elements of his life is often as essential as his control of the mixture of pigment on his palette. And it is in the life of one of the most celebrated artists of our century that we can observe this need to control his environment as well as his Jennifer.

Françoise Gilot met Pablo Picasso in 1943, when she was twenty-one and he was sixty-two. At the time, she was an aspiring artist and he was a legend, who had gone through a series of stormy relationships with considerably younger women. During the next ten years, Gilot would be his lover, his model, and the mother of two of his children. In her book *Life with Picasso,* Gilot describes her infatuation and her passion for him, and her sorrowful awakening when she was unable to tolerate the controlling emotional tyranny that characterized their last years together.

At first she was prepared to devote herself to him, knowing "I should expect to receive nothing beyond what he had given the world by means of his art. I consented to make my life with him on those terms." But she came to realize he had never been able to stand the "company of a woman for any sustained period and that I would get nothing more than what I had been willing to settle for at the beginning: whatever joy I might receive from devoting myself to him and his work. . . .

"He had insisted that I have children because I wasn't enough of a woman . . . now that I had them, it began to be clear that he didn't care a bit for it. He had directed this metamorphosis in my nature and now that he had achieved it, he wanted no part of it."

She tried to devote herself to him and their children and to her own work as a painter, but when he began going off with other women, even though she loved him "as much as anyone can love somebody else," she writes, "I had waked up and I was disenchanted. . . . His constant dread of death had moved into a critical phase and as one of its effects . . . he was anxious to appear youthful whatever the cost."

Similar to other women who experienced less than happy times with older men, in the end Françoise Gilot survives, stronger and self-aware. Flexing her once-underdeveloped muscles of independence, she's enriched instead of embittered by the experience. She concludes, recalling Picasso's words to her on their first visit, "My coming to him he said seemed like a window that was opening up and he wanted it to remain open. I did too, as long as it let in the light. When it no longer did, I closed it much against my own desire. From that moment on, he burned all the bridges that connected me to the past I had shared with him. But in doing so he forced me to discover myself and thus to survive. I shall never cease being grateful to him for that."

For fifteen years Connie White played Jennifer to one of Boston's most distinguished surgeons, and like Françoise Gilot, after a number of years she, too, woke up "disenchanted."

Connie is a redhead, the kind who defiantly wears tangerine lipstick, shocking-pink blouses, and burgundy skirts. Her hair is pulled back in an ersatz ponytail, but layers of spray and lacquer give it a fixed, rigid appearance that destroys the *jeune fille* impression she is trying to convey. With her eyes circled in kohl-black pencil, and her fiercely long, blood-red fingernails, she is a throwback to the fifties. We met in her dress shop in a Boston suburb, where, between customers, she told me her story:

"I fell in love with him the first time I saw him, couldn't take my eyes off his hands, imagining them all over my body. You see, he was also a sculptor, and while I was only twenty-four, I had a vivid imagination, and I was dying, craving, to be the clay he molded beneath his fingers.

"In his late fifties he was a great-looking guy, and I was a very pretty little girl. I was impressed; he radiated charm. He was an extraordinary man, brilliant, worldly, a first-rate athlete."

Connie was studying a customer who had paused in front of her window, eyeing an expensive alligator bag. The woman continued walking past the shop, and with a shrug, Connie looked at me and merely said, "Pity."

"Was his money part of his attraction?" I asked.

"Because I had my own successful career as a fashion consultant, making a nice six figures, I was perceived as more than just a young chick, so his kids were happy for us, even happy when he left his wife. His money wasn't all of it or even the main thing, but"—Connie paused, smoothing away a wisp of hair that had somehow escaped from her tortoiseshell barrette—"I didn't mind the idea that a life with him would include a marvelous life-style. He was lovely to me until I became his wife."

"What happened then?" I asked.

"After I became his wife, I had to be perfect because I *was* his wife. I realize now you must deny your feelings to be happy with older men. It took me fifteen years, then I realized what was happening. I had to be an ornament, a dear little doll. Oh, I was wrong, so wrong. This was not a good daddy; he was a cruel parent. It was tyranny, not strength, but I didn't know that then."

Two teenage girls had entered the shop, rifled through a pile of sweaters, and left, leaving them in disarray on the counter. As Connie folded them, stacking them neatly on the shelves, she said rather matter-of-factly, given the emotionally loaded nature of the subject, "Everyone I ever met who was a younger woman with an older man is somebody who in some way feels worthless. Later they recognize they had to deny their feelings to stay in the marriage, and then they realize there's nothing for them. It's all domineering, controlling; they're treated like dirt. The trips and the furs and jewels aren't worth it, but you don't know that until you've been in it for a long time."

"And then?" I asked.

"I finally realized that for fifteen years I had felt worthless, and it was he who was making me feel this way. I got out. Remember, I had a lifetime of being deprived of any caring from anyone—two selfish, unloving parents—and all of a sudden I was told one lie and really went for it."

"Why do you think it took you so long to see what was happening?"

"It's incredible masochism; the woman has to believe the man is strong when in fact he's a tyrant and she's just simply recapitulating what she knew as a child: being with an unloving parent and thinking it's wonderful."

As she started back toward her desk near the rear of the shop, she suddenly laughed. "Funny, you asked me if I liked his money," she remarked. "I remember he especially liked that I was making lots of dough; that left him money to give his ex-wife and assuage his guilt."

"And sexually—was that a good part of your relationship?"

"He performed incredibly sexually," Connie answered, and then, with enviable confidence, she added, "but that's because I was great in bed. I would arouse him to the point where he could perform miracles. This was terribly important for his ego. I made him feel he was in his twenties, and I knew just how to do it."

Picasso once told Françoise Gilot that living with someone young helped him to stay young, but years later he complained, " 'Seeing someone young around all the time is a constant reproach for being no longer young oneself.' The idea that he was now past seventy was something he hurled against me as though I were responsible for it. I used to feel that the only way I could atone for it was by making an effort to become suddenly seventy years old myself. . . . I recalled how he had told me at the beginning, 'Every time I change wives I should burn the last one. That way I'd be rid of them. . . . Maybe that would bring back my youth too. You kill the woman and you wipe out the past she represents.' "

From his vantage point as a divorce lawyer, Raoul Felder sees another downside aspect a younger woman may present to an older man. While Felder's views betray a rather harsh estimation of Jennifers, it's of particular interest to remember that they come from a man who sees so many men and women going through midlife divorces because of Jennifer Fever.

"Hemingway said somewhere that a man is really only a man for five minutes after he makes love. Now what happens after that?" he asked. "A Jennifer may be beautiful to look at, even better-looking because the lights are low. And she smells nice and everything. And you do the in-and-out business, and then what happens?"

I hoped Raoul Felder's question was rhetorical and he didn't expect an answer, because I was still laughing at his description of the mystical act of making love, but he continued; his pause had been only for emphasis. "One thing we know about Jennifers, they're replaceable. Imagine the depression that must set in after a succession of Jennifers."

Lifting a pen from his desk, he toyed with it, aiming it this way and that as he continued. "All right, so you have a wife who is a little overweight and she washes out your dirty underwear, and then you've got this wonderful creature who smells perfect, who oohs and ahs over you. And she says you're wonderful. So you go to bed with her three or four times, and you exchange her three or four times, and you've taken up eight months of your life. What happens then?"

"You tell me," I replied.

"You either marry her or say you've lost," he answered, tossing his pen aside. "OK, so she doesn't know Pearl Harbor. And you put up with that. But we're talking twenty-four hours a day. We're talking about when it's snowing outside; we're talking about when you come back from the theater; we're talking about when you've got indigestion. What are you going to do with her then?"

Connie White knows precisely what men do with them then. They enjoy doing what her husband did. "He wanted to parade a much younger woman who was twenty-four in front of his friends," she said, scowling. "It's a guy with low self-esteem who has to show off an object and count the number of forks that drop when he walks into a restaurant, as a measure of his self-esteem."

"Can you recall any pleasures in the years of your marriage?" I asked.

"Initially you get a kick out of being the object that everyone hates and all his friends' wives can't stand and won't accept because they're scared to death their husbands will do the same thing. And then you realize it's absurd. Why does anyone just want to parade you like an objet d'art? It's not for you. I hated it, loathed it."

"And today you're still angry?"

"There's no point in being angry; you can't solve it."

From her desk drawer she removed a bottle of nail polish, and as she stroked the fiery-red polish on her nails, she continued without looking up, her voice betraying the anger she didn't want to feel. "You can't do anything but look for people who don't have that perspective. If someone hates blacks, or women, or women of a certain age, you're going to get nowhere, because they have a checklist in the back of their sick little minds."

Holding her hands away from her, she blew on her nails to help them dry, and now she looked at me, the pain in her eyes matching the bitterness of her words. "They want someone who will live in never-never land and restore their potency," she said coldly. "If a woman has needs and expresses them, that's the end of the ball game." She paused only for a second, inhaled deeply, and continued with her flow of words, each of them etched in anger. "It's consummate narcissism on their part to have this grandiose fantasy that everyone's really envying them for having this wonderful young thing. Remember, the woman's self-esteem is every bit as low as the man's, or else she'd look for a man her own age to have a loving, caring relationship with, as opposed to a guy who will use and dominate her."

Though sociologists report that many men enjoy the ego-bolstering satisfaction of the trophy factor—the oohs and ahs that having a young, attractive woman on his arm can bring an older man—few men mentioned that to me as an asset. Although, if they were questioned about it, few denied it was pleasurable.

Movie agent Joe Pollock lives in Beverly Hills, where being an important cog in the Hollywood social wheel is crucial, not just for ego bolstering but for business.

A short, rotund man, he had a well-tended December tan, in vintage condition, and his face was lined with creases that seemed to have been etched by laughter rather than the grief of failed love affairs. But over the phone he had told me he was eager to talk about his experiences with Jennifers, which were definitely, most definitely, on the debit side of his romantic ledger. Still he went on undaunted, though lately a little less blithely, from one Jennifer to the next. Maybe talking about it would clear things up.

"It's a mixed blessing," he began, his voice surprisingly serious for a man who represents some major comedians. "For all that trophy business—you know she looks great on your arm when you walk into a restaurant, all the staring and admiration—but sometimes it works in reverse."

"I don't understand," I said.

"You get resentment," he said, trying to explain. " 'Why doesn't he grow up?' That kind of thing. And they show it by not inviting you to a lot of dinner parties where there are grownups."

I repressed a laugh, because although I found him amusing, I knew part of him was very serious. We were sitting at an outdoor coffeehouse near his office, and a pair of Jennifers walked by, tan and gorgeous, in that golden, outdoorsy, California way they have of being gorgeous. His look of dismay was so apparent, I realized that for him, living in this town with its abundant Jennifers must be like being diabetic and working in a bakery.

Joe shrugged as he poured Sweet'n Low into his iced tea. "You pay the price; you get socially isolated," he continued. "It's fascinating, the kind of social ostracism that comes after you get divorced if you left your wife for a younger woman. And even if your wife dies, you cannot bring a young girl to dinner parties. If you do, they'll strike you dead socially."

"They?"

"All those women who give the dinners, make the parties, run the benefits; the word goes out, and they will kill you socially. You're never invited anywhere again."

"That's not so terrible," I observed. "I mean, if you're in love and she's in love with you and you're happy, what's a dinner party?"

"In this town, baby, trust me, that *is* terrible."

Then he was off. One downside of his Jennifer experience having been considered, another rushed to mind.

"And then there's no escaping that sometimes, even if they are great to look at, vivacious, spunky, all that, they may not be playing with a full deck, or at least the amount of cards they'll have when they ripen."

I was lost somewhere in the mixed metaphor of cards and ripening. He explained: "For example, I came home one night after working at the office, and there by the phone, on the note pad, in her writing—which I had come to know well because I was so damned astonished at how childlike it was—she had scribbled her name, Caroline, ten or twenty times on the paper."

"Joe, that's not a capital offense—"

"Wait." He shook his head and, with a curious smile, continued. "After her name she had written Redford, then on the next line Newman, then Hurt, and Cruise, and on and on, trying out her name with ten of Hollywood's biggest stars. I wish I represented any one of them."

"No Pollock?" I asked.

He looked at me imploringly. "Don't you get it? I was with a teenybopper trying out movie stars' names. My daughter, who has now made me a grandfather, did that years ago. Well, that night I told her gently she had to leave. I found her a place, a job. Sometimes it's spooky; after a while, I even try to see that my younger women get dates with appropriate guys."

"And now?"

He shook his head grimly, rubbed his eyes, and, with an expression of resignation bordering on defeat, remarked, "And now I'm sixty-eight. And I know, I *know,* I would have had a quieter crossing with a reasonable lady of my own age. But I didn't want that."

And who's to blame him? Few of us embarked on the journey of life are interested in a quieter crossing.

Some men are caught in the middle, desirous of a Jennifer but skeptical it can work. One man who had left his wife of twenty-seven years for a Jennifer ended the relationship recently because she wanted to get married and have a family.

"It's depressing," he told me, heaving a giant sigh. "I don't like where the older ones have been, and I don't like where the younger ones are going."

Motherhood is one of the directions the young ones are going, and it's that wish on the part of a Jennifer which creates the greatest problem between her and her older husband, and sometimes the greatest joy.

17

"Please Let Me Have This Little Companion"

Of the many jokes that exist about older men who lust after Jennifers, many involve the man we've met before—the man who goes to his doctor and boasts about the fact that he's married a much younger woman.

In this version, the doctor suggests to the older man, "Why don't you get her a companion, someone younger to keep her company. After all, you are sixty and she's only twenty-eight."

"Good idea!" says the man.

A year later the man visits his doctor, and the doctor asks, "So how is your young wife?"

"Wonderful," the man tells him. "She's pregnant."

"Ah." The doctor smiles slyly. "You took my advice. You got her a young companion."

"That's right," the man says, his own smile broadening. "And she's pregnant too."

Unlike the man in that story, for many men who are already fathers and grandfathers when they marry younger women, the reaction to the idea of having more children is frequently very simple. They don't want them, and insist their Jennifers agree. Often the Jennifers comply with their wishes. They promise not to want them.

But sometimes, after a year or two, even those women who had agreed, or had convinced themselves their husbands were right, hear the ticking of their biological clock. Despite the adoration, the security, the fulfillment of deep and intense needs that their older

husbands provide, many Jennifers cannot ignore the insistent toll-
ing of the clock, measuring out the hours, days, and months left in
which they can satisfy their desires to nurture and mother. If they
choose to ignore it, many believe they pay a price.

Men who already have grown children and have lived through
both the joys and the discomforts of raising children are often
aware that despite their Jennifers' promises, the desire to mother
may be too great to resist. They frequently insist, as an ultimatum
before they marry, that their young wives agree: there will be no
children.

Attorney Bill Zabel, who is an expert on premarital agreements,
says men may try to codify, in a prenuptial contract, the stipulation
that the wife must not get pregnant. However, since a prohibition
that binds a wife contractually to *not* have children may be held to
be against public policy, it would be difficult to enforce, even if
agreed to by both parties in a legal document.

Zabel suggests, though, that if a man feels strongly about the
matter, "He could legally stipulate in an agreement that if the wife
breaks her promise, and *does* get pregnant, and insists on having the
child, should they divorce or if he dies, she will only receive ten
thousand dollars instead of the two million she would get for herself
if there were no child.

"That," Zabel suggests dryly, "is a pretty good way of ensuring
that the Jennifers live up to their promises."

But without resorting to legal documents, many men simply
rely on their powers of persuasion to convince young wives that at
this point in their lives, having a child would be wrong for them and
detrimental to the marriage.

Stan Gershun, a sixty-four-year-old Chicago salesman, was so
opposed to the idea of children that when his thirty-six-year-old
wife, Rachel, became pregnant, she had an abortion. Money was
only one of the reasons.

"I think women are full of shit. They want to have all these
babies, they should have one when they're fucking around when
they're younger. Don't come on late in life and then decide you
want to have babies. I say there's a time for having babies."

Stan Gershun is of medium height and portly build, his most distinguishing feature being his thick, snow-white hair, which frames his face like the mane of a jungle lion. Hard-nosed, sometimes primitive in expression, he made it clear that his feelings about late-life fatherhood were deeply felt. We were in the kitchen of the Gershun apartment, and as he slammed the ice cube trays against the sink, he said angrily, "Look, kids aren't that rewarding anyway. First of all, they want every goddam thing there is in the world. And I'm not talking about my children, I'm talking about children in general; they are a large pain in the ass.

"I'm sure I was a pain in the ass and a disappointment to my parents," he admitted, as he delivered our drinks to Rachel and me at the kitchen table. "I'm sure Rachel's pissed at her mother; she didn't have a father to be pissed at. It goes on and on. Blame your mother for everything you've screwed up; blame your father for everything. It's a lot of crap.

"Blame *yourself* if you screw up is my theory!" he exclaimed, his face flushed with emotion. "This idea of having children is nuts; they're only a burden and extremely costly. Who the hell can afford them? Who the hell wants them? And what do you do in a crappy apartment with a kid running around? Besides, a kid doesn't even know who you are till she's ten years old. I'm sixty-four; I probably won't be around in ten years."

Although Rachel Gershun had her abortion ten years ago, her eyes filled with tears as she told the story:

"We had a scare. Stan came home with the letter from the doctor that said he had an inoperable spot on his lung. I was very pregnant when Stan presented me with the facts and asked me, 'At this point in life—my life, your life—are you prepared to raise a child alone? The doctor has assured me it's possible for you to become pregnant again, and if it turns out that this isn't just a scare, that I'm dying, this is the worst possible timing of all for you to have a child.'

"He also said, 'Because of our tremendous age difference, I really don't think it's a good idea.' He never really was for it, even though when the subject came up he had said to me, 'If that's what you want, we'll have the child.'"

Rachel fixed her eyes on her husband as she relived this dark time in their marriage.

"I was over thirty-five, and my doctor said I could have a child up to the age of forty-one. I only had one ovary, because I had surgery in 1955, but you can become pregnant with one ovary, obviously."

For a moment there was silence, as Rachel struggled to maintain her composure, then, after sipping her drink, she inhaled deeply and continued.

"A week later we found out Stan was fine; his doctor had been sent the wrong X-rays. We decided not to have the abortion; I was to continue with the pregnancy. But then I started to bleed, and the doctor said the baby wasn't seated properly. He recommended I either terminate the pregnancy or stay in bed for the next six months. With Stan's business problems and the health problems, I saw it wasn't meant to be.

"Whether you're eighteen or thirty-five, there is something very basic in the female psyche that wants a child, and it had been touched in my psyche in a way I had never experienced before."

Battling her tears, Rachel stiffened in her chair and added, "It was a very upsetting time emotionally. I was married to a man I loved very much and carrying a child that I wanted. I wasn't pregnant as a single person having to have an abortion. When I was single, I had spent years avoiding becoming pregnant, and here I was officially married and everything was legal, but everything in all the other aspects was wrong."

Sally Rollins is thirty-four, married to a sixty-five-year-old Seattle real estate developer for whom the idea of having a child is out of the question.

"It's a big issue in our lives," she said. "I've always told him that if I die tomorrow, God forbid, it's the only thing in life that I felt I would have missed out on. Now, there's a lot of things in life I haven't done, but I told him there's only one thing I would regret, and it's the fact that I never had my own children. But he was dead set against it; he's set in his ways and has a child of twenty-six and another twenty-four, so he doesn't want any more children."

She snapped open her alligator bag, carefully protecting her long fingernails, and fished out a shining gold cigarette case and a shining gold lighter to match. Sally had the aura of wealth about her. Whatever price she had paid, it was apparently worth it. And I think she fingered the cigarette case as a reminder to herself and to me that she hadn't given up *everything.*

"Does your regret about not having a child ever get in the way of your feelings for him?" I asked.

"I could have tried to get pregnant to get him to marry me, and I didn't," she answered. "Even now I wouldn't do it, but that doesn't take away the fact that I want a child. I do understand and respect his feelings, and lately I tend to feel he is right at this stage of life. I can't say it doesn't bother me. If I found out today I was pregnant, I'd be the happiest person in the world. It's not going to make me hate or reject him because he didn't give me the one thing I wanted. He gives me so many other things."

Sally lit her cigarette and toyed with the lighter in her hand as she continued. "At first he didn't even want to have a dog. He told me dogs require brushing and loving and training, and he was worried it would take time away from us. It took me a long time to convince him. I said, 'Please, please let me have this little companion, please let me have her. Honest, you won't have any responsibility.' "

Then, with a broad smile, she told me about her hard-fought victory. "Finally he gave in. But I kept my word; he had no responsibility. I trained the dog, slept with her in the kitchen because he didn't want her in the bed and I didn't want her to be a yapping dog trying to get into the bed. But it paid off; she goes to her own bed. Six months later, he was begging to walk her.

"She's gorgeous, she's not a pain in the ass, and I say, 'What did I tell you?' "

"Why do you think he was so opposed to it in the first place?" I asked.

"Oh, he lived through raising kids, raising dogs, and he didn't want to get involved in all that again. I knew it came with the territory before I married him."

Sally Rollins lowered her eyes; her smile of only a few minutes before vanished like a mask, and she brushed away her tears and said softly, "Still I would have loved to have little children I could have grown with."

If some midlife men are adamant about their wish not to have children with their young wives, others are eagerly pursuing the idea. Cary Grant, Charlie Chaplin, Telly Savalas, John Ehrlichman, and Ed McMahon are just a few well-known men who became fathers in their fifties or sixties.

Bill Epstein, a fifty-eight-year-old Denver dentist, eagerly wants to begin a new family, even though he has three grown children from his first marriage. Ironically, he and his young wife, Sara, are currently consulting a fertility specialist, since after three years she has been unable to conceive.

When he left his wife, he explains, he thought his children were lost to him. Bill and Sara discussed having children when they were dating.

"She's twenty-four, I'm fifty-eight. When we met she was actually astonished I hadn't had a vasectomy, because I already had three children. I went through a bitter divorce. My ex-wife wanted the kids to hate me. For many years I thought I had lost them. It's taken five years, but at last the kids have come back; now all the kids have moved in with us. How many women would do that? Take all my kids in without reservation? I love her for it; it's more than a gesture."

I asked why he decided he wanted to have more children at the age of fifty-eight.

"It took a long time to establish my career; I didn't have time to see my kids grow up. Now I have more time; I don't work seven days a week anymore in this office. We'll have a child, and both parents will take care of it. It will be better for me and the kid to find out what life's about, rather than just working seven days a week building a practice and making a lot of money."

"But did you have doubts at first? Did Sara have to persuade you to accept the idea?"

"No, not at all," he replied. "When Sara talked about having a child, I thought it would be a wonderful experience to actually participate one hundred percent, not the way I did when I had my first children. At the time, my own kids weren't speaking to me. We've been trying but we don't know if she can have a child. We're trying very hard. It's very important to us. We'll try in vitro fertilization if we have to."

Maureen Richardson was thirty when she married the sixty-five-year-old widower who is editor in chief of a newspaper in the Southwest. When they married he had five children, three grandchildren, but was not vehemently against the possibility of having more children.

With a pale complexion, dark-brown hair worn in a classic pageboy, she has the natural good looks of a woman in an Ivory soap commercial.

Maureen was feeding their two-year-old daughter, Patty, as she explained their decision to have a child.

"I wanted a child; and we had discussions. He wanted to make sure it was the right thing to do for the child. He was worried that at his age, maybe it would lead to a birth defect or some other trauma for the child. So he spoke with the pediatrician, who told him, 'Mike, you might not see your son graduate from graduate school; that's the only problem I can see.' Mike said, 'So what?' Then we decided to have a child.

"After we married he was rejuvenated, and after Patty's birth he was even more rejuvenated. He even looked younger. He's been under a lot of pressure; there's a lot of controversy in the city and scandal, and the paper's getting a lot of heat. So it's wonderful for him to come home while all the shit is flying, walk in the door, and for this little person to run down the hall and say 'Dadada.' It's a source of great comfort."

"With all the stresses of his job and the demands on his time," I asked, "what kind of a father is he, now that he's almost seventy?"

"He's a terrific father, and it's a whole new life. When he was a father to his older kids, fathers weren't really parents in the same way they are today, changing diapers, bathing the baby. One night the mayor called, bristling about an editorial Mike had written that day. I simply told him Mike was diapering the baby, and the mayor said, 'Have him call me later; that's more important.' "

Certainly many men who become fathers in their fifties and sixties are less driven, less consumed by their work or by trying to climb the proverbial corporate ladder, than they were in their twenties or thirties. They have generally attained the level of achievement they will maintain for the rest of their lives. That, plus a sense of guilt about the little time and attention they may have invested in their first set of children, often makes fatherhood the second time around more than a badge of virility and potency.

Although movies, television, and national magazines present idealized pictures of young fathers diapering babies and taking children to school, it is far from being the norm in most American families. Even if it is more myth than reality, it's easy to understand that some older fathers are eager to feel part of the modern world, intimately involved in the sociological changes that have swept the land since they sired their first brood. For the man who is plagued by middle-age fears, pushing a baby carriage down the street can be a powerful antidote.

Ernest Freed, a stocky, rugged cattleman from Oklahoma, picked me up at my hotel in a gleaming new Jaguar. But that's where his flashiness ended. He was wearing faded jeans, a flannel shirt, and he used his battered pipe as a pointer as we drove through his city.

"When I met Matty I was fifty," he told me, "she was twenty-nine. I already had two grown kids, and I had problems with both of them and didn't want any more. As a matter of fact, one of the preconditions of our marriage was that we wouldn't have children. I had even considered having a vasectomy to ensure it."

"What changed your mind?" I asked.

"My oldest son was killed in a car accident, and my wife convinced me that the best thing to do was for us to have children of our own. I'm happy we did. Today we have two beautiful children, and I'm convinced my kids and my wife keep me young."

"How, exactly, do your children keep you young?"

"I'm busy constantly taking them to classes," he replied, "involved in their schools, conferences with their teachers, in a way that I never was in my first set of children. I think we would be bored with each other without kids. I don't know if we'd still be married. The kids have become the center of our attraction; they enrich us. It's a mistake, I think, for men to think they don't want to have kids again."

But Todd Rappaport disagrees. He was sixty-two when he married a thirty-six-year-old woman.

"She *did* want to have children," he told me. "I said, 'If you're willing to change your life, move to a smaller apartment so we can afford help with the baby, give up the maid and cook, OK. Of course, we won't be able to travel, but we'll have a child if you insist.' But I knew what she would say. We have a wonderful, exciting life, always traveling, for business or pleasure. I knew no matter how deeply she wanted a child, she wouldn't want to give up our life-style. And I was right. We don't have any kids."

Dan Rennet became a grandfather the month before his young wife gave birth to twins. His wife, Carol, said, "In a strange way, his daughter and I have something in common for the first time since we both became mothers. You see, his ex-wife looked to his kids for sympathy, so at first his kids were antagonistic to me and closer to her.

"At first we weren't going to have a child. At twenty-six I felt it wasn't a necessary part of my life. I could be fine without them. Or so I thought. At thirty I started feeling that maternal instinct. I told him that since he wasn't having such a good relationship with his own children, it might be nice to have a child."

Her husband, Dan, agreed. "She changed my mind about children when she said, 'Because of the age difference, I'd like to have a son for when you're not there, a child of my own.' " He hesitated before adding, "I was so scared. Am I going to be around for them? Will I be able to take care of them? Now I deal with it. I think she was right. And it's ironic—she went and had twins."

Gordon Alcott became a father to a baby boy. His thirty-two-year-old wife is close in age to his older son and daughter. Unlike other men I spoke with, Gordon Alcott had no doubts about starting another family at the age of sixty-seven. Beginning his career as an electrician, today Alcott is president of his own computer company. A soft-spoken black man with laughing eyes, he said he loved being a father.

"I was a good father the first time around; now I'm even better. I want to make my boy happy, and if I last long enough, I'll be around to see him pretty grown. Of course, I have made a new will, but I didn't forget my first set of children."

"How is becoming a father in your sixties different from the first time?" I asked.

"It's all different," he said, smiling. "With this child, I went into the delivery room, I watched my son being born, the cord being cut. I heard my son's first cry, saw his first gasp of air on his own. Ten minutes later he was sucking away at my wife's breast as if he had done it all his life. It was fantastic. A miracle. It never entered my mind to do that when I was thirty.

"I'm so wrapped up in this child, and it's wonderful that I'm at a point in my career, have enough money, so I have the time to be with the child as much as I am."

Women who raised the first batch of children for men who later discover the joys of fatherhood at midlife may view this sudden conversion of their ex-husbands with a trace of irony, and sometimes bitterness.

"These men I'm afraid seem to be turning into the fanatical mothers of days gone by," writes Linda Stasi, author of *A Field Guide to Impossible Men.* "If women were criticized for losing themselves in what was called 'the boring tasks of motherhood,' what can be said of fathers who lose *themselves* in the boring tasks of motherhood?

"These men are now media stars who are elevated to the rank of prince for doing precisely what women have been criticized for doing. And women always took the short end of the stick without discarding any families on the road to self-fulfillment.

"I find it crazy . . . in these post-liberationist days that men are revered for grinding baby food and cutting cloth diapers! Meanwhile, their grown children have access to Papa and his teen queen only on visiting days."

Was there a downside? Did midlife fathers have doubts, worries, or fears? I asked Gordon Alcott if he had second thoughts about becoming a father in his sixties.

"Occasionally my wife verbalizes *her* fear that she'll be left alone with a child," he answered. "All I can tell her is I can't promise I'll be here forever, but I take such good care of myself, there's no reason for me to die soon. I'm sixty-seven, not a hundred and two. But if I do die, I tell her, financially she'll never have to worry."

Gordon Alcott accompanied me to the elevator just outside his office.

"I don't have living parents," he commented, "and I know I'm closer to the end than the beginning." He hesitated and, grinning, went on to say, "Once I met a man in his nineties, and when he was asked how he felt about being so old, he said, 'It's not so great. I'm in pretty good shape, I can do a lot, but I really can't make plans. For example, I don't buy green bananas.' "

I entered the elevator, and as I stood facing him, Gordon quipped, "Luckily, Barbara, I can say, 'I still buy green bananas.' "

"I would give a second marriage another name," Joanna Ansen was saying as she poured coffee from a gleaming silver pot.

Everything about Joanna is gleaming—the rings on her fingers, long gold earrings, sunbursts bouncing off the paintings and sculptures that fill her studio. Born rich, she became even richer by virtue of her talent and shrewd investments. After her husband left her for a Jennifer, she floundered, went through every available man in Denver. Today she views their marriage and the image of her gray-haired former husband pushing a baby carriage with a mixture of bemusement and irony.

"A second marriage should be a different kind of relationship, with a whole different meaning; it's freedom," she continued. "It's companionship, none of the worries of getting up in the middle of the night, of worrying what people will think. The minute you make it a *marriage* and try to copy the first marriage, then you're destroying all the absolute benefits of the second marriage.

"I've seen many men in their fifties or sixties marry younger women who wanted children. So now these guys are getting up in the middle of the night." She laughed and, shaking her head disapprovingly, added, "And now they've got to go through all that crap and annihilate the very reason they married the young woman. And they are back to square one."

For many men, if it means being at square one, that's a small price to pay for life with a Jennifer. A younger woman, it seems, offers a man a second shot at something more than being a wooer, a lover, or merely having his virility proclaimed. Giving a second set of children the love, time, and money he didn't share with his other children offers a man a kind of redemption. It represents a second crack at immortality.

Maureen Richardson explained her feelings about mortality, immortality, and the hard truths that become part of your life when you are married to a man thirty-five years older than you are.

"It's a very painful point to have to realize," she said, "but when you're married to a man who is sixty-eight, things like career and money, all those things that are so important when you're forty or fifty, are less important."

She wiped Patty's mouth carefully, kissed her on the cheek, and carefully handed her a glass of milk, which the baby grabbed eagerly. "You have to treasure the moments you have together; you have to be very philosophical and rise above things. You have to remind yourself that some people drop dead suddenly of a heart attack at forty.

"You can't think that life is over at sixty-five. For us, his life really began at sixty-five. So you can't be influenced by things like reading of someone who died at sixty-five, or of people being washed up and old at seventy. You have to realize that is not *your* life."

Patty threw the glass on the kitchen floor and shrieked with laughter. Fortunately it was a plastic glass, and as Maureen sponged the floor, she shook her head at Patty, gently chiding her daughter, saying, "No, you shouldn't do that."

"There are no guarantees," she went on, "and anyone with an older husband isn't telling you the truth if she says she doesn't worry about being left. You have to become philosophical and figure that age is not a function of chronology. Age is a function of who the person is, what his anatomy is, what his attitude is to a certain degree.

"Indeed, my husband may be sixty-eight, but as far as I'm concerned he's fifty or less. I think of him as a fifty-year-old man, that he's going to last a long time, and I try to do things that make him happy. A lot of younger couples fight more and take fights more seriously, because they know they have the time."

I asked if her husband was concerned about the age difference, and what it meant for her and their daughter.

"Of course, he asks me all the time, 'Will you love me when I'm old? When I'm medically incapable of making love?'

"I say, 'You're the greatest, and I'll always love you. I feel in love with *you.* You're a nice-looking man, but I didn't fall in love with your looks or your body.' He says, 'Are you sure? What if I got sick?'

"I tell him if he got sick, I'd take care of him. But I also take good care of him now. Since we married, he takes such good care of himself, watches what he eats, jogs. He's in better shape now than when I met him."

Sally Rollins said her sixty-five-year-old husband asks the same question:

" 'Will you love me when I'm old?' I assure him of course. 'But what if I can't make love anymore? Will you love me?' I tell him of course."

Carol Rennet assures her husband she will always love him, even when he's older and grayer and less able to enjoy the vigorous sex life they have today. But she has concerns of her own:

"I have to tell myself there's a real possibility I'll be alone for a long time. My mother warned me when I married him I might be a young widow. But I have him now, and take very good care of him. When he does leave me I'll have the twins; I won't be alone."

Some men believe that a Jennifer is like the magic air of Shangri-la, offering them renewed virility. Others believe that when displayed, a Jennifer will win them increased admiration from their friends. And some believe that a Jennifer, with her unvarnished, worshipful adoration, provides a powerful antidote to midlife fears and doubts. Now I realized that on top of all that, some men believe Jennifers offer a man a second shot at fatherhood and another crack at immortality.

To many women, that may sound like so much bad news, and who needs it?

But there is good news too.

18

"And Here's to You, Mrs. Robinson"

It was shocking when a young college graduate, played by Dustin Hoffman, became involved with the older but terribly attractive Mrs. Robinson, portrayed in a stunning performance by Anne Bancroft, in the film *The Graduate.*

But that was twenty years ago. Today it would be less shocking. Recently Joan Collins's celebrated affair with a younger man, rock singer Peter Holm, grabbed headlines even as it foundered on the perilous rocks of the divorce courts; and Cher claimed her own headlines when she and a noticeably younger man were seen together in many nightspots in New York. It's so unshocking that author Francine du Plessix Gray has noted, "The younger lover is becoming as fashionable among American women as jogging and home-made yoghurt."

But what about the Mrs. Robinsons? Apart from the ecstasy of sexual union and the joy of being with a perpetually erect, chronically ready young man (admittedly more fun than either jogging or yoghurt), is something else going on? Are the women enjoying something more than sex? And is that "something" similar to the "something" older men talked about experiencing with their Jennifers? How did the benefits and risks of these relationships compare with those of Jennifer Fever?

I was once a Jennifer, and while I had never been through the experience of Janets who were left, I could easily understand the wrenching sense of loss that comes when a man leaves for a younger woman. But I've never been a Mrs. Robinson. Not because it's unthinkable or a taboo; it's just that I've never been in a situation where a younger man and I connected in a romantic fashion. Except once, with a man I will call Brad. He was simply wonderful to look at, and with him there was no cultural chasm. At thirty, he knew Pearl Harbor was not an actress, and he also knew the movies of the forties and fifties, and the books of the sixties. He was smart and clever and tender, and for a while I entertained the idea that we might have an affair. But it turned out that we both so enjoyed the friendship, I think neither of us wanted to risk losing it, always a possible side effect when friendship is transformed into something more.

Still I have an idea of how the fantasy of an affair with Brad made me feel. Younger? Not really. Rather hyper-alive. I can imagine that for an older man who is fearful of waning sexuality, a Jennifer may seem like a tonic. But for a woman who doesn't feel the same need of sexual performance, it's different. It's as if, when I'm with Brad, I feel like myself squared or cubed. Is that because he is all future, heading inexorably toward the prime of his life, and that makes me feel, by some kind of proximity or osmosis, that I, too, am further away from old age and death? Maybe.

I know he doesn't judge me, nor is he threatened by my being a writer; implicit in our friendship is the fact that I have been around longer, and from there we can go on and enjoy each other. It's possible that because of my years and experience, he felt he didn't dare make a sexual advance. I don't know. I do know it remains a delicious friendship of mutual caring and shared thoughts.

Today there are hundreds of thousands of Mrs. Robinsons out there, and for many of them it may be good news to learn there are also increasing numbers of Graduates eager to enjoy their special charms.

Whether Jeffrey Fever in a woman is a response to the dearth of available middle-aged men, or less a response than an active, conscious choice by women, is not clear. It may also be the result of the evaporation of the cloud of sexual taboos that usually blankets such relationships. Whatever the reasons, women are doing it, and both they and their younger lovers are more than happy to talk about it.

"Turning to young flesh as a source of renewal has always been the privilege of the wealthy and/or powerful . . . so it is not startling to read that Jeanne Moreau, Estelle Parsons, and Louise Fletcher are married or keeping house with men twelve or twenty years their juniors."

What seemed new to Francine du Plessix Gray writing in 1978 is not news to anyone today: "less renowned but equally successful professional women" and women who are not particularly successful in their professional lives are now enjoying relationships with younger men.

Once the taboo is stripped away, the participants are joyfully discovering what sex experts have known for years: that the most favorable time for sexual pleasure is when men are in their early twenties and women in their forties, since it is then that they are both at their orgasmic peak. (It is a peculiar irony that when older men link up sexually with young girls, neither are in their sexual prime, physically or emotionally.)

Still, as Gray observes, "In our society with its taint of puritanism such a relationship is bound to remain taboo because it is too much fun, just as it is inevitable that in France, in that pleasure-laden world of Colette, it would flower."

But in Colette's world, traditionally, young Europeans like Chéri had to turn to older women because any sexual contact with contemporaries was taboo. Ironically, "young Americans are now said to be turning to older women just as access to their contemporaries has reached an unprecedented level of permissiveness.

"Could it be," continues Ms. Gray, "that the sheltering warmth of a Mrs. Robinson can be more mysterious and reassuring to some recent Graduates than the jovial available classmates in striped pajamas whom they encountered in the shared dorms of Yale, Wisconsin and Penn State?"

Yes, it could.

For answers, I didn't have very far to search. Many women contacted me, eager to talk about the sudden wellspring of happiness that came when they discovered the joys of a younger lover. Most intriguing, almost half of the women who had been abandoned for Jennifers were now having relationships with younger men.

Coincidence? Chance? At first I thought so. But psychoanalyst Harvey Greenberg says it's not a coincidence at all. It may be, he suggests, "a form of identification with the aggressor—a way of women gaining control over their lives by replicating the form of trauma their husbands exhibited which so drastically disrupted their lives."

Few women appeared to be even dimly aware that they were copying their husband's model. And they would probably agree with psychologist Lillian Rubin, who dismissed Greenberg's theory as "a male therapist's analysis which disregards the sociological reality that often an older woman turns to a younger man because he is the only man available who offers her intimacy and friendship and who will not be threatened by her experience or success."

Still it's interesting to note that taking a younger lover is one response to losing one's husband to a Jennifer that appears to be working positively for some of the Janets.

Listening to them, it is clear and inescapable—the women are having the times of their lives and believe they are enjoying the most fulfilling, carefree, problem-free relationships of their lives. Occasionally some of their comments parallel the views of older men toward younger women. Yet the immediate differences seemed to be more significant.

The most apparent is that for women, the younger man is a more recent option than the millennia-old tradition of older men and Jennifers. Unlike the men, they are acutely aware of breaking a time-honored taboo, and when they speak of their liaisons with younger men, it is with a rush of excitement, unleashing a torrent of emotions very much like an epiphany.

Tina Ross greeted me at the door of her home, a bungalow a few blocks away from the ocean on Long Island. She wore tight stretch pants, and her auburn hair fell to her shoulders. Only the deep creases in her forehead and an intermittent grave expression in her eyes gave away her fifty-eight years. She guided me to the patio, and as we chatted she was engaged in repotting her begonias.

"I have a terrible problem with age," she confessed, tying a large-brimmed straw hat around her head. "I hate getting older. I've been very vain all my life, and when I was young, people said to me, 'You're going to have a miserable time when you get older.' Of course, that was meaningless to me then."

Pouring soil from a burlap bag into a row of ceramic pots, she continued. "I didn't get together with Tim to feel younger at all. I have my own thing about age and my looks; whether it was Tim or Shmim, none of it makes a difference. Tim is accepting of my age. Maybe it's because he's only twenty-eight. But I'm the one who pisses and moans about the way I look."

None of the older men had alluded to feeling much social pressure or that they were violating the rules of sexual behavior. I asked Tina if when she and Tim are seen together in public she feels strange, aware people are judging them, that they are breaking a taboo.

Tina nodded. "You bet. There *is* a taboo about an older woman with a younger man. They make fun of older men and young girls. They say, 'Oh, yeah, he thought he was getting older so he dumped his wife and picked a young chick and he kidded himself he was younger too. And she'll dump him when she gets his money.' But all of that is still *accepting.*"

"And an older woman and a young guy?" I asked.

With a frown and a narrowing of her eyes, she replied, "I think there is something deeper, a revulsion. I think it goes back to Freud and the taboos on incest. The mother image is sacred, and people think it's violated when a woman is with a younger man. The incest taboo between an older man and younger woman may be there, but it isn't as strong."

I wondered if Tina meant the taboo was greater for older women because, unlike a daughter and father, a son is born from the flesh of a woman. Perhaps because he was a part of her, having lived inside her for nine months, if an older woman is seen with a younger man it's too heavy for people to absorb. It's as if she's loving, consuming, a part of herself.

I also wondered, since Tina's children are grown, off leading their own lives, if she was aware of wanting, or of his wanting her, to be a mother, to live out some mentor role for him.

"A mother?" she asked incredulously. "I have two children, and that's the last thing I want to be to Tim."

Taking a red begonia from a box, she placed it in one of the ceramic pots and carefully covered the roots with soil. Then she wiped the dirt from her hands and announced, "I'm not interested in molding him. I want him to get all molded. I want him to wake up tomorrow and be all done, all evolved. I don't want to teach him or anybody. I have a passive, old-fashioned, female approach toward sex. Let him be the initiator; it's not my job.

"And he doesn't want me to take care of him. Neither of us have much money, but naturally I have a little more. In that respect, I guess you could say I take care of him. But he contributes whatever he can."

"And your concerns about the future?"

She drew her chair close to mine, removed her hat, and after a few moments of silent reflection, she spoke in a more serious tone. "I never worry about it. I don't deal with it and I can't. I live wholly in the present. People warned me I was crazy. My daughter asks about what's going to happen in ten years. I can't relate to ten years. I don't know what I'll be like then, either.

"At fifty-eight, I can't have children, and today he says he doesn't want them. But he could change, and if that's what happens, it happens. Who knows where I am going to be in ten years? *If* I will be?"

"Tell me, Tina," I asked, "what's special about Tim?"

Her entire expression brightened as she described her young lover. "He has an openness to new experience. I like that; it turns me on. I remember the first time we went in to New York; he was so fascinated. It was terrific. Aesthetically it's wonderful. It's pleasing to look at a young, beautiful man with a gorgeous body all day. I never liked the oldness in older guys' bodies, and if Tim and I were to break up, it would be more difficult for me now than it would have been before to go back to an older guy.

"Also I would miss the affection. Most men aren't like Tim, almost like a child, constantly hugging, touching, holding my hand.

It's childlike, and wonderful. I don't know if he'll keep that as he gets older. I don't know if that's part of his youngness, if it will go away. But I love it."

San Francisco interior designer Teresa Scatti moved easily through the crowded restaurant, and when she got closer I was impressed. She was wearing a long sweater over bleached jeans; her hair was pulled back in a braid. There was a no-nonsense freshness about her that didn't necessarily make her look younger than her fifty-three years but rather gave her a timeless quality: hardly the mother of a twenty-six-year-old son and a nineteen-year-old daughter, and the lover of a twenty-five-year-old man.

"Since you called, I've been thinking about how Michael differs from other men I've dated since my divorce," she said, slipping into the booth. "With a younger man, I think the main difference is there is more fun. The lack of judgment, and no fear of being threatening. What a joy!"

The lack of judgment. How many times had I heard that from men about their Jennifers?

"By definition," she went on, "a younger man is proud of your accomplishments, is happy to live in your reflected light. Not like with older men. With them, if you cast the light, they are threatened. I'll be so happy when Michael makes it, and I can live in his reflected light, but now, now I cast my own shadow.

"But that's no problem. I can be with him without condescension, without criticism, without judgment. And of course, sexually it's wonderful, you know."

Of course I knew. A small secret smile, a knowing look, were enough to remind me of all those sex experts who said Teresa and Michael are in the prime of their collective sex lives. If the experts could see the bliss radiating from each pore on her un-made-up skin, they would enshrine their findings in stone.

The smile became less private when she added, "His relationship with his mother is great, so he has a positive image of older women. Michael says things to me no man has ever said, such as, 'I will do anything to have you. I want to spend the rest of my life with you. I want to make you happy. You make me very happy.' "

Adoration, but it had a slightly different cast from that which the Jennifers expressed in "Oh, Johnny, You Park So Good."

"He is honest," Teresa went on. "He's not playing games. He wants me, and he tells me this. He never lies. And he hasn't been injured by the past, so I don't have to pay for it. It's all fresh and new, because he's not scarred by other women or by life."

Parallel two. The scarring factor had been mentioned time and again by older men. Now I understood that as they age, both men and women prefer being with people who are not scarred, who haven't been damaged, injured by lovers or life, who don't build a shrine to their hurts, daring the rest of the world to meet their impeccable, impossible standards.

"Friends say, 'You've always been a teenager; you look at life with the wonder of a young person.' " Teresa paused, then went on, with obvious satisfaction: "I do get along with young people. I like my own kids, and their friends have always liked me in a special way. My kids always told their friends, 'You'll like my mom, she's not like a mother.' "

"Why do you suppose that is?" I asked.

"I love a youthful outlook on life, and I have one," she explained. "If I could have met a contemporary man who had that outlook, I'd have been pleased. I don't expect to meet men my own age who are right for me. I'm content with Michael.

"I see the humor in almost everything; so do younger people. Michael kids about himself. Most men my age take themselves extremely seriously. They lose their playfulness."

I asked Teresa to tell me more about the middle-aged men she encountered before Michael. What was wrong with them, from her point of view? With her, from theirs?

She had a rapid-fire answer to describe why at fifty-three she was incapable of playing a Jennifer game, even if she tried. "I find most adult men—say over forty—are quite stuffy. They have their guard up. They think everything I say is an insult. I speak up. I contradict. I have opinions. I think this turns them off. Their ex-wives had opinions.

"Most older men are afraid of me," she said coolly, "inflexible about their politics, uninterested in my life, only want to talk about themselves. If I offered to pay the check, some scoffed. Others were shocked, because no woman had ever offered to pay."

Across the room she spotted a table filled by a group of those older men she was talking about. Shaking her head in mock sympathy, she pursed her lips, saying, "Poor things. Life is hard on them, and they need someone who will massage their egos and compliment them. One older man I dated married a woman eight weeks after we broke up. He hadn't even met her before our breakup. I hear she hangs on his every word, thinks he's a genius, compliments him all the time. Rose-colored glasses? I don't wear them."

Teresa frowned, fixed her eyes on me, and continued. "Here are some of the social consequences of marrying a younger man: My women friends are envious, contemptuous, or distant. The married ones are the meanest. I think that's because they haven't had a date in twenty-five years. Only one married friend was supportive. Another said, 'This relationship with Michael makes you look desperate.' Most single friends say, 'Wow, go for it.'"

"And taboos?" I asked.

"Unsettling things happen all the time," she replied. "At a party, a woman who met Michael said to me, 'You're so lucky; your son is really smart.' I can handle it. He *is* smart.

"Yet in the beginning I couldn't let myself take him seriously. Then he was there, calling, visiting, coming to old movies with me—and old movies are my passion.

"After a month of being friends we became lovers, and he's never left my side. Now he wants to marry me. No one has ever treated me so well, with such love and devotion. He loves my work. He thinks women his own age are silly, easily influenced, easily led. He loves the past, he loves the fact that I'm connected with the past."

In Paris I met Lili, who lives with a man twenty years younger. Lili at forty-five does not exude a particularly youthful persona. She is chic, and like many European women, Lili has a soft, natural quality. To her, being accepted without judgment, being loved for who she is without condescension, without criticism, is crucial. But even in France, where Mrs. Robinsons have flourished for centuries, Lili paid a price.

"He is the son of a friend of mine," she told me, "and even though we've been together six years, she will not speak to me."

"Is that because she feels you've replaced her by becoming another mother figure to him?" I asked.

"Am I a mother to him? No more than any woman. There's always a role of mother in relationships with men. Whatever their age, it's normal.

"Living with a vital, younger man keeps you on your toes. It can also be tiring. I did begin with him as a mentor or a muse. We're both interested in painting. But now we're more equal."

"What about the future?" I asked. "Will he want to leave you for someone younger? Or if he decides he wants to have children?"

"Who knows?" She shrugged. "I don't think of it. I think only of now. We have friends my age, his age, friends of all ages, and that's wonderful too.

"I have learned one thing from all this," Lili said as she looked at her watch. "You have to know what it is you value in life. If it's money and prestige you want, don't have an affair with a younger man. If it's companionship, love, affection, adventure, creativity— you can have all that with a younger man. As a woman you can give of your experience, and you find a new value to yourself."

As she slipped into her jacket and started for the door, she hesitated and smiled. "My older son was worried that it wouldn't last, that I'd be left." She nodded, signaling her understanding. "After all, there's only seven years between them. I told him that's my concern, and I'm not worried. You see, my lover was trapped in a mold when he met me. I represented things that helped him break the mold, his sense of adventure. He liked that I'd just get up and do things. He liked my vitality and that with me he could fight against the social roles defined for him by his family and his culture.

"Oh, and one last thing," Lili added. "He accepts me as a woman; he doesn't want to mold me."

At fifty-nine, Joanna Ansen has a younger lover. She called me from Denver with the news. A few days later we met for lunch in her studio.

"He's thirty-one and a half, and it's the half I'm grateful for," she said, laughing.

She told me more about her new boyfriend and her life in Denver. Active in Jewish philanthropies, she is on the go constantly—luncheons, dinners, charity balls; and dwelling in her rarefied world, a woman like Joanna could easily meet a man closer to her own age, even a man who might usually prefer a Jennifer.

But money, attractiveness, social access, and power can make women ageless in the eyes of some potential suitors; can make a man blind to the charms of a Jennifer. Similar to other women who possess her heady combination of attributes, Joanna has frequently had to fend off the advances of men who are too eager to partake of these assets. Today Joanna Ansen finds herself with a lover closer to her son's age than her own.

Possibly because she's stronger and richer and more uncompromisingly sure of herself than most people, male or female, Joanna's attitudes toward her younger lover are unique. She isn't afraid of judgment, and probably even the middle-aged men who are the most judgmental and most in need of adoration are dazzled by her beauty, success, and money—her combination of glitz and gloss.

"It never was my idea to be with a younger man," she began. "When I think about it, it's ridiculous. I always went for a man because of his intelligence, his brilliance. I've been a collector of brilliance. This man is a *jock*—literally a quarterback—so his macho aspect has been well sated. The 'Me Tarzan, you Jane' thing gets to me, because I've really been Tarzan all my life." She chuckled. "I don't need someone to make me Jane because he's a man and I'm a woman.

"I've graduated from college, had children, made deadlines, had to support my husband and his career, put my ass on the line in exhibitions. I think I've had it all." Joanna paused, as if she was considering her next words carefully. Then she continued. "I don't see why I have to be subservient. I'm in total control. I don't know if it's my age or attitude, but if he stays or goes, I don't care. It's nice if he stays. Why should I force myself into being what I'm not? How can you be that way with an older man who wants Jane?"

"Why do you think Ron is attracted to an older woman?" I asked.

"He's *always* been attracted to older women," she answered, "and he appreciates my glamour and elegance. After seeing women running around in tennis shoes all the time, it's fun for him to see me dressed the way I do. He has a strong aesthetic sense, and if he likes a shirt of mine he'll try it on. He's in touch with his female side. It's nice for me; I can get out a lot of my fantasies too."

While few of the older men said they experienced signs of social taboos with their Jennifers, a number of women were aware of the frowns and the whispers and the tsk-tsking that traveled in their wake as they walked through supermarkets or airports, sat side by side with younger lovers in restaurants or theaters. Had the world given Joanna and Ron a hard time?

"Naturally," she snapped brusquely. "With older men and young girls, it's easy. People consider it natural. Laughable, perhaps; foolish, perhaps; but natural. But Ron and me? At first I was self-conscious, sure someone would say, 'Is this your son?' It happened, and when it did I said, So what? Once you give up the idea of what's appropriate, letting society dictate who you should be with—height, money, religion—once you give up all that you're free."

Suddenly she stood and paced around the large studio, circling in on a large piece of sculpture, obviously a work in progress, that sat in the middle of the room.

"I'm free in other ways," she said. "He's romantic and wants to talk about romantic things, about *us,* all day. Sometimes I'm not in the mood, and I can really see where men are coming from when they come home from work. I don't want to hear all that when I'm worn out from a day of business or art.

"He's nothing like other men—doctors, lawyers, playwrights.

This is completely different. Intellectually, I miss that, but you can miss that with girlfriends too."

Joanna was the only woman who mentioned a sense of joyful retaliation in doing what her husband had done to her with his Jennifer.

"On our trip to Europe there was a certain satisfaction when I'd see all these older men with young girls and the older men would glare at me," she said. "Being a little competitive, which is probably an understatement, I must admit it was nice to be able to show them, 'OK, I've got it too!' "

A number of men shied away from talking about the sexual pleasures they experienced with younger women. But those who did spoke with a strange combination of adoration, sexual redemption, and gratitude. Older women didn't have to be asked. All of them talked eagerly about the sexual fulfillment they shared with their young lovers.

Rather than the gratitude that many men, including Benjamin Franklin, believe to be the core of older women's sexual experience, I found they either purred contentedly, or revealed a sense of startled and joyous discovery. As if they were saying, "Me? At this time in my life? Making love all night? With a man who's always hungry to make love? I hadn't planned for this. It's so unexpected. It's wonderful."

Possibly the difference is due to that old biological trick. For men, every night is opening night. Men are always burdened with having to perform. As they age, they dread the inevitable diminishing of their sexual performance. This may create a self-fulfilling prophecy: Anxiety about performance can lead to occasional performance problems, creating even more anxiety, which can lead to failure. His worst fears are realized; he is a flop.

For women, it's not the capacity for sexual performance they fear. It's the loss of their fertility—the dreaded menopause—and all the emblematic losses of femininity associated with it. It's the *fact* of aging itself. And the double standard of attractiveness by which they know they will be judged.

As far as I could tell, Joanna Ansen had never feared anything in her life. I wondered about the sexual side of her relationship with Ron.

"If you've never had a younger man as a lover, you forget how it was when you were young and had a young man," she said. Her eyes widened and her enthusiasm was obvious; she was delighted— no, eager—to talk about sex with a younger man. "He's extremely sexual, always turned on. Sometimes I feel captive, he's after me all the time. It makes me feel good; the sex act is different. There's a freedom sexually in this age group that allows you anything. Not that anything is kinky. Everything is open; you don't feel shy or inhibited."

"Some women told me a sexual relationship with a younger man made them feel older," I told her. "They dreaded daylight, bright lights, anything that might betray their age."

"The myth about wrinkles and looking older is crazy, because with a younger man you're so accepted," she replied. "It's the older men who see the signs of age faster, because they see it in themselves and will identify with it. In a sense I feel younger with Ron. Not like they do in movies—lyrical walks on beaches, Ferris wheels, all that hype. Maybe it's just a bounce in your step, an agility of spirit."

She began working on the sculpture as she talked. "I see women wheeling men in wheelchairs, always women. You know that's part of the deal, the trade-off. Many of these guys want a woman who'll take care of them as they get older. Men become so effeminate in middle and old age. I wondered if my husband got sick, would I take care of him? I would, but emotionally I wasn't there. The irony is I got sick and Ron took care of me."

Discussing her husband, she said sharply, "Let's face the fact there are no young girls with poor middle-aged men. They go for a daddy and for money. You can't have a daddy without money."

"Do you have similar fears about Ron?" I asked. "If some Jennifers grudgingly admit the scent of money and power is very much part of an older man's appeal, might not a younger man also be after the same thing?"

Scowling at the sculpture, Joanna grabbed a hunk of clay and began working it around the neck of the torso. "I've got two talmudic scholars arguing in my head all the time," she told me. "One old Jew is saying, 'What are you doing? A younger lover? Are you mad? You've got money!' And the other says, 'Who cares?' And then I wonder, 'Is he a gigolo? Isn't he a gigolo?' I didn't need people asking those questions; I was doing it to myself. I know he's not a gigolo, and if he were, so what? He couldn't take from me that which I wasn't willing to give.

"Then I began to see that the notion they're after money like Jennifers is really a myth. Maybe some are. But for most of these men's lives, they've been with dominating women who are in superior positions to them—the teacher, the mother—so it's a natural thing for them."

"And today which part of your brain is winning the argument?" I asked.

"Today the talmudic scholars are less noisy." She laughed. "We're happy; there aren't any 'should's' or 'have to's.' I insist he keep his own apartment. I play it day by day, and when you learn the knack of that, there's no other way."

Joanna stepped back from her sculpture and, frowning, cocked her head to one side, and then, discovering the problem, she returned to her work, reshaping the expression around the eyes. "Once I was in a restaurant," she went on, "and a young man walked in and I thought: Aren't they Young Turks? The stride, the look, and the way they think they have life by the tail, or are certain they're about to get it. I think for men who have sons, see them in college, see them with younger women, the men feel they've lost out. When they see the vitality and sensuality of their sons, they remember themselves, because their memory would probably deal with sex more than anything.

"Instead of enjoying all the pleasures they can reap in their lives, these men could become the new poor. Such a waste," she said, standing poised before her sculpture. "Paying alimony and child support, they become gray-haired fathers with young kids, and can't have the freedom their money and time provide at this time of life. I think it's uncreative to live your life this way."

She examined her work once again, and, pleased, she returned to where she had been sitting and sighed. "I'd like to be creative about my relationship," she continued. "If only I could assassinate these voices in my head, it would be terrific. Why shouldn't I live the life I want with this man? Because society says I should live on what he can afford? Screw society!"

For young men who are involved with older women, "Screw society!" is an attitude they must adopt as well. For they arouse more curiosity and censure in other people than do their counterpart Jennifers. Jim Wright is twenty-nine, and has been involved for two years with a woman twenty years older. He sums up the attitudes of many of these young men when he says, "She's twenty years older, that's true. To say the age doesn't matter is not true. It does matter, and it's why I feel the way I do about her. I love her experience. I love that she knows more. Has her own mind about things. Girls my own age? They're so diffident, so laid back, so unsure.

"For example, Carla makes plans for the weekend, she's not wishy-washy, there's none of that 'Whatever you want to do' kind of thing. She knows. It's fun; she has more sense of adventure than any woman I've ever known."

Joanna Ansen's young lover, Ron, told me, "Sexually, we're perfect. We can feel things in each other without saying a word. I never met a young girl who knew things about sex that Joanna does. And it's that knowingness, about sex, movies, food, life—*everything!* I love it. As a young kid, I always preferred being around grownups. I still do. I'm growing faster than I would with someone younger. It's great."

It's not growing faster that young men are seeking with older women, psychologists suggest. They share Freud's view that frequently these relationships, as with a man and a Jennifer, involve "an infantile object choice . . . a fixation of the infantile feelings of tenderness for the mother or father that were held in infancy. . . . For Freud, this infantile object choice constitutes one of the deeper disturbances of psychosexual development."

None of the younger men or their lovers seemed concerned about the mother-son aspect of their relationship, that the man might be perpetuating his dependency, the woman her mothering role. Oblivious of or unconcerned with what experts have to say, they either regard it as so much psychobabble or, if it strikes a note of recognition, feel it is not a major chord, not the central theme of the relationship.

Undoubtedly there is a darker side, which Tennessee Williams explores masterfully in *The Roman Spring of Mrs. Stone.*

Her beauty fading, her career as an actress in decline, the recently widowed Karen Stone is in Rome, where she meets Paolo. She knows he's a gigolo, but she is helplessly obsessed with him. Karen has invited Paolo to her apartment for a drink. They've skirmished; he has made an undisguised pitch for money, claiming it's for a friend. Karen knows better and says, "When the time comes that nobody can desire me for myself, I think I would rather not be desired at all."

But anticipating Paolo's making love to her, Karen is filled with raging emotions, "incontinent longings, and while they repelled her they gave her a sharp immediate sense of being. . . .

"It was not like anything she had felt one time or two in the past. The past was of course the time when her body was still a channel for those red tides that bear organic life forward. Those rhythmic tides had now withdrawn from her body. . . . And all at once Mrs. Stone did not need to wonder what the difference was. . . . What she felt now was desire, without the old implicit distraction of danger. Nothing could happen now but the desire . . . and its possible gratification."

For Karen, there is a price for the gratification of these "incontinent longings." He has treated her badly, and Karen cries out to him: "I am not a wretched old fool of a woman with five hairs and two teeth in her head and nothing but money to give you. . . . In America, Paolo, I still have the reputation of being a woman of talent and beauty. Fashion magazines are still eager to have portraits of me. . . . Plays have been written for me and books about me."

But Paolo reminds her he has had his own picture taken, and has gone with a woman more photographed and probably richer than Karen.

Finally Mrs. Stone says, "You are right, Paolo. It is not a dignified subject and I think the worst thing about love between a very young and a somewhat older person is the terrifying loss of dignity that it seems to call for."

In the end Paolo is gone, along with her dignity. But another young Italian gigolo is on his way up in the elevator.

For some women, the idea of playing Mrs. Robinson is only superficially appealing. Acknowledging that the aesthetics might be pleasing, they believe that intellectually and emotionally it wouldn't work. They know they would feel maternal, or like Karen Stone, end up feeling they were with a gigolo. As one woman told me, "It would be like living in the outskirts of your own life."

Most women I interviewed who were involved with younger men don't see themselves as being in love with a gigolo, even if it is the women's money that is the main source of income in the relationship. Joanna is happy to pay the bills, but she told me that lately, the rather sudden happiness she discovered with Ron has been slightly diminished.

"It's a little boring," she said over the phone. "I'm not interested in being Henry Higgins. In bed, it's divine, but as they say, you have to get up sometime."

Still the affair has brought some unexpected side effects. Her bitterness toward her husband's marriage to a younger woman has finally begun to diminish. Today she's philosophical and happy.

"Life is just moments," she observed. "If these guys can get it up for a couple of months, and they couldn't for a couple of years, why shouldn't they take it? If they think it's all because of a young girl, so be it. It's all illusion, isn't it? Everything we perceive as reality is only *our* reality.

"Yet it's ironic. My ex-husband is trying to give her what he didn't give me—time, intimacy. But that's not what she *needs*. She wants to duplicate our life: have children, throw dinner parties. She doesn't want him to feel deprived. I hear she has a brass bed and a Louis Vuitton traveling case for her dog. Doesn't that tell you everything?"

A few years after her divorce, Francesca Grayson began having an affair with a man twenty years younger than herself. I asked if on any level she believed she was doing precisely what her husband had done.

"I know, you mentioned that on the phone," she replied, "but I don't think so. When I met Larry I was with my daughter, who's twenty-four. I spotted this attractive young man and I thought he would be great for my daughter. Then he and I became friends and remained just friends for six months, until one night we were having dinner and he said, 'I want to go to bed with you. Not now, not tonight, just think about it, and we'll see.' I went home and realized I wanted to, and"—she laughed—"we've been together ever since.

"Remember, Barbara," she said, her voice filled with deprecating wistfulness. "I was this dependable, reliable, nice person, good hostess, good mother, but in these two years with Larry I've changed. I've never known such spontaneity, such tenderness, and the joy of doing things for myself as well as others. I've become more accepting of myself and others as well. We appreciate each other.

"With another kind of man I don't think I would have ever trusted very easily after all that happened. But with Larry, trust and friendship, as the song goes, that's the one thing we've plenty of, baby."

"Do you think you fill some mother role for him?" I asked.

"I knew you were going to ask that," she said. "No, although he does have a terrible relationship with his mother. Maybe as an approving, uncritical, older woman, I'm the good nonjudgmental mother he never had. But that's where it ends—the mother thing.

"I'd find it hard to be with an older man. I've dated a few because Larry and I believe we should see other people from time to time."

"You do?" I hadn't known about that.

"Of course," she said, eager to dismiss this aspect of their relationship, "and these older men—I mean men my own age—oh, it's so dismal, depressing."

A shadow of displeasure crossed her face, reminding me of the Francesca of five years ago. Comparing other men to Larry clearly upset her. "Their problems, their children, their business, this heavy, heavy load," she explained.

"Men aren't so thrilled with our problems, either," I said. "Everyone's looking for someone who isn't scarred, right?"

"What do I need it for?" she replied airily. "I'm fifty-six and I had seventeen good years of marriage. I don't need to be married. We have something better than marriage."

We have been friends for many years. Seeing Francesca so happy, the pain of those dark days of five years ago diminished by time, was very good news indeed.

I hoped there was more good news. And there was.

19

In Buddy's Eyes

> In Buddy's eyes
> I can't get older—
> I'm still the princess,
> Still the prize.
>
> —Stephen Sondheim, *Follies*

We've all met them or know them, men who remain married to one woman for twenty or thirty years, forty or fifty, and as the years tumble by—with their accretion of births, deaths, graduations, wrinkles, diets, illnesses, awards, bifocals, christenings, and funerals—they remain attached. Love, perhaps of a different kind than they shared at first, has evolved between them and their wives. But they are still together, not merely hanging on or feeling suffocated in some sort of stifling connubial trap.

Why were these men Jennifer-proof? Were they ever tempted by the dewy complexions or vivacious spirits of younger women? How did they remain unmoved by the seductive powers of youth and beauty?

Perhaps a truly Jennifer-proof man is one who not only stays involved with one woman for many years but also, in his fifties and sixties, after a divorce or the death of his wife, chooses for his second wife or companion a woman closer to his own age, defying the statistics that such men generally marry women ten years—or, as we have seen, more—younger.

Of course, I was looking for what was supposed to be the norm, men who don't feel they need a younger woman to enhance, revitalize, or boost their libidos, sagging egos, or failing spirits.

Last year columnist Liz Smith reported that when Mike Wallace remarried, it was to a woman much closer to his own age than any Jennifer would have been. Citing Henry Grunewald, former editor of *Time,* and A. M. Rosenthal, of the *New York Times,* who had both eschewed the many Jennifers who doubtlessly had been available and willing, and instead married "women of a certain age," Liz Smith wrote, with apparent glee, that this had all the makings of a trend.

With this encouragement from celebrityland, I began the search for less famous Jennifer-proof men, and when I found them, it felt as if after months of dwelling in a chilly, antiseptic, airless, soulless chamber in a glass-and-steel tower, I had walked into a cozy, inviting, sun-filled room in a traditional, slightly run-down but well taken care of, highly regarded inn: flowers everywhere, a brass bed with fresh, cool linen, lace curtains flapping as a soft breeze poured through the open windows. I had come home. At least to a spiritual home.

I strained to listen to these men as if they spoke another language, one I had once known but hadn't heard in a long time.

As they talked, they often alluded to the accumulated bounty of their marriages, and my eyes surveyed the rooms of homes or apartments or offices, which were filled with the combined treasures of the years spent with their women—pictures of *their* children, or of *his* children next to *her* children; the rug purchased in India twenty years before; coffee mugs, relics of a Vermont honeymoon twenty-five years earlier. Or, smiling from picture frames, photographs of grandchildren they may suddenly have acquired, inherited in a new midlife match.

I hoped to discover what bound them to each other, and what distinguished them from the men who had extolled their Jennifers, lavishing on them all the life-enhancing, life-extending virtues men have bestowed on younger women since King David fell under the spell of Bathsheba.

Finding them was not difficult, and they were happy to tell me their attitudes toward Jennifers, as contrasted with the older women in their lives.

After his wife died, fifty-nine-year-old Max Crawford married a woman of fifty-seven. Now in his early seventies, Max is a jovial, almost jolly sort of man. His pink complexion is framed by a head of wavy white hair. His pipe is a recent appendage, since after a serious operation his doctor insisted that he give up cigarettes. We were talking in his Boston apartment. I asked him what he thought was the characteristic that distinguished him from men his age who are only attracted to a younger woman.

"I didn't want a Jennifer," he began thoughtfully, "and I think it has to do with confidence, a quiet confidence my parents had. I got it from them. My mother was securely in love with my father. If a man lacks confidence and views his work, his sports, sex, everything as being performance-oriented, and if he feels sexually diminished with his wife for whatever reason, he may panic."

"But it's natural for men to experience some sexual diminishment as they age," I observed.

"Yes, but it's worse for men who view sex as the most crucial part of the relationship," he replied, "not just one of the list of nice things to share with your woman. To me, it's part of the list," and, smiling, he added, "a marvelous part, but only a part. And I don't view it as a performance.

"At our age, Lydia and I still have sex," he said with a wink, hoping to dispel the notion of people in their seventies living sexless lives. "But now, really for the first time in our lives, sex doesn't have us by the throat anymore. Thank God! For the first time in our lives it's not as acute, as consuming, a need. In a way it's a wonderful relief."

He reached into his jacket, took out a packet of tobacco, and deliberately filled his pipe, lit it, drew on it. After a moment of reflection, he continued. "When we wake up in the morning, if I have an ache, or she has a pain, we laugh and say what a joy it is that we're with each other. That neither of us is with someone younger. Then we'd be ashamed, have to hide our aches. We'd want the shades down so one of us wouldn't see the other's wrinkles."

The shades were *not* drawn, and late-afternoon sunlight filled the sprawling living room of the Crawfords' rambling apartment.

"Hers," he explained. But when they married and he moved in with sixty years of possessions, it quickly became "ours."

"After thirty-five years, my wife had died suddenly of a cerebral hemorrhage," he continued, speaking slowly, carefully. "When I began seeing women again, there were so many available women around, it became a joke with a friend of mine, and I called her Candy because it was her job to screen all the candidates. I never thought about seeing an older or a younger woman; frankly it didn't enter my mind."

"How did you meet Lydia?" I asked.

"We met on the Cape, where we both had summer houses. I helped her load some groceries into her car. I didn't think she was old or young. She had a charm, a certain kind of tenderness that for many contemporary sophisticated women is a no-no. I think charm in a woman is the same thing as confidence in a man. Just as impor-tant.

"My mother had great charm," he explained, "even though she was uneducated. Lydia has it, charm, elegance, but not the kind of elegance that waves a flag, calls attention to itself. That puts me off. I trust her. . . ."

His voice trailed off, and he tapped his pipe in an ashtray. Again deliberately filling it with tobacco, he lit it and, slowly inhaling, leaned deeply back in his chair. "I trust her," he said. "Lydia's not afraid to be pure woman. And she's not a scorekeeper, she's not judgmental. There's no nervousness in the air with her. I've always trusted my vibes with women."

"Were you *ever* attracted to younger women?" I asked.

"I've seen that kind of worshipful adoration young girls give older men," he answered, shaking his head with disapproval. "I wouldn't like it; I would feel it's false. Just as some men can look in the mirror, knowing they are wearing a toupee, and even though they know it's false they still like the way they look, they still feel better, younger, whatever. They're the same way with a young girl: They may realize all that adoration is false, not be so stupid as to *not* know it's false, but they still like it. Or need it."

I told Max about the men I had met for whom adoration was as essential as oxygen.

His pipe still clenched in his mouth, he grinned, saying, "I met an analyst once who said most of the men he saw in his practice were those who leave their wives to marry a young girl. He said the trouble comes when those girls then try to prove to all his friends they are even more proper than the first wife was. If they had the courage to fool around a little, that would refresh them, add to their confidence. Then they could go back to their wives. But the wives get so angry, they don't understand. It's who he comes *back* to that counts. I was married for thirty-five years and never tired of my wife.

"I don't want someone judging me or looking up at me adoringly. And I couldn't tolerate her not knowing what I was talking about. Who wants to be explaining things all the time? I want to have the same point of reference."

At fifty-nine, Dick Reinert is recently divorced. Tall, thin, with engaging blue eyes, he is by any standards a catch. But Reinert is very clear about the kind of woman he wants the second time around.

"Jennifers?" he asked. "What do they talk about with these women? What do they see in them? These men can't be very sexual men, for if they were sexual they would know older women are much more sexual.

"And if they have daughters, how could they sleep with a much younger woman? It's too close, too sick. It tells us something about these men, and what it tells me isn't nice."

Irv Fromson has been a widower for just over a year. When I asked about the women he's seeing now, his answer was straightforward. "I'm sixty, I did the young-girl trip, and it was OK. But now I think I want to get married again. And for a relationship, and for the rest of my life, I don't want to marry someone younger."

"Why is that?" I asked, slightly surprised.

"These young girls don't know what's up," he replied crisply. "Whether to commit or not. Marriage or not. City or suburbia. Continue working or not. I'll marry a woman close to my age because, as I always say, I prefer doing business with an established firm."

Several men echoed the thoughts of sixty-year-old Bud Allen, who has been married to his wife Ellen for twenty years. She is just a few years younger.

Bud Allen radiates a paradoxical expression of perpetual merriment and chronic fatigue: the former, a result of his innate curiosity about everything—life, books, art, psychology; the latter, the exhausting result of a medical practice that requires hours in the operating room of a large Los Angeles hospital, and then more hours in a free clinic, where he devotedly treats those who can't afford his Beverly Hills rates.

We were sitting in the hospital coffee shop. His tired, owlish eyes peered out from behind wire-rimmed glasses; then he removed the glasses and rubbed his eyes, making even more tiny red hemorrhages appear, obliterating whatever traces of white in his eyes I had been able to see before.

"It's really very simple," Bud said wearily. "Look over there." He pointed toward the window, through which we could see a group of young women walking briskly toward their cars.

"Aren't they great?" he asked, smiling a sad smile. "Aren't they something? Tan, and those figures! And that bouncy silky hair that moves when they walk, just like in a commercial! They're everywhere, particularly in Los Angeles.

"There isn't a man alive, fifty or sixty, no matter how much he loves his wife, or his woman, or his lover, or his lady, or whatever the hell they're calling it these days—there isn't a guy who doesn't imagine what it might be like in bed with a woman like that. Wondering if he's still attractive, wondering, 'Could I do it? Could I perform adequately for her?' Then he asks himself, 'And if I could, would I?' "

"Would you?" I asked.

"My answer is simple. No. Your book is about the differences between men who act out that fantasy and those who don't. That's what you're trying to find out. Why do some guys want it, need it, *have* to have it? Not just for a night or two, but guys who are willing to throw away everything they thought mattered or held dear, for the fulfillment of that little fantasy. I'm not one of them."

"Is it because of a personal ethic," I asked, "a sense of morality, that you don't act on it?"

"I couldn't handle it," he said, shaking his head. "It wouldn't be right. It's not due to religion, although ethics are probably part of it. But Ellen's my best friend. I couldn't jeopardize that, not for a minute. But that doesn't mean I don't think about it. And because I think about it and don't act on it, don't imagine I feel trapped. I think about a lot of things."

When it comes to action, sixty-year-old Mel Howell of New York is Jennifer-proof too, but like Bud Allen's, his imagination isn't immune to the fantasy.

"Of course, I think about it," he told me. "They're out there—Jennifers are everywhere. I see ten a day in my office. But then I think: If I did it, and it didn't work, didn't work for the girl, or I couldn't perform, how horrible it would be. How stupid, how awful! How could I face Erica? We've been married thirty-five years. We're grandparents, for Christ's sake.

"Then I get cocky, and think of course it would work, and maybe it would be divine in bed, me and a young girl! Then I get *really* frightened. What if I liked it sexually? And I was great sexually? What if she liked it? And what if she was fun to talk to and do things with? What would I do then? Would I leave Erica for her? Never."

"So either way," I suggested, "if you enjoyed it or didn't, performed well or didn't, you wouldn't do anything, wouldn't change anything?"

"How could I risk never being able to look at Erica the same way again, because I wanted to test a fantasy?"

Most men agreed they had the fantasy. But what were the other reasons some men can leave it at that, a fantasy, while others turn it into a reality? In explaining why they chose Jennifers when they reached fifty or sixty, some men told me that being with their wives of twenty or thirty years made them feel old. They needed someone new, who didn't know dark little secrets, weren't aware of foibles, illnesses, imperfections. Yet other men believe it is precisely being with women who have known them for years, through many incarnations, that makes them feel young.

At fifty-seven, Burt Topping is a man of medium height, with thinning gray hair, who says being religious about his daily jogging keeps him fit. Married for thirty years, he can't even imagine beginning again with a younger woman.

"In Beth I see myself at twenty-seven," he said, "just beginning, carefree, not burdened with a mortgage or this potbelly." He pointed to what I thought was a reasonably solid middle. "She remembers me when I had hair, dreams—even some that didn't come true."

There is another category of Jennifer-proof man that is worth mentioning. Although it is not that common, there are men for whom similarities in upbringing, economic circumstance, and social connections are more important than youth.

Joshua Whiteside, fifty-five, recently divorced after twenty years of marriage, is representative of this admittedly narrow group. Slim, tall, he is a quintessential Main Line Philadelphia banker. No flashing gold chains, no bright-colored shirts; everything about him is quiet, subdued. Polish without the sheen.

"I just got divorced, and it's not because I had a young girl on the side," he commented. "My wife and I both wanted it. The marriage was tired; we were tired. We both wanted another chance."

"And are you seeing anyone special now?" I asked.

"Yes," he answered quickly, "I'm seeing a woman who also just got a divorce. We've known each other for years. Before she moved with her husband to Indianapolis, we went to the same schools, the same parties, the same country club.

"We travel each weekend to be with each other. Until we decide whose work will allow us to move most easily, we'll keep flying back and forth to spend time together. But with all the traveling, the chaos a move will cause us, I'd rather be with Myra than any young girl."

"Could you tell me why?"

"It's very simple," he said matter-of-factly. "I don't want to have to explain myself. We know the same people, have the same values, there won't be those awkward moments of introductions, gaps in experience. We have the same frames of social reference."

"Would you be more specific about those frames of reference?" I asked.

"I'd rather not," he replied. His eyes narrowed, and there was a new edge to his voice when he said, "Regrettably, they may represent a tiny closed group—rich, perhaps overly conservative in politics, overly prejudiced toward others of different religions, different economic status. But it's who we are. I want to spend the rest of my life with a woman from that world, small as it is, rather than with some young thing who says 'Wow.' "

Most of the married men who seemed to be Jennifer-proof sounded more like Chuck Vitale, a wrestling coach at a small Northwestern college. A former street kid from the roughest streets of Chicago, he told me, "I flirt on campus with these girls every day. I flirt outrageously, but if one ever made a move or responded to me, I'd run for the hills.

"Never thought I'd be able to say it or do it, but twenty years and I'm faithful. Why? Betty's my best friend. With those girls, I'm all talk; I just couldn't handle it."

"Do you ever fantasize having a relationship with a younger woman?" I asked.

"It would be nice to know I could get it up," he answered, "really get it up and please the socks off one of these chicks. It would make me feel great. But even if it worked, and I did, and the sex was great, where the hell would I be? No, I couldn't handle it."

Ken Avnet, a fifty-eight-year-old accountant from Denver, has been married for thirty years. His Jennifer-proof status, he explained, is due to other factors. "Maybe it's because I was the youngest son of nine children," he told me, "and I've always been treated as the youngest, that I never went through a midlife crisis, never felt the need for a Jennifer.

"I hear guys talking about shacking up with a Jennifer, as if it's a B_{12} injection. For me, when the kids left home for college, that was my injection. After twenty-five years of marriage, my sex life with my wife is the greatest."

Unaccustomed to speaking so openly to a woman about the intimacies of his marriage, Ken blushed, and I sensed that he didn't wish to appear boastful; rather he was proud of his successful long-lived marriage. "We're both turned on all the time," he explained. "Sex has never been better, freer. In the past I worried that she was more preoccupied by the kids and their needs, and sometimes so was I. Today it's different. We are having a ball, better than when we were first married."

Women have their own answers to the question of what makes one man Jennifer-proof and another not. My dear friend Lisa has never, *never* been without a man. Although some of her relationships are short-lived, I can attest to the fact that this good-looking fifty-four-year-old redhead is sexually alive and well in Chicago. When I was there, I called her, and since she was leaving for Europe with Marvin, yet another contender for husband number three, we agreed to meet for a drink at O'Hare.

"Tell me about Marvin," I began.

"He's separated," she answered crisply.

"Ah, Lisa, watch out," I warned. "That generally means that when his wife is in the kitchen, he's in the bedroom."

Lisa laughed and, staring at my tape recorder, asked, "So what have you discovered?"

"Some men are Jennifer-proof and some aren't," I answered tersely.

"Ridiculous," she said. "Any man is Jennifer-proof if you're clever."

"Clever? This has nothing to do with intelligence."

"It does," Lisa insisted. "Listen, these guys forty, fifty, you have to know how to play them. I always meet men, you know that, and while you might not want to marry any of them, they're not bad, and at least I'm in the game. What you don't realize is that we have an advantage."

I stared at her blankly.

"You're damned right we do," she went on, "and don't look at me like that. With Marvin"—she waved her Concorde ticket to London in front of me so I'd know who Marvin was—"I know what he needs, what his dreams are, what his fears are, what he thinks he's missed, what he'd like to do in bed that he never dared ask his wife to do, and I feed right into it."

"Maybe Jennifers can do all that and without wrinkles or cellulite," I suggested glumly.

"Are you crazy?" she cried. "If I were a Jennifer, I'd be too busy filling my own insecure little needs, or my yuppie ambition. I'd be searching for my identity and concerned about my still under-developed sexuality. And if I were a Jennifer I'd be jealous of his four daughters. You think I like him traipsing everywhere with them, and his whole bloody family?"

I shook my head. The picture of Lisa living some Norman Rock-well existence was rather unbelievable.

"But I do," she said. "I shop for their gifts and their husbands' gifts and his grandchildren's gifts, and endure those endless birth-day parties and family reunions. Tell me, what Jennifer would do that?

"You see, we have a psychic advantage. Marvin's relationships with his family have never been better. And he believes it's all due to me. And it is."

"Sounds exhausting; it's a full-time job," I told her.

"It is. Men *are* work, and women today, for all their vaunted liberation, have ignored the fact that they have to devote as much time to the care and feeding of their relationships with men as they do to nurturing their precious careers."

Her flight to New York was being called, and I was flying on to California, so we walked through the frenetic airport until we reached her gate.

"We can compete, Barbara," she told me, "but women have to draw on all the strengths and knowledge that time and experience have given them. I have problems with men, like every woman, but I don't think any of them have anything to do with my age and the fact that I'm not a Jennifer."

Lisa kissed me, or the air near my cheek, and hurried off. I followed her with my eyes till she disappeared on the ramp to the plane, then I started toward my gate.

Perhaps in some ways she was right. But I wondered about women who have full-time jobs, who work not to feed their yuppie ambition but because they have to feed themselves and their chil-dren, women who have neither the time nor the money to devote to looking as good as Lisa does at fifty-four. How could they com-pete?

I knew that despite all Lisa's cunning and craftiness, with all her

Machiavellian plotting, and despite her glamour and elegant good looks, there are men, unlike Marvin, who would still prefer a Jennifer.

The question remained. Why do some men act on the fantasy, while some don't? Why are some married men immune to the need for a Jennifer? What about boredom, sexual staleness? How does a man not succumb?

I turned to the marriage of Will and Sheila Albertson. For twenty years, she stayed home and raised the children, living primarily for and through her family; he struggled his way from poverty to a successful, glittering career. Sounds ominous—fertile territory for a Jennifer. Yet Will doesn't feel he has outgrown Sheila, and she is neither challenged nor threatened by his glamorous professional life. An editor of a national journal, he meets dignitaries, movie stars, celebrities all the time.

They live in a rambling, comfortable, two-story shingled house, located in a suburb of New York. There we sat down to dinner. Grace was said, the children helped with the dishes. Except for the computer in their son's room, it was as if I had walked into an obsolete dream; still I sensed that this was how it always was for the Albertsons. All this normalcy wasn't laid on for my benefit.

Will and I settled down with coffee in the living room. Sheila disappeared, saving her comments for later. Although we had worked together, Will agreed to talk about his personal life. We were both a bit anxious; this was new turf for us. He gazed deep into his cup and then looked past me into the den, where Sheila was helping their daughter with her homework.

"I cannot define myself without Sheila," he began slowly. "Sheila *is* me. We're both different than we were when we married, but we've changed together; we're part of each other. I can't imagine life without her.

"What it comes down to is I *like* Sheila. She's my friend, and I trust her; that's more important than anything. I wouldn't run to a chippie and violate our friendship. Everyone needs someone who loves them, to be touched and needed. But it's more important to love. I know this is what gives us joy."

"After so many years together, how do you maintain a sexual interest in each other?" I asked.

"Sex is important but less important than when we first married," Will replied, "but you don't run away from commitment. Sheila is the best friend I have in the world; I couldn't violate that. How could I violate my children's trust?

"When we met we both went to work, me at the paper, she at the phone company. I took courses at night, so we only saw each other weekends. Today I'm successful, but it's Sheila who handles the money, the investments. I don't need to control everything; I'm happy for her to do it.

"Twenty years." He shook his head with wonder. "I'm forty-three, she's forty-two; we've shared so much joy—the birth of our children. And tragedies—I was with Sheila when her father died. What on earth could I have in common with someone my daughter's age? How could I make love to a woman my son's age? My son is my son forever. I'm going to be his father till the day I die. I'm amused when people say, 'I'd die for my child.' I say, 'Are you willing to live for your child?' "

Will pointed to a row of pictures in the hall, pictures of him with senators and Presidents.

"I meet all kinds of celebrities—actresses, models—and they make goo-goo eyes at me at parties. But the men who make goo-goo eyes, who need sex from them—that only shows their own weakness. That sort of man can't deal with a real woman," he said, scowling with disdain. "I can't imagine myself with them. I would have nothing to share with a younger woman." He grinned and added, "Even the music wouldn't be the same."

"Where did this security with yourself come from?" I asked.

"I had a strong mother," he replied, "and an alcoholic father, a man who brutalized my mother and me, a man who was uncontrollably violent. I learned from women in my life. Not just my mother, but my two aunts and grandmother. All four survived their husbands. They had tough times but hung in. I have no model for divorce, and not because of religious reasons. I just grew up around four incredibly strong, marvelous women. I respect women."

Because I have known Will for five years, and have written for his journal, I've been able to observe the way he treats the women in his office, and I concur. He *does* respect women. While he had described the origins of his respect, he hadn't quite explained what he looked for in a woman in his personal life.

"I don't seek a mother or a daughter in a woman," he explained. "I seek a partner. I have a mother, I have a daughter."

"What do you think the men who *do* leave their wives for Jennifers are seeking?" I asked.

"These guys feel a thrilling guilt with their Jennifers," he answered. "They are cheating Mommy with a twenty-two-year-old girl. A twenty-two-year-old girl is not my intellectual equal; there's very little we can share, very little she can add. You can find pleasure in the arms of a young woman, but you can't find joy. For a while you smell the daisies, but it's the child in her you are responding to. I couldn't respond to a young girl like that."

Silent for a moment, Will seemed to be thinking to himself, then he looked toward the hallway where Sheila was saying good night to the children. "Men who leave for young girls aren't family centered," he said softly. "If your center is your business, you'll wake up one day and discover the hollowness. You'll see it's not that you have a job, or a great job; you're just a caretaker. When men see that, if their whole life has been their work, with no joy at home, they try to find happiness with a young girl as an aphrodisiac to their spirits. If you have a solid home, a foundation, it can't happen."

"He makes it so easy to be married to him," Sheila said. Without either of us noticing, she had joined us. Smiling, she took a seat facing her husband.

"We have a wonderful life, but there are problems," she began slowly. "I *am* intimidated by the kind of people I meet with Will. Each time I fear I'll blow it. I took a Dale Carnegie course, and it helped me."

"I never worry," Will interrupted her. "I don't care one iota for them the way I care for her. She couldn't blow it. All these highfalutin people call her as often as they call me."

"It was tough during the sixties and seventies," Sheila continued, "when the women's lib people were putting down being a housewife and mother. Now I'm not intimidated. When they ask if I have a job, I say, 'Yes, I'm a housewife.' "

Sheila glanced at her husband, and I sensed she had never told him these things this way before. Her expression was one of sheer pleasure when she said, "He never pressured me to go back to school or get a job. With my daughter in high school and my son off to college soon, I'll start thinking about it. But when I think of work, I say how can I live up to Will's job? Can I sell things at Macy's? It's always been clear—if I'm happy at home, I stay at home. It's up to me."

With her eyes fixed on her husband, Sheila continued. "He gives me the confidence, because with all his success, he hasn't changed. We still have friends from my days at the phone company. The husband's a butcher; we're godparents of each other's children. Will is still Will. He can meet with Gorbachev next month—and it looks like it's going to happen—but he'll still be Will to me, the children, and our friends."

Will, taking obvious pleasure in all Sheila had said, added, "My core hasn't changed; I've become more polished, skillful. Sheila isn't the girl from the Bronx anymore. She can talk to anyone. The things she does, the people she meets, she couldn't have done twenty years ago."

Sheila, pleased with his remarks, said, "How can it get dull? There's never a dull moment. He fills the void—the trips, the job, the house."

"I can't stand being bored," Will added, "so I make changes on the boat, the house, but I don't change the fundamentals—my wife, family. At work, I like to mix things up, change the philosophy, keep it fresh."

Both agreed that they are equals in the marriage.

"My father was dominant, made all the decisions," Sheila explained. "I expected Will to be like that, and it upset me at first when he wanted a partnership, not a power trip. Now I treasure our equality."

"Do either of you worry about aging?" I asked.

Sheila laughed. "I'd love to lose ten pounds," she said. "I do twenty minutes on the treadmill each day. Other than that I'm not worried."

"I swim and run," was Will's reply, "and last year I entered my first triathlon, but I'd be upset if you didn't take care of yourself," Will said to Sheila firmly.

"You must be able to have eye-to-eye contact with women," he continued, "without treating them as a mommy or a daughter. What is a man? A man lives with women and children. To feel joy, you need a family. It's what bonds us psychologically, physically. It's like poverty. You can throw money at the ghetto, and there's no poverty. But money can't help the poverty of spirit that comes from not having a family."

In talking with psychiatrists and psychologists, as well as with the men themselves, it seems to come down to a question of inner security, a man's confidence in himself, being comfortable with himself. If he is secure about who he is and what he is, apparently a man is less driven to seek outside confirmation of his worth.

For men suffering from a narcissistic personality disorder, there may always be a gnawing hunger within, one that is exacerbated by aging. Frequently it can be only temporarily satisfied by a new woman, a new young woman who will tell him and the world that he's "somebody."

As several psychologists observed, we are living in narcissistic times. "I want mine now" has become the national mantra, and women as well as men are increasingly reaching for whatever is their perception of happiness.

Dr. Harvey Greenberg puts it this way: "Since the late sixties, therapists have begun noticing an increasing prevalence of narcissistic character disorders in our practices. We've seen more narcissistic parents, then more narcissistic adolescents.

"Although it's impossible to assign any one cause to this, I think it's at least partly born out of affluence in the middle and upper classes, people reaping the benefits of an affluent society. From a leftist perspective, it may very well be a function of the excesses of late twentieth century corporate capitalism manifested at an individual level—an 'I do my own thing, even if I have to do it on you' sort of thing. 'And I don't have to give anything back.'

"As time does *its* thing, the envelope of the self shows the changes that come with aging. The narcissist takes this assault personally. It can lead a guy to a plastic surgeon, or a lot of guys to refurbish their failing self-image with a young girl. What you might call a 'trophy' complex.

"Not all these men are narcissistic bastards by any means. But certainly at the extreme—and it really is awful—is the man who leaves home for a Jennifer, then cuts off his wife, has a kid, and becomes indifferent and cruel to the original wife and children. He amputates himself from them emotionally and financially. He doesn't want to remember his old life where he was growing old. He's too involved with his new, narcissistically fueled life-style."

Echoing the thoughts of other psychologists and sociologists, Dr. Greenberg believes that narcissism is created by cultural factors as well as by the early constellation of the family—the events, the personalities, and the interaction of the mother, the father, and the child.

Jennifer Fever is only one manifestation of this narcissism, this greed, emotional or monetary. Examples can be found everywhere in our culture—in toxic wastes being dumped in rivers, in stock market scandals, on television, in our universities—on Main Street as well as Wall Street.

As Kay Prothro and Rosanna Murray, the psychologists who have treated gay men and women, emphasized, any persons, gay or straight, male or female, who have faced up to who they are, and to their own sexual identity, are, after that internal struggle, complete, in touch with their own identity, their own power. And when they choose a partner, they are looking more for shared values and shared interests than for completion, or enhancement of their own view of themselves.

But for those who have not experienced that internal struggle, and who require external accoutrements to fill their inner void, words like "loyalty" and "responsibility" are meaningless.

Will Albertson echoed the thoughts of other Jennifer-proof men who believe emotional responsibility and loyalty to the family are sadly lacking at this time in our history. I asked Will what would make men less vulnerable, would let them find satisfaction with their wives, not needing Jennifers.

"Only if men change the way they define women, and how they are defined by women. Women are the foundation of society. They raise the future. They mustn't allow themselves to play unnatural roles. I don't mean having a job or a career. That's natural. Women can't allow themselves to play mama or daughter to satisfy a man's ego. They can't let themselves be defined badly or debased, and should leave men who treat them badly."

"And men?"

"And men who are driven and consumed by their work should remember: All jobs end."

It was almost eleven. Will had ordered a car to take me back to the city, about an hour away. Mercifully, the driver wasn't talkative.

Suburbia sped by, then the rough and rugged outlines of the tenements of the Bronx, the hard lights of the ghetto where Will had been brutalized as a young boy. Through the strength and love of four determined women, he had somehow miraculously survived.

I remembered that he always delighted in William Faulkner's distinction between those who merely survive and those who prevail.

Really, Will was a miracle of surviving. I had always known he prevailed in his work, in his glittery, globe-trotting, gutsy journalistic career. But love? With Sheila and those kids, wasn't that prevailing too?

Yes—in a major-league way.

I could still see the four of them—a nuclear family, that dinosaur of contemporary sociology—seated around the dining room table saying grace. It wasn't an obsolete dream; it was real.

The car pulled in front of my building, and as I said good night to the driver and headed for the elevator, I thought: How sweet it was to see Will and Sheila. Just what I needed.

Will and Sheila remain in my mind, a memory, sunny and warm, blotting out a darker, chillier world of premarital agreements, power games, trophy factors, and adoration factories. Timeless as it is, Jennifer Fever today is a reality. But for women, there is another shining reality: There are men, not all of them, but lots of them, who have a protective antibody, which makes them chronically, and steadfastly, and delightfully immune.

Afterword

As I was nearing completion of this book, I went to the theater to see a preview of a play called *Fences.* I knew nothing about it, except that the advance word was marvelous. I had no idea that the play would in any way have anything to do with the book I was working on. All I knew was that the playwright, August Wilson, was said to have written a powerful drama, and James Earl Jones was supposed to be giving the performance of a lifetime.

It was both of those things. August Wilson's biting drama pivots on the life of fifty-three-year-old Troy Maxson, a proud and angry black man who lives with his wife, Rose, in Pittsburgh, circa 1957.

Although *Fences* is about many things, and Wilson deals with each of them eloquently, the central plot concerns Troy's falling in love with a very young woman, who becomes pregnant with his child. Finally Troy makes his confession to Rose, who is stunned and outraged by his words.

"It's just she gives me a different idea . . . a different understanding about myself," Troy explains. "I can step out of this house and get away from the pressures and problems . . . be a different man. . . . I ain't got to wonder how I'm gonna pay the bills or get the roof fixed. I can just be a part of myself that I ain't never been. . . .

"I can sit up in her house and laugh. . . . I can laugh out loud . . . and it feels good. It reaches all the way down to the bottom of my shoes. Rose, I can't give that up."

Rose protests, "You should have stayed in my bed, Troy. . . ."

"Then when I saw that gal," Troy continues, "she firmed up my backbone. . . . Rose, I'm trying the best I can to explain it to you.

It's not easy for me to admit that I been standing in the same place for eighteen years."

Rose, filled with hurt and disappointment, rages at him, "I gave eighteen years of my life to stand in the same spot with you. . . . Don't you think I ever wanted other things? Don't you think I had dreams and hopes? What about my life? What about me? Don't you think it ever crossed my mind to want to know other men? . . . But I held on to you, Troy, I held you tight, you was my husband, I owed you everything I had. I wanted to be there with you 'cause you was my husband, 'cause that's the only way I was gonna survive as your wife."

Suddenly I was flooded with memories of that June afternoon at the swimming pool high in the sky, as I watched the men watching the Jennifer. I remembered how, compared to hers, my own body felt sluggish and unsleek. I also remembered wondering how women like Rose survive the devastation of knowing their husbands prefer making love to a younger woman.

I went back to the club, and instead of Jennifers, it was filled with Janets—exercising and treadmilling and bicycling, lifting weights and applying weights. I wondered what they were thinking. What had I learned in two years? What did I know now that I hadn't known that day when it all seemed like a matter of older men and young flesh? He has money, he needs youth. She has youth; she wants money.

It wasn't merely or totally a matter of flesh or money. Now I knew about some men's need for adoration, unresolved attitudes about their mothers, and their terrors about midlife passivity. I also knew there was nothing in the health club, with all its high-tech equipment and treadmills, that could fix the inside of me or of anyone, if he or she was a sour, complaining, angry scar tissue of a self which men found so unpleasing in middle-aged women. And which, not so incidentally, women disliked in older men and found refreshingly absent in younger men.

As I worked on this book, I realized with a startling sense of irony that there was a time when the stigma of being an unattached midlife woman was as intense as any stigma I had faced in the past. I am not unfamiliar with being in a stigmatized place. I described in a book I wrote ten years ago the types of stigma I encountered after abruptly ending a long relationship with a prescription drug. I had landed in a hospital, not the kind that sets bones or stitches up appendixes, but one that is supposed to help us patch up our souls. I discovered then that my self-stigmatization was as great as any I would face from friends or colleagues who knew what had happened to me.

Still a societal battle is waged against that stigma every day. Speeches by Presidents and senators, television public service announcements, and newspaper editorials urge us on a daily basis to be kind to those who, rather than suffering a physical injury, have had the poor taste of incurring an affliction of the spirit.

Problems remain, but those atmospheric exhortations help stigmatized people from being too hard on themselves and strengthen them when they actually confront stigma from unenlightened quarters in society. In some quarters, there is so much societal support that it has developed a kind of cachet.

But this Jennifer thing was different. For me and the millions of women like me, there was little cachet.

There were moments when I pictured myself, tape recorder in hand, arriving to interview another fifty-five-year-old man about his Jennifer, as analogous to a black reporter in 1950s Little Rock who has wangled an interview with Orval Faubus: sitting there with a tape recorder and a straight face, asking the governor why there are no blacks in his cabinet; sitting there asking for the truth, the facts, the lowdown. As the governor, also with a straight face, ticks off the alleged deficiencies of blacks and the superior virtues of whites, I see it all clearly: Through the particular prism of the racist, the blacks' purported intellectual lacks—my wrinkles; their alleged shiftlessness—my cellulite; their passion for watermelon—my inability to prolong life; their propensity for tap-dancing—my desexualized matronliness.

Of course, the man with a Jennifer is neither a racist nor a bigot, and frequently he isn't a sexist, in feminist terms. But he, too, picks up what has been in the atmosphere and part of the water supply for years—the conviction that youthful women are sexy, sexier, sexiest, and older women are not.

Like many women, I, too, internalized the values of my society, inescapably picking up what's in the atmosphere. As I watched the Janet on the treadmill, and the one lifting the weights, and another jogging around the running path, I hoped they would never make the terrible mistake of ascribing every wrong, even their manlessness, if they are manless, to their age.

Admittedly many women are dealt a bad hand. Some of us, however, play the cards we are dealt better than others. Of the women I met, only a few remained embittered and wore their scars of lousy relationships with men, or their loss of a man to a Jennifer, like badges of dishonorable service. Only a few of them were defiant, daring other men to atone for the sins of the men who preceded them. I know that many men disagree; they think too many women vent their frustrations and their hurts from previous relationships on the next man—and they hate it. And why shouldn't they hate it? Don't we hate it when men make us the object of all their anti-female wrath, projecting their mothers, aunts, ex-wives—or any female who has wounded them—onto the blank slate of a new relationship?

If women want a crack at those few available Jennifer-proof men who pass through their lives like fireflies in the night, they ought to consider removing their scar tissue. If they were, indeed, just victims of bad luck and bad circumstances, they should resist to the death the awful lure of becoming a perpetual victim. Rather than making a career out of victimhood, they should deal with their rage, be wary in the future, and move on.

Certainly harsh realities may impinge, re-igniting those old wounds. The man who ignores his financial and emotional responsibility to his first family because all his resources are now devoted to a second makes it difficult for his first wife to deal with her anger, bury her hurt, and move on. But she must. For either a man or a woman, to cling to rage only perpetuates the sense of injury and stigmatizes them in a far more toxic way than age—it makes them unloving and unlovable.

As I left the gym, I thought about the new generation of women growing up in an atmosphere less clouded with sexism and ageism. These are the women who, with their young husbands, rewrote the marriage vows, replacing the promise to obey with words about equality and partnership. Can they be as fearful that their husbands will fall prey to Jennifer Fever as were women of the previous generation? And if their husbands do someday come down with a case of Jennifer Fever, will these young women be more insulated because less of their identity is tied up with being Mrs. Somebody?

Yet one young woman told me that while economic emancipation and professional equality offer women a better shot of surviving their husbands' bouts of Jennifer Fever, she would be just as devastated as her mother.

"Why?" I asked.

"Precisely because I *wasn't* housebound, precisely because I worked and raised our children and lived a fuller life than my mother, how could he then leave me, or say, as some men do, 'I outgrew her'? Women's liberation is not insulation. I think that in some ways, for us it would be worse."

After I left the gym, I wandered through the quiet Sunday streets of Manhattan. All the emotions of the past two years were available on the surface, not blurred by time. I remembered the joy of knowing there are men, terrific men, who in their relationships crave equality and partnership.

I could still feel the buzz of pleasure I experienced interviewing the men who knew that mature women may have been through a dark or lonely time but now were at the best time of their lives, with the most to give and the knowledge of how to give it, their minds sharp, their abilities most developed.

My interviews with these women, these Janets who had survived, filled me with profound respect and admiration. In the journey of these two years I had learned much, and it had changed my perception of myself. Never again would I feel neutered or alien, nor would I feel a member of a separate species.

And Jennifer Fever? It is a fever. The emotions it produces are hot. Never the chill of indifference, always the heat of lust, of craving flesh, of battling death, of struggling to stay young, and sometimes the gnawing pangs of guilt.

Unlike some fevers, this one doesn't induce a doctor to tell a man to take two aspirin and get into bed, and it will disappear in the morning. A doctor, particularly if he is a male doctor, is more likely to give him a knowing wink and that special male "I was there" smile of understanding. And he may also tell him to get it out of his system and enjoy himself, and he'll be fine in the morning.

In the 1940s movie *Mr. Peabody and the Mermaid,* just before his fiftieth birthday, Mr. Peabody, played by William Powell, goes bonkers over one and almost drowns. A mermaid—so perfectly emblematic of what many men are seeking. Far from being judgmental or even a peer, she cannot speak. Far from being too assertive or independent, she has no legs and cannot leave him.

Forty years later, the mermaid reappeared in the popular film *Splash.* Only this time, unlike William Powell, this hero, Tom Hanks, doesn't come to his senses and feel better in the morning. When we last see him, he is happily swimming beside his mermaid as she guides him toward her kingdom beneath the sea.

In forty years the world has progressed, but when it comes to the lure of a Jennifer, not much. The fact is many men are fine in the proverbial morning. Others, who succumb, will give up everything, and do anything *not* to vanquish the fever but to prolong it.

Although it may only be a delusion, the fever talking, they may even convince themselves that they can learn how to live underwater.

Acknowledgments

There are so many people to thank who were so generous in their support and assistance throughout the writing of this book, I fear I may neglect to mention someone. If I do, you are remembered and appreciated in my heart, if not on these pages.

I cannot find adequate words to thank my dear friends and associates who made so many contributions to the manuscript. I appreciate all of you and send my heartfelt thanks to:

My friend Georgeanne Heller, for being Georgeanne, for being wise and funny, and for the secrets contained in the universe of her highly prized Rolodex.

Louis Schumaci and Vincent Zito, who believed in me and my book from the first day we met, for their friendship, and for *always* offering the gift of laughter,

Peter Dunn, Sidney Bergen, Herb Stavisky, Bruce Rattray, Toni Lopopolo, Lynn Levenberg, Barbara Howell, Linda Stasi, Barbara Seaman, Edie Selman, Barbara Ansen, and David Currier, for their support.

And to Betty Jean Lifton, Harry Frolich, Barbara Victor, Sara Ravis, Barry Richmond, Tom Holzbog, and Stephen Dembitzer for the very special help they offered on the manuscript.

To Ann Boggan for her tireless research, and Lois Trager, Candy Rubin, and Carol O'Leary for their assistance.

And Burton Beals, whose comments on the manuscript were so valuable.

To the librarians at the Donnell Library Research Department in New York and those in the drama department of the Lincoln Center Library of Performing Arts.

And to my many friends at Harper & Row for their encouragement as well as their professionalism, my thanks for their insights, suggestions, and all the contributions they made during the writing of *Jennifer Fever:* Bill Shinker, Florence Goldstein, Linda Michaels, Joseph Montebello, Dolores Simon, Roz Barrow, Brenda Segel, Scott Manning, Lisa Berkowitz, Lucia Kelly, and Lisa Morrill.

To Anne Sibbald and Cynthia Cannell for their encouragement.

How can I begin to thank the many people who asked that their names not appear, who were willing to make flashbacks into their own pasts, who dipped deep into their memories, reawakening old hurts, and generously shared with me the thoughts and emotions of their past? To all the Janets, Jennifers, and men who shared their dreams and terrors, I thank you for the hours you spent with me and for your courage in being willing to face one more time the thornier moments of your lives . . . and also for sharing your happiness.

As always my thanks and appreciation to Dan Harvey, Jim Fox, Roger Straus III, and Peter Elliott, not only for reading my pages but for touching my heart with their friendship.

To Walter Anderson for his encouragement and friendship.

And to Jerry Traum and Buz Wyeth who, after ten years and three books, are always there, often suffering through my primal doubts, but always, always believing in me and the book that is struggling to be written. Their wisdom, judgment, unwavering loyalty, and inimitable sense of humor enrich my life and my work. I thank them for being there.

And to my family, Lewis and Sally Loeb, Eddie and Melinda Loeb, David, Jason, and Michael, my love and my thanks.

Notes

PAGE

37 "Virginity became exalted for . . ." Murstein, *Love, Sex and Marriage Through the Ages.*

CHAPTER SIX ◇ *A Woman's Time Is Short*

42 "He will look up . . ." Ransohoff, *Venus Over Forty.*
   "inescapable effect on the . . ." Ransohoff.
43 "A little boy must come . . ." Ransohoff.
   "As in Pygmalion, he . . ." Ransohoff.
44 "Psychoanalytic criticism of classical . . ." Pomeroy, *Goddesses, Whores, Wives, and Slaves.*
45 "He taught that male . . ." French.
46 "Not as a woman . . ." Aristophanes, *Lysistrata.*
   "You . . . you've filled your . . ." Aristophanes, *Ecclesiazusae.*
   ". . . And if a lover . . ." Aristophanes, *Ecclesiazusae.*
47 "Before she was lovely . . ." Richlin, *Garden of Priapus.*
48 "You'll find he loves . . ." Babson, *Roman Women, Early History and Habits.*
   "demanded marital fidelity, while . . ." Richlin.
   "That the Romans appear . . ." Murstein.
49 "smells like an octopus . . ." Richlin.

CHAPTER SEVEN ◇ *"Oh, Johnny, You Park So Good"*

53 "I'm beginning to get . . ." Chayefsky, *Network.*

CHAPTER TEN ◇ *. . . And Sometimes She Doesn't*

78 "Thy nobler parts which . . ." Wilmot, "Song of a Young Lady to Her Ancient Lover."
81 "For the young, sexual . . ." Perrin, "Middle-Age Dating."
82 "We have demonstrated that . . ." Sigal & Landy, "Radiating Beauty."
   "It is very tempting . . ." Sigal & Landy.

CHAPTER ELEVEN ◇ *It's Moonlight Madness*

89 "He'd tell me, 'I . . ." Goldsmith, "Dark Inheritance."
   "as if he were a . . ." Goldsmith.
   "as he became weaker. . ." Goldsmith.

CHAPTER TWELVE ◇ *A Whole World Lost*

104 "Get out. Go anywhere . . ." Chayefsky, *Network.*
105 "If your husband is . . ." Euripides, *Medea.*
106 "You thought that reason . . ." Euripides.
113 "if Martians ever . . ." Lurie, *The War Between the Tates.*

PAGE

CHAPTER THIRTEEN ◇ *Survival*

129 "i smiled your smile . . ." Previn, *Bogtrotter.*
130 "Beware of young girls . . ." Previn.
135 "inadequate, unpaid and uncollectable . . ." Weitzman, *The Divorce Revolution.*
136 "She becomes increasingly . . ." Weitzman.
 "The woman who lived . . ." Weitzman.
 "personally better off than . . ." Weitzman.
140 "in the nineteenth century . . ." Rosenberg, *Disorderly Conduct.*
 "It therefore is most . . ." Rosenberg.
 "menopause could become woman's . . ." Rosenberg.
 "Since the days of . . ." Banner, *American Beauty.*
141 "The Renaissance of the . . ." Banner.
 "powerful role in standardizing . . ." Banner.
148 "literate American women . . . were . . ." Banner.

CHAPTER FOURTEEN ◇ *"La Vie Est Courte, Il Faut Suivre la Magique"*

150 "Only a deeply feminized . . ." Gray, "The New Older Woman."
 "won from French society . . ." Bree, *Women Writers in France.*
151 "Surely a woman like . . ." Colette, *Chéri.*
152 "I thought one day . . ." Melamed, *Mirror, Mirror.*
153 "I have never come across . . ." de Beauvoir, *The Coming of Age.*
164 "feels a certain antipathy . . ." de Beauvoir, *Brigitte Bardot and the Lolita Syndrome.*

CHAPTER FIFTEEN ◇ *Breaking the Rules*

177 "The Athenian man had . . ." Murstein.
 "the aging male is . . ." Richlin.
 "The genital area of . . ." Richlin.
 "Adult homosexuals are the . . ." Richlin.
178 "typically faces the crisis . . ." Berger, *Gay and Gray.*
 "more likely to have . . ." Berger.
 "maintaining a masculine . . ." Berger.
183 "The aging process is . . ." Marmor, *Homosexual Behavior.*
184 "What affects them is . . ." Adelman, *Long Time Passing.*

CHAPTER SIXTEEN ◇ *Pearl Harbor's Not an Actress*

185 "Like the ghost of . . ." Gidlow, *Elsa: I Come with My Songs.*
186 "Crabbed age and youth . . ." Shakespeare, "The Passionate Pilgrim."
195 "I should expect to . . ." Gilot & Lake, *Life with Picasso.*
 "He had insisted that . . ." Gilot & Lake.

PAGE

195 "I had waked up . . ." Gilot & Lake.
     "My coming to him . . ." Gilot & Lake.
198 "Seeing someone young around . . ." Gilot & Lake.

CHAPTER SEVENTEEN ◇ *"Please Let Me Have This Little Companion"*

212 "These men I'm afraid . . ." Stasi, "David's Dad."

CHAPTER EIGHTEEN ◇ *"And Here's to You, Mrs. Robinson"*

217 "The younger lover is . . ." Gray.
219 "Turning to young flesh . . ." Gray.
     "less renowned but equally . . ." Gray.
233 "incontinent longings, and while . . ." Williams, *The Roman Spring of Mrs. Stone.*
     "You are right, Paolo . . ." Williams.

CHAPTER NINETEEN ◇ *In Buddy's Eyes*

237 "In Buddy's eyes I . . ." Sondheim, *Follies.*

AFTERWORD

256 "It's just she gives . . ." Wilson, *Fences.*

Bibliography

Adelman, Marcy. *Long Time Passing: Lives of Older Lesbians.* Boston: Alyson, 1986.

Aristophanes. *The Complete Plays of Aristophanes.* New York: Bantam Books, 1984.

Babson, John. *Roman Women, Early History and Habits.* New York: Barnes and Noble, 1962.

Banner, Lois. *American Beauty.* New York: Knopf, 1983.

Berger, Raymond W. *Gay and Gray.* Boston: Alyson, 1982.

Bree, Germaine. *Women Writers in France.* New Brunswick: Rutgers University Press, 1973.

Chayefsky, Paddy. *Middle of the Night.* New York: French, 1977.

———. *Network* (Simchah Productions, directed by Sidney Lumet, released by United Artists).

Colette. *Chéri and the Last of Chéri.* New York: Ballantine, 1982.

Dante. *The Divine Comedy.* New York: Columbia University Press, 1931.

de Beauvoir, Simone. *The Coming of Age.* New York: Warner Books, 1970.

———. *Brigitte Bardot and the Lolita Syndrome.* New York: Arno Press, 1972.

Euripides. *Medea and Other Plays.* Middlesex: Penguin, 1954.

French, Marilyn. *Beyond Power.* New York: Summit Books, 1985.

Gidlow, Elsa. *Elsa: I Come with My Songs.* San Francisco: Bootlegger Press and Druid Heights Books, 1986.

Gilot, Françoise, and Carlton Lake. *Life with Picasso.* New York: McGraw-Hill, 1964.

Goldsmith, Barbara. "Dark Inheritance," *Vanity Fair,* October, 1986.

Gray, Francine du Plessix. "The New Older Woman." *New York Times Book Review,* January 15, 1978.

Gutmann, David. "Individual Adaptation in the Middle Years." *Journal of Geriatric Psychology.* 9:1 1976.

Horner, Tom. *Sex and the Bible.* New York: C. E. Tuttle, 1974.

Horney, Karen. *Feminine Psychology.* New York: Norton, 1967.

Hrdy, Sarah. *The Woman That Never Evolved.* Cambridge: Harvard University Press, 1981.

Koestler, Arthur. *The Heel of Achilles.* New York: Random House, 1974.

Legman, G. *Rationale of the Dirty Joke.* New York: Castle Books, 1968.

Lurie, Alison. *The War Between the Tates.* New York: Random House, 1974.

Marmor, Judd. *Homosexual Behavior.* New York: Basic Books, 1980.

Melamed, Elissa. *Mirror, Mirror.* New York: Linden Press, 1983.

Murstein, Bernard. *Love, Sex and Marriage Through the Ages.* New York: Springer Publishing Co., 1974.

Norwich, John. *Christmas Crackers.* Middlesex: Penguin Books, 1980.

Perrin, Noel. "Middle-Age Dating," *New York Times Magazine,* July 6, 1986.

Pollitt, Katha. "Being Wed Is Not Always Bliss," *The Nation,* September 20, 1986.

Pomeroy, Sarah. *Goddesses, Whores, Wives, and Slaves.* New York: Schocken Books.

Previn, Dory. *Bogtrotter.* Garden City: Doubleday.

Ransohoff, Rita M. *Venus Over Forty.* New York: Macmillan, 1980.

Richlin, Amy. *The Garden of Priapus.* New Haven: Yale University Press, 1983.

———. "Invective Against Women in Roman Satire." Reprinted from *Arethusa,* 17:1, Spring, 1984.

Rosenberg, Carroll Smith. *Disorderly Conduct.* New York: Knopf, 1985.

Shakespeare, William. "The Passionate Pilgrim." XII. Edited by George Lyman Kittredge. New York: Ginn and Co., 1936.

Sigal, Harold, and David Landy. "Radiating Beauty." *Journal of Personality and Social Psychology.* Vol. 28, 1973.

Staples, Robert. *The World of Black Singles.* Westport: Greenwood Press, 1981.

Stasi, Linda. "David's Dad." *Beauty Digest,* January, 1987.

Tanner, Nancy. *On Becoming Human.* Cambridge: Cambridge University Press, 1981.

Trible, Phyllis. *God and the Rhetoric of Sexuality.* Philadelphia: Fortress Press, 1978.

———. *Texts of Terror.*

Weitzman, Lenore J. *The Divorce Revolution.* New York: Free Press, 1985.

Williams, Tennessee. *The Roman Spring of Mrs. Stone.* New York: Ballantine Books, 1950.

Wilson, August. *Fences.* New York: New American Library, 1986.

Index